JE 238.3926 W

KEEPING MINIBEASTS

Beetles

This edition first published in 2005 by
Sea-to-Sea Publications
1980 Lookout Drive
North Mankato
Minnesota 56003

Copyright © Sea-to-Sea Publications 2005

ISBN   1-932889-16-7

Printed in China

Library of Congress Control Number:
2004103608

2 4 6 8 9 7 5 3

Published by arrangement with the
Watts Publishing Group Ltd, London

Design: Edward Kinsey
Consultant: Michael Chinery

KEEPING MINIBEASTS

Beetles

TEXT AND PHOTOGRAPHS: BARRIE WATTS

CONTENTS

What are beetles?........6

Habitats 8

Collecting beetles.......10

A pitfall trap 12

Handling................14

Housing 16

Feeding 18

Useful beetles 20

Life-cycle 22

Completing the cycle 24

Releasing your beetles ...26

Unusual facts...........28

Index..................29

SEA-TO-SEA

Mankato Collingwood London

What are beetles?

Beetles are found in all shapes and sizes.
Most of them can fly but keep their wings
under their wing cases when they are not
being used.

Some kinds of beetle live on the ground or even under water, whereas others, like ladybugs, climb plants to look for food.

Habitats

Beetles live in all kinds of habitats. They live in forests, in freshwater ponds and streams, houses and gardens. In the home, carpet beetles can cause damage to carpets and fabrics.

However, many beetles do good, especially those that feed on pests such as aphids. Some even feed on flower pollen and in doing so pollenate the flowers so that they can bear fruit.

Collecting beetles

You can collect beetles in any small plastic or cardboard box. Put only one beetle in each box because some beetles could easily fight. Some even eat each other.

The best time to look for beetles is on a sunny day. Flying beetles will be looking for food and can easily be found. Look under stones and rocks and you could find ground beetles.

A good way to collect ground living beetles is to make a pitfall trap. You can set the trap in a wood or even in a garden. All you need is a jar or a plastic cup, four stones and a small piece of wood.

Bury the cup level with the surface and cover it with the wood and stones. Compare beetles caught at different times of the day.

Put some food in the cup and see what attracts certain species. Always remove the traps when you have finished.

Handling

Beetles are easy to handle. Use a small paintbrush and a paper cup with the smaller ones because you can damage them if you pick them up in your hand.

Larger ones can be picked up but always be gentle. Do not worry if they give off a smelly fluid. This is their protection against predators.

Housing

An old aquarium with a net cover is the best container to keep beetles in. Ground beetles need a layer of earth in the bottom as well as pieces of wood and stones under which to hide.

The lid must have plenty of holes and the earth must be damp or the beetles will dry up. Make sure you put in a good supply of food.
If you are keeping more than one beetle, make sure they are the same type, so they do not eat each other. A shady windowsill is the ideal place to put your beetle home.

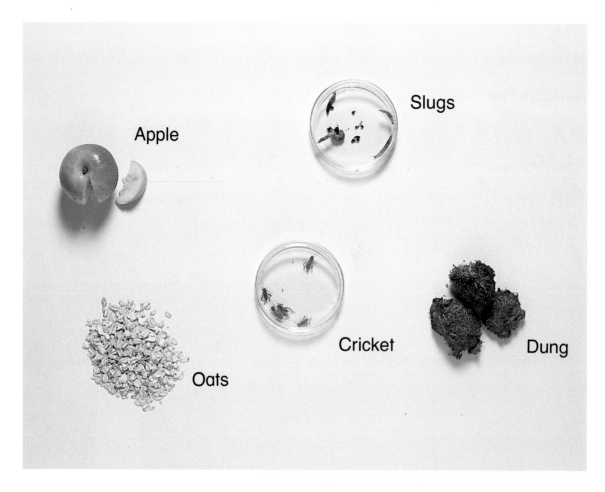

Apple

Slugs

Cricket

Dung

Oats

If the beetles are to stay healthy you must provide the right food for them. Sometimes it is difficult to know what they eat so watch them carefully before you collect them.

Ladybugs will eat aphids and dung beetles will eat horse manure. Black ground beetles are generally carnivorous and eat slugs and worms. You can also give them small pieces of meat.

Useful beetles

Some beetles are a great help in controlling pests in gardens and on farms. Ladybugs and their larvae eat a large number of aphids. A ladybug larva eats up to thirty aphids a day.

Dung beetles help to get rid of animal dung.
Some roll the manure into balls and bury it.
Then they lay their eggs in it so that the larvae
will have a ready supply of food when they
hatch.

It is easy to study the life-cycle of a beetle. Buy some mealworms from a pet shop and put them in an old plastic container with holes in the lid. Give them some dry bran and oats to feed on and then leave them.

From time to time check to see how they are growing and put more food in if it is needed. Eventually you will see the mealworms, which are larvae, turn into pupae and finally into the adult beetles.

After the mealworm beetle has emerged from its pupa it is a light brown color, but will get darker as it gets older. The female will lay her eggs on the food. The eggs are like dust and almost too small to see.

When the eggs hatch, the larvae that emerge
are what we call the mealworms. They are
very small, just like cotton threads. They soon
get bigger and need to change their skin just
like a caterpillar. When they get to 1 1/4 in
(30mm) long they are ready to turn into pupae.

When you have finished studying the beetles always return them to the same habitat. Do not release any foreign beetles or ones that are likely to become pests, such as the mealworm beetles.

If your garden has too many aphids in it, add some ladybugs to eat them. If you have too many slugs, release some ground beetles. They will eat them every night — it is much better than using chemicals.

Unusual facts

The heaviest insect in the world is the Goliath Beetle from Africa. It weighs 4oz (100 g).

The oldest beetle was found in Southend-on-Sea in Essex, England. It was a Splendor Beetle and it had spent 47 years as a larva.

The smallest insects in the world are the Hairywinged Beetles. They are only 0.2mm long and weigh only 0.005mg.

The glow-worm is a beetle. The wingless female uses the light in its tail to attract male beetles so that they can mate.

Index

aphids 9, 19, 20, 27
aquarium 16

Carpet Beetle 8

Dung Beetle 19, 21

eggs 21, 24

Flying Beetle 11
food 18, 19

glow-worm 28
Goliath Beetle 28
Ground Beetle 11, 19

habitats 8, 9
Hairywinged Beetle 28
handling beetles 14, 15

ladybugs 7, 19, 20, 27
larvae 23, 25

mealworms 22, 23

pitfall trap 12, 13
pupae 23, 25

releasing beetles 26, 27

slugs 19, 27
Splendor beetle 28

wings 6

Winston Churchill

THE CROSBY KEMPER LECTURESHIP

The Crosby Kemper Lectureship was established in 1979 by a grant from the Crosby Kemper Foundations of Kansas City, Missouri. It is intended to provide for lectures by authorities on British history and Sir Winston Churchill, himself, at the Winston Churchill Memorial and Library on the campus of Westminster College. The Lectureship has been established under the auspices of the British Institute of the United States and the Winston Churchill Memorial and Library.

Winston Churchill

Resolution,
Defiance,
Magnanimity,
Good Will

Edited by

R. Crosby Kemper III

University of Missouri Press
Columbia and London

Copyright © 1996 by
The Curators of the University of Missouri
University of Missouri Press, Columbia, Missouri 65201
Printed and bound in the United States of America
All rights reserved
5　4　3　2　1　　00　99　98　97　96

Library of Congress Cataloging-in-Publication Data

Winston Churchill : resolution, defiance, magnanimity, good will / edited by
    R. Crosby Kemper III.
        p.　cm.
    Includes index.
    ISBN 0-8262-1036-8 (cloth : alk. paper) BT 24.95 |18.56 |96
    1. Churchill, Winston, Sir, 1874–1965.　2. Great Britain—Politics and
government—20th century.　3. Prime ministers—Great Britain—Biography.
I. Kemper, R. Crosby, III.
DA566.9.C5W52　1995
941.084'092—dc20   95-36100
                                                                         CIP

♾ This paper meets the requirements of the
American National Standard for Permanence of Paper
for Printed Library Materials, Z39.48, 1984.

Designer: Stephanie Foley
Typesetter: BOOKCOMP
Printer and binder: Thomson-Shore, Inc.
Typefaces: Minion and University Roman

For R. Crosby Kemper Jr.

Who inspired and funded this series of lectures and in his resolute character exemplifies the finest Churchillian virtues.

In War: Resolution
In Defeat: Defiance
In Victory: Magnanimity
In Peace: Good Will

Contents

Acknowledgments   xi

Introduction   The Rhetoric of Civilization   1
                R. Crosby Kemper III

1.   The Origins of the "Iron Curtain" Speech   34
      Martin Gilbert

2.   The Dominion of History   62
      Sir John H. Plumb

3.   Churchill and Europe in 1944   80
      Sir William Deakin

4.   The Personality of Sir Winston Churchill   108
      Sir John R. Colville

5.   Churchill, the Man   126
      Robert Rhodes James

6.   Churchill and the Conservative Party   140
      Lord Blake

7.   The Transfer of Power in India   158
      Philip S. Ziegler

8.   Churchill: Prophet of Détente   176
      Sir Michael Howard

9.   Winston Churchill: The Great Human Being   190
      The Lady Soames

10.   Churchill as I Knew Him   202
         REGINALD V. JONES

11.   Winston Churchill: His Art Reflects His Life   222
         EDWINA SANDYS

12.   Memories of Churchill and How He Would
         Have Seen the World Today   234
         THE RIGHT HONORABLE LORD AMERY

Acknowledgments

T he nominal editor wishes to thank the real editor, Ms. Beverly Jarrett, the incomparable Director and Editor-in-Chief of the University of Missouri Press. He wishes to be on record as promising to, in future, respond promptly to her letters and calls, having not done so heretofore in recognition of the traditional, historical role of authors and editors. Thank you also to Jack Marshall, who has been the ramrod at Westminster College for this lecture series and much else; to Harvey Saunders, former President of Westminster, who enthusiastically responded to the idea; to Russ Jones, Judy Pugh, and the other members of the faculty and staff at Westminster who have made this a delight as well as an inspiration.

Also many thanks to Martin Gilbert, our inaugural lecturer and constant counsel and Ambassador; Robin Winks; Lord and Lady Blake; Jack Plumb; Edwina Sandys, who has many muses and is mine; Lin Dreis, who wishes I would stop with the muses, already; and especially Hilary Kemper.

Winston Churchill

Introduction

The Rhetoric of Civilization

R. Crosby Kemper III

"Was greatly moved by your splendid speech." So Randolph Churchill telegraphed his father from Italy on May 8, 1945, after hearing Winston Churchill's radio address on the Allied victory in Europe. So have we all been moved—those of us fortunate enough to have heard most or all of the addresses published here which began their lives as Crosby Kemper Lectures on Churchill and His Times at Westminster College in Fulton, Missouri.

The lectures commemorate another splendid speech, the "Iron Curtain" speech delivered in Fulton in the Westminster Gymnasium on March 5, 1946—and before a world weary of war but confused about the uneasy peace created by constantly bickering allies.

It is a provoking curiosity of the world's attention to this speech, which did indeed reverberate around the world and far beyond Fulton, that the three newsreel companies covering it managed enough footage for a creditable reprise of the entire speech with one astounding exception: there is no film of the "Iron Curtain" section itself; the visible record of one of Churchill's most memorable, indeed epitomizing, moments is lost.

Yet in many ways it is found again and again as these lectures attest. Churchill's power with words has become legend. And no legend is more powerful or comes closer to the truth than that the "Iron Curtain" address alerted the world to the second great encounter between liberal democracy and totalitarian tyranny. Churchill's speech was a defining event in the history of the Cold War and perhaps the first event with world-changing consequences ever to take place in the state of Missouri. It was a defining moment in the history of a small liberal arts college whose sense of self and mission was forever changed on March 5, 1946. Before this probably the most reverberating event on the banks of Stinson Creek in central Missouri had been the publication of *King's Row,* a kind of prewar Peyton Place, whose fame as a small-town soap opera was enhanced by the film version starring Ronald Reagan in his best and most melodramatic role.

Small towns of Missouri, Kansas, Iowa, and Nebraska have sometimes been places where cultivation of the virtues has been corrupted by too inward a focus. The soul stagnates when the comings and goings of a small-town social hierarchy become that town's exclusive focus. In Henry Bellamann's novel one character escapes this fate by looking to Dr. Freud's Vienna for a doctoring of the soul and another character (played by Ronald Reagan in the movie) transcends his fate through suffering and tragedy. His soul grows in adversity by touching the light, deeply buried within, which when liberated leads him to become . . . a real estate developer!

Willa Cather looks at this world with greater artistry and chronicles many anguished journeys. The soul struggles, aspires and seeks for sustenance outside its little world. One thinks of Captain Forrester, in Cather's great novel *A Lost Lady.* He is a railroad builder who is once "greatly taken" with a hilltop overlooking the Sweet Water River. Planting a willow tree to mark it he returns many years later with his bride to find his willow tree and build his house. The house becomes something of a shrine to the character of this good man. And here is how he describes it and his life to his friends.

> My philosophy is that what you think of and plan for day by day, in spite of yourself, so to speak . . . you will get it more or less. . . . *Because a thing that is dreamed of in the way I mean, is already an accomplished fact.* All our West has been developed from such dreams; the homesteader's and the prospector's and the contractor's.

We dream the railroads across the mountains just as I dreamed my
place on the Sweet Water. All these things will be everyday facts to
the coming generation. . . .

Even on the prairie there are places that are the products of our thoughts
and dreams. Invested with enough of the romance of our dreams they will
come to represent for future generations the ideas behind those dreams.

It was, then, with pleasant surprise that I found myself approached by
President Harvey Saunders and Jack Marshall of Westminster College to
join in supporting a mission of the college that appeared to an outsider
to be resolutely anglophile, international and traditional in serving up the
history and literature of the West and celebrating one of its twentieth-
century giants, Winston S. Churchill.

The landscape around Stinson Creek and the small hill where sits the
campus of Westminster College is pleasant but undistinguished. That is
until one comes up Westminster Avenue from the creek and sees the
spire of St. Mary Aldermanbury. St. Mary Aldermanbury! Christopher
Wren in Missouri! Christopher Wren wrought a small masterpiece in
1677 in the city of London, in the wake of London's great fire of 1666.
Eighty-seven parish churches were destroyed by the five-day fire that
started in a baker's shop on Pudding Lane. Though it took eleven years
to accomplish, St. Mary rose from the ashes—and not for the last time.
Again substantially destroyed in the blitz during World War II, it was
slated to be razed by the London County Council, this last of England's
Christian soldiers to crumble and die, victim of the Nazi terror bombing
of London.

But there were those who saw a great opportunity in this. Trustees and
friends of Westminster, led by Neal Wood, supported by President Larry
Davidson, raised funds to prevent the razing of St. Mary. And so they
raised a church in the foothills of Missouri that was to be a memorial to
Winston S. Churchill and to the great friendship between two English-
speaking peoples and to a transforming event. They restored the church
stone by stone, with love and determination. And when they finished they
had transferred a little of the soul of the city of London and Christopher
Wren and Winston S. Churchill to Fulton, Missouri.

The beauty of the memorial, the liberal arts mission at the college, and my own belief in the historical and *moral* importance of Churchill's speech led me to propose this lecture series to my father. Then, as now, chairman of the largest bank holding company in Kansas City, Missouri, a reader, a civic leader, a lover of the fine arts and of the history, traditions, and landscape of his native state, my father was sure to respond as I had to the idea of honoring Churchill, the principles behind the Iron Curtain speech, and the men and women who built the memorial.

Honoring also the man who invited Churchill, whose presence at Fulton and whose ultimate agreement with the message given there led to the first decisive victories of the West in the battle with its new enemy. Harry Truman had his first political experience attending the 1900 Democratic National Convention in Kansas City as a guest of my great grandfather W. T. Kemper when he was sixteen. At age eighteen, his first job was as a clerk for W. T.'s Commerce Trust Company. He worked in the basement office, was mistreated by his immediate supervisor, and did not last long. Otherwise, he might have made a fine banker—for, like Churchill, Truman was a great judge of men's character.

Like Churchill and like my father, Truman could judge the virtues but, more importantly, he exemplified them. Crosby Kemper Jr. likes to say there was no prouder moment in his career as a banker than when Harry S. Truman named him, or rather the bank (though that has been much the same thing for thirty years or so), trustee of his estate. Truman was an angry partisan when my father abandoned his Democratic roots and ran for the U.S. Senate as a Republican in 1962. W. T. Kemper had been Democratic National Committeeman from Missouri for many years and a close friend of Jim Farley. Crosby Kemper Sr.'s younger brother, W. T. Jr., had been Truman's senate campaign treasurer much as Crosby Jr. was later a treasurer for Senator Stuart Symington. The apostasy led to harsh words and estrangement.

Thus there was surprise as well as pride in his heart when my father was invited to the Truman Library oval office in Independence to discuss the terms of Truman's estate. When he was ushered into the oval office, Truman was nowhere to be seen. While looking around the room, he heard the rumble of rushing water and Truman popped out of a door disguised in the wall. He was drying his hands and as he looked up he said, "Crosby, it's the one God damn thing you can't delegate."

Churchill, Truman, the Iron Curtain speech, an elegant, awe-inspiring Wren church, and the liberal arts in a small Missouri town: it was irresistible to associate our family name with this honored, even glorious, concatenation of virtues. I knew my father would leap at the chance to sponsor a lecture series likely to celebrate and exemplify the virtues, for it would celebrate and exemplify Churchill.

And for one moment of filial piety, just and true, let me celebrate the man who exemplifies the virtues to me. It is originally a Greek notion that man's highest existence comes in seeking excellence, seeking what is truly essentially good in each activity of mind and body. I have known three men, in varying degrees of intimacy, who have seemed to live in such a spirit, William F. Buckley, Brendan Gill, and my father. They have each in my presence made of the moment a world and found in the world its soul. It is my father whose nobility of heart and soul speaks most deeply to me and to the community in which I live. He has had the courage to fight for his convictions in the political and civic arenas, without regard to which side the big battalions are on. He has sought justice for the weak when it would have been easier and more profitable to do otherwise. He has run for the Senate, built a museum, and developed a bank all on the principle of encouraging the best. Like Churchill he can be immovable in seeking that which is just, but is always magnanimous after the battle, win or lose. He always remembers the principles for which he fought and forgets the injury done him in the fight. As we both grow older, more and more I see the wisdom of living life on one's own terms or as one of his favorite Victorians has it.

It is today, and has been for a long time, unfashionable to speak of the soul in terms of Victorian piety. It seems Emersonian vapor or Hegelian hogwash. To establish a lecture series that seeks to celebrate a great soul's virtues would seem to foolishly stand athwart the zeitgeist. As the reader will forgive this son his filial piety, so will he and she excuse the piety of Lady Soames to her father and Edwina Sandys to her grandfather. They will be surprised, however, if they have not read her biography of her mother, at the eloquence with which Lady Soames describes Churchill's enthusiasm for commanding his daily life at Chartwell as he drained ponds, laid bricks, and sought for peace and hope in the light and color of his painting—making of the moment, a world.

Beyond these lovely moments there is more: "the nobler, larger view of life . . ." in which two words loom large: *duty* and *liberty.* Duty to one's country was at the core of Churchill's view of the world, and his great magnanimity to enemies, from the Boer War to World War II, in Parliament and abroad, had much to do with his empathy for men who felt and acted upon the same call.

There are no more moving lines in these lectures than Lady Soames's "I, too, see Winston Churchill with infinite pride and wonder as a hero-figure. For am I not an Englishwoman? Do I not cherish liberty more than life?" This is reminiscent of one of the last letters written by Lady Soames to her father—with which Martin Gilbert closes his magisterial biography: "In addition to all the feelings a daughter has for a loving, generous father, I owe you what every Englishman, woman and child does—Liberty itself."

Duty and Liberty, the great combination that England has given the world. It was Simone Weil who most memorably said as the first line of her program for the French Resistance in World War II, "Obligations precede rights." Rights indeed are founded in obligation, in duty, in the honor that guarantees, and will fight for, the charters, contracts, and covenants of men.

Churchill is the last great figure in a long line of British statesmen, extending back beyond Burke, but whose highest expression is found in Burke, who linked notions of freedom and responsibility. He saw the mission of the English-speaking peoples to be a great paternal spreading of the rule of law and its offspring, liberty. It was paternal in that it involved a Burkean concept of trusteeship and a Platonic concept of rule by the best.

His greatest failures as a politician in the 1930s, his opposition to the swift devolution of power in India and his defense of the King in the abdication crisis, were also the finest expressions of his idealism. They were failures largely because actions that Churchill himself found ignoble, British brutality in India and the private misbehavior of the King, put the legitimacy of the King-Emperor's crown in question, with no noble course on the horizon to resurrect it.

As three of our lecturers (Blake, Ziegler, and Rhodes James) have pointed out, Churchill pursued his opposition to the India policy of successive Labour, National, and Conservative party governments "to the bitter end." He ridiculed Dominion status for the subcontinent. He predicted that civil war would result from devolution. He accused Gandhi of being a "seditious Middle-Temple lawyer" and a "fakir." He saw the Congress Party as a western-trained, socialist-inspired, Brahmin elite that would rule with much greater partisanship than the British Raj ever had. As Rhodes James says, "He had debased the language of alarmism."

How did the master rhetorician become so "extreme" and "inflexible"? It has been suggested that these are merely the defects of his virtues (a romantic caricature of his ideas), that he was "truly in character" only when faced with the real evil of Hitler's Europe. While offering no opinion as to the inevitability or even the timing of the transfer of power in India, I would argue that too little attention has been given to the positive program of Churchill's ideas about India. Though there may be elements of a wispy, romantic paternalism born on the late Victorian battlefields of the Northwest Frontier there is also a notion of the Good, of justice and statesmanship that is consistently present in Churchill's attitude toward India, and that is at the core of the Churchillian character. These ideas are not the defects of his virtues but those virtues themselves at work in circumstances resistant to all virtue.

British legitimacy in India received its most serious blow, as Churchill recognized, not from failing to recognize or recognizing too swiftly, the Indian right to self government. Rather India began to be lost to the Empire in a true philosophical sense in April 1919 in an Indian city called Amritsar. There British General Dyer opened fire on an unarmed crowd killing nearly four hundred and wounding thousands more. As Churchill recognized in his July 8, 1920, speech, on the disciplining of General Dyer, it was "an extraordinary event, a monstrous event which stands in singular and sinister isolation." It was an outrage on the rule of law, and on the restraint that power must always show to maintain its legitimacy. Above all, Churchill said, the "British way of doing things," the "lawful authority" descending "from hand to hand and generation after generation" of the "venerable structure of the British empire is absolutely foreign to this kind of frightfulness."

The foundations of British power in India, the foundations of British imperial *legitimacy* in India were based on the "British way of doing things," which implied "cooperation and good will." It was not physical force that kept the British empire intact but moral force, the force of "civilization" as he quoted Macaulay; the "most frightful of all spectacles" is the "strength of civilization without its mercy."

These phrases about magnanimity and goodwill were in another context to become the watchwords of Churchillian greatness in the Second World War. In his distance from India (he never went back to the scenes of his youth on the Northwest Frontier) Churchill missed the moral force of Gandhi and the Congress Party, the moral force of nationalism on the Indian subcontinent. The frightfulness that he objected to in General Dyer's actions and predicted about the transfer of power did indeed come to pass when the British left India. Whether or not there was any true alternative as Churchill suggested there might be in a more federal India with a greater role for the Princes and a greater role for local authority is not my purpose to discover. I merely point out that like Burke, Churchill had a notion of trusteeship and civilizing mission whose core was resistance to any tyrannizing idea.

Churchill's empathy, the root of his magnanimity and goodwill, never ceased to be engaged with India. As postwar Prime Minister he received Prime Minister Nehru of India. After showing him to the door at the end of his visit Churchill was in tears; "we put that man in jail for years and he bears us no malice!"

At his best Churchill in his Indian speeches presented a vision of the goods of government as compelling as any of those from his youthful period as a reformer, the prewar prophecies on the tragic failures of the Europe of the dictators, or his great wartime addresses as Prime Minister. Churchill was ever the democrat and a believer in the virtues invested in the peoples of the English-speaking countries, but he was a firm believer (in Lord Blake's epitomizing phrase) in the difference between self-government and good government. He was wrong about the ability of the Indian political classes to perpetuate democracy after British withdrawal and wrong about the depth of Indian desire for a true rule of law, but right to assume that these were the questions to ask.

Throughout the 1920s and 1930s Churchill was concerned with the false utopias of both left and right, whether Mosley's brown-shirted imitation fascism or Labor's affiliation with the socialist international. "The British way of doing things" is a phrase that recurs. It is his shorthand for the virtues he admired and the ideal of good citizenship within an imperial, European, and Atlantic civilization that he believed in. In a speech of 1919 to a group interested in the idea of a center party built on the wartime Coalition government Churchill evoked the memory of his father, Randolph Churchill, and his notions of Tory Democracy. Lord Randolph had described this Tory Democracy as animated by "lofty and liberal ideas" taken by his son to mean mitigation of the "severities of a laissez-faire policy," a mitigation desired so that the party of order—then the Tories and now the Coalition—might maintain "the prestige necessary for the guidance of the people." Goodwill, expressed "not so much in principle as in the application of principle," is to be contrasted with the Bolsheviks' "most wonderful utopian ideals" and their "most wicked behavior."

> We must recognize that good citizenship must be the foundation of a good, well-organized State. With good men in decent homes, working hard, doing their duty, being anxious to give something to their country, or town, or village, or their fellow-men, it is on a basis of citizenship of that kind and of that order rather than in the mere formulation of fantastic idealism that the safety, the health, and the glory of nations reside. . . .

Here Churchill echoes Burke in the unity of ends and means, in the rejection of the fantastic and notional in favor of the customs of British civility. The ideal starts in the little platoons of good men in decent homes doing their duty in family, town, and village first. This is the "common inheritance and . . . common purpose." It begins in obligation and ends in duty. Churchill would feel in 1931 about Indians, in 1939 about the Poles, in 1940 about the French, in 1944 about the Greeks, in 1946 about the Iranians as he felt about his fellow Englishmen in 1919: "we are the trustees for the whole people of this island . . . it is a sacred trust."

Churchill's speeches touched mysterious chords in the hearts of so many in World War II because of this consistent—*insistent*—return to principle. Much as Burke in his great speech on Fox's East India Bill traced the descent into the cave of politics, the East India Company's descent into a "plentitude of despotism, tyranny and corruption," under a trust derived from Parliament. As the ultimate cause of the evil Parliament must be responsible for redress. "All political power . . . being wholly artificial [and] a derogation from the natural equality of mankind . . . ought to be . . . exercised ultimately for their benefit . . . in the strictest sense a *trust* . . . [we cannot] passively bear with oppressions committed under the sanction of our own authority."

For Burke the rights of men "affirmed and declared by express covenants" are "positive engagements" against power and authority. Burke said, and Churchill echoed, "The very essence of every trust [is] to be rendered accountable."

Richard Weaver, the rhetorician and moralist, once wrote to a student: "Rhetoric is compulsive speech having to do with the human condition. A rhetoric without some vision of the order of the goods is actually a contradiction in terms . . . this is a world of action and history, and . . . all policies involve the choosing between better and worse." In his magnificent essay, "The *Phaedrus* and the Nature of Rhetoric," the best I know on the subject, Weaver says there are really only three affects of language: "it can move us toward what is good; it can move us toward what is evil; or it can . . . fail to move us at all." The Western democracies, including America, were led by those embodying the last type, a "rhetoricless," "emasculated," businesslike group of calculators. They were no match for Hitler because Hitler knew, as Churchill knew, as Plato in the *Gorgias* and the *Phaedrus* and Aristotle in the *Rhetoric* knew, that men are not moved without passion, and passion without the good is incoherent. World War II was (in Weaver's formulation) a "contest for souls which the nobler won. But the contest could have been lost by default."

Churchill's greatness, like Hitler's evil genius, lay in the power of words. These words moved and brought in response movement of whole nations and peoples. Churchill affected after the war that he was only the roar of the lion. But he was more. As John Lukacs, in one of the best books written about 1940, *The Duel,* has said, "Ideas matter only when men incarnate them," and hence "the fascination of this duel, which was, of course a duel of minds." As Lukacs says, Churchill understood "that words are not merely the symbols of things; they are the symbols of meanings."

He quotes Metternich's distinction between idea and principle, saying: "a categorical idea is like a fixed gun. It is dangerous for those who stand or move along the line of its trajectory. Principles, on the other hand, may be compared to a gun that can turn around and fire at untruth in every direction." Churchill had no Leninist or German romanticist Philosophy of History. There were no fantasies of capitalist or Jewish conspiracies, no inevitabilities beyond influence of men, and very few demons. His quality of empathy saw even in the war, even in Hitler, tragic humanity, the fallen angel in Lucifer.

Both Hitler and Churchill had visions of epic quality but where Hitler's was Götterdämmerung Wagnerian, anti-Semitic, fanatic, shrill, and based on resentment, Churchill's had the quality of coherence available only to someone with "feeling for and fidelity to the great tradition for which he assumes a personal responsibility, a tradition that he bears upon his shoulders and must deliver embellished . . . to successors worthy of accepting the sacred burden," as Isaiah Berlin puts it so eloquently. It is Winston Churchill in our century who has had the courage to say that some things are worth fighting for not because they are German or British, inevitable or rational, but because they are good.

It would be a shock today to hear a politician defend "a specific world order" (Isaiah Berlin's words, again) and call it civilization, as Churchill did in 1938 in an address as Chancellor to the University of Bristol, or to hear him contrast the inheritance of freedom "bequeathed by valiant men," the rule of law, love of country, goodwill between classes, to tyranny and arbitrary power and to talk of the collapse of right principles without the "qualities of civic virtue and manly courage" to support them. It seems a quaint return to the age of chivalry when Churchill contrasts these British ideals with the gnostic "non-God religions" of the dictators of the Right and the Left.

What is striking about the "non-God religions" of Communism and Nazism is "their similarity. They substitute the Devil for God and hatred for love." Hitler, Stalin, and Mao based their religions on hatred, raised in a soil of peasant and lower-middle-class resentment. Churchill based his chivalric ethic upon love, love of the character of the people he led, love of the mission he felt they had in the world, love of their inherited traditions of the law and liberty. Churchill portrayed himself as a man of action and a realist politician, but he had read Plato and Aristotle along with his Gibbon and Macaulay in the barrack rooms on the Northwest Frontier of India. "A man's life," he said, "must be nailed to a cross of Thought or Action." But in him there was a harmony of the two. About his "socratic moods" he spoke with irony but not without truth.

Richard Weaver says, again in his essay on *Phaedrus,* "a term of policy is essentially a term of motion, and here begins the congruence of rhetoric with the soul which underlies the speculation of the Phaedrus . . . motion . . . is part of the soul's essence . . . terms of tendency—goodness, justice, divinity, and the like—are terms of motion and therefore may be said to comport with the soul's essence. . . . education of the soul is not a process of bringing it into correspondence with a physical structure like the external world, but rather a process of rightly affecting its motion."

Hobbes's *Leviathan* is the classical location of the notion of education in the body politic as an attempt to achieve correspondence with the physical motion of the world. Its heirs from Locke to the present include the various scientisms of the seventeenth century, sensationalist psychology of the eighteenth century, the various materialisms and monisms of the nineteenth century, and all those academic theories from Nietzsche to Foucault that seek to reduce history to a history of power and philosophy to a description of its hidden mechanism; and to all those materialists from Mach to Edward Wilson who seek a basic movement of atoms or genes or race or will to explain the world.

In the *Phaedrus* Socrates says of Pericles that he was the greatest and most complete speaker who has ever lived because he studied the nature of things with the philosopher Anaxagoras; he studied the nature and excellence of the soul. The purpose of speech, says Socrates, is to influence the soul. But first the nature of the soul must be ascertained. The key words are *truth* and *nobility;* they define the soul. There is a circular argument here, perhaps *the* circular philosophical argument. The soul cannot be influenced without direct knowledge of its truth and yet the influence of speech is what moves the soul to be just and true. Plato rescues us from paradox with poetry. Allegory in the poetic mode from the cave myth of the *Republic* to the charioteer in the *Phaedrus* is the way to Plato's full truth. The Charioteer holds the noble horse and the wild horse together to move the chariot. Perhaps the horses are mind and body or divine truth and human truth, reason and passion. Whichsoever, what moves *us* in Plato's myths of the chariot-soul or the soul-slave moving out of its cave in the *Republic* (which had power in Churchill's universe) is the vision of the soul's struggle and the need for and difficulty in achieving the soul's truth—such difficulty that Socrates says at the end of the *Phaedrus* that he is not a wise man but, simply, a lover of wisdom.

And so Winston Spencer Churchill was a lover of wisdom. As Isaiah Berlin sums him up:

> The Prime Minister was able to impose his imagination and his will upon his countrymen, and enjoy a Periclean reign, precisely because he appeared to them larger and nobler than life and lifted them to an abnormal height in a moment of crisis. . . . [He] did turn a large number of inhabitants of the British Isles out of their normal selves, and by dramatizing their lives and making them seem to themselves and to each other clad in the fabulous garments appropriate to a great historic moment, transformed cowards into brave men and so filled the purpose of shining armor. . . . Churchill's unique and unforgettable achievement was that he created this necessary illusion within the framework of a free system without destroying or even twisting it; that he called forth spirits which did not stay to oppress and enslave the population after the hour of need had passed.

Winston Churchill was a truer student of Socrates than his actual student, Alcibiades, the follower who was too much in love with physical love in *The Symposium* and too much in love with the unreal fantastic utopia of the Sicilian expedition.

In the second volume of his memoirs of the Second World War, Churchill describes the discordant scenes leading up to his assumption of the leadership. It was a close-run thing. India and the abdication, a history of strong antisocialist rhetoric and antistrike action left him vulnerable to attacks by partisans of both major parties. But the strength of his rhetorical presence was undeniable. Even during the darkest days of the 1930s Austen Chamberlain had written to Baldwin, the Conservative leader, that Churchill waited in the wings to become the prime minister. It is now a universal assumption that Churchill was kept from power in the thirties because of his extremism, intemperate language, and overly developed egotism. On the contrary, he was kept from power because his speeches increasingly identified him as the only possible alternative to the shams of appeasement.

In writing of his accession to power Churchill ended his chapter with the much-quoted dictum, "facts are better than dreams." Rarely, for him, Churchill was just off. The fact of his becoming Prime Minister, of his being in the unique position to unite the British—indeed the West— was the consequence of his dreams, the great vision of law and freedom handed down as a way of doing things over generations to a people blessed by their past and ready to defend the common inheritance against the common danger.

Churchill's own sense of what was noble is revealed in his rhetoric in the great war speeches. Two remarkable facts stand out as we read them fifty years on: They look backward every bit as much as they look forward and they are full of a kind of tragic grandeur and simplicity—achieved through an unblinking assessment of the failure of arms and overwhelming might of the enemy coupled with the deep belief in the rightness of the cause.

As Aristotle said, history is what Alcibiades did and suffered. Pericles said as much in his great funeral oration, which like Churchill's speeches, is at its strongest when explaining to Athenians why sacrifice is worthwhile— why in a good cause it is equally good to live or die.

They gave their lives for the common good and thereby won for themselves the praise that never grows old, but where their glory remains in eternal memory, always there at the right time to inspire speech and action. For the whole world is a burial place of famous men . . . the unwritten memory . . . of their spirit . . . lives on within each person. Now it is for you to emulate them; knowing that happiness requires freedom and freedom requires courage.

Churchill in 1938 at Bristol had described civilization as "freedom, comfort, and culture." This version of happiness is what free men fight for and why "the eternal memory" of the deeds of the "happy few" were so important an inspiration to the fundamental virtue of courage.

The great speeches of 1940 are remarkable for their frank discussion of the collapse of the French, the failure in Norway, and the triumph throughout Europe of the Nazis. In the midst of the Battle of Britain with Hitler's invasion forces gathering on the other side of the Channel, Churchill gave one of his great speeches (September 11, 1940). He did not avoid the description of the "cruel, wanton, indiscriminant bombings of London," which were "killing large numbers of civilians, and women and children."

But he asserted that Hitler did not know

the spirit of the British nation, or the tough fiber of the Londoners, whose forebears played a leading part in the establishment of Parliamentary institutions and who have been bred to value freedom far above their lives. This wicked man, the repository and embodiment of many forms of soul-destroying hatred, this monstrous product of former wrongs and shame, has now resolved to try to break our famous Island race by a process of indiscriminate slaughter. . . . What he has done is to kindle a fire in British hearts, here and all over the world, which will glow long after all traces of the conflagration he has caused in London have been removed. He has lighted a fire which will burn with a steady and consuming flame until the last vestiges of Nazi tyranny have been burnt out of Europe, and until the Old World—and the New—can join hands to rebuild the temples of man's freedom and man's honor upon foundations which will not soon or easily be overthrown.

These are days, Churchill said, that will rank with those when England opposed the Spanish Armada, or when Nelson stood between England and Napoleon's grand army. He looked to the past and his phraseology— "Let God defend the right," "every man will therefore prepare himself to do his duty"—all looks back to the glorious days of Queen Elizabeth or Wellington and Waterloo and Queen Victoria, before it looks forward to the "long and better days that are to come." And it looks backward and forward through "the heart of suffering."

Hitler perceptively said of Churchill that he was a man of the sixteenth century. The great movements of Churchill's rhetoric are to look back and show that the past has glories worth defending, to look into the heart of suffering and to find there something worth suffering for, and finally to paint a picture of "the broad sunlit uplands" that will seem a fine resting place for virtues so strenuously exerted.

There are echoes in Churchill's speeches of the great moments and the great speeches of England's past. His famous August 20, 1940, reference to the RAF—"never in the field of human conflict was so much owed by so many to so few"—shows the undisguised influence of the great St. Crispin's Day speech from Shakespeare's *Henry V*, "We few, we happy few, we band of brothers." Defiance in defeat seems hardly a modern concept: "Death and ruin have become small things compared with the shame of defeat . . . we are sure of ourselves and of our cause and that is the supreme fact . . ." is surely Victorian, perhaps classical. Admitting to the "cataract of disaster," to an entire "period of horror and disaster," Churchill quotes the Victorian poet and tells his fellow islanders they are still "masters of our fate . . . with the conviction of final victory burning unquenchable in our hearts." Never have defiance and resolution had a more powerful expression.

The Iron Curtain speech is often credited with inaugurating the Cold War. I would suggest that it did more than that: It was directly responsible for the first and most important victory in the Cold War. Churchill, the master rhetorician of the twentieth century, faced with a spiritual scene of great confusion in which a seemingly irresistible movement of the historical forces of international socialism was triumphing throughout Eastern Europe, in Asia, and in the heart of Western Europe itself, saw the "common danger" to our inheritance in the totalitarian ideas of the Left just as he had those of the right in the thirties. And the forceful movement of Churchill's rhetoric was itself the key weapon in our first victory of the Cold War.

Harry Truman's personal invitation to Winston Churchill was a handwritten note on a more formal invitation from President Franc McCluer of Westminster. The source of this invitation was Harry Vaughan, Westminster alumnus, veteran of World War I, and military aide to the president. He had brought McCluer to Truman's office in October 1945.

There was no geopolitical strategy in Truman's invitation. Eight months after assuming the presidency, Truman was still in a quandary about the direction of the grand alliance of the United States, Great Britain, and the Soviet Union. New Deal leftists like Henry Wallace and Harold Ickes were still a powerful part of the cabinet. James Byrnes had yet to achieve any definite strategic direction as secretary of state. Joseph Davies, Joseph Kennedy, and others were forceful advocates for either pro-Soviet or anti-British points of view. The State Department was a hive of conflicting voices. Though never as deeply charmed as was Roosevelt, Truman still felt he could handle "Uncle Joe" Stalin on a one-to-one basis. The Russian police state methods in Eastern Europe were unsettling to the administration. But there was also strong anti-imperialist, and therefore anti-British, sentiment as well. Walter Lippmann perhaps best expressed the current of opinion among those who considered themselves the foreign policy elite when he wrote Byrnes:

> I have been more disturbed about the conduct of our own policy than I have thought expedient . . . to say in print. Though the issue here has apparently been drawn between the Soviets and ourselves, this alignment is not inherent in the nature of things but is due to inexperience and emotional instability in our own delegation. There is a far deeper conflict of interest between the British and the Soviets than between the USA and the Soviets, but we have allowed ourselves

> to be placed in the position where instead of being the moderating
> power which holds the balance, we have become the chief protagonists
> of the anti-Soviet position.

Lippmann was referring to the disputes at the San Francisco Conference over the seating of the Polish delegation—in effect the question was
whether one of the first official acts of the United Nations would be to
ratify the Soviet conquest of Poland. Why the British should have a greater
interest in preserving a truly democratic and plural Poland than the U.S.
cannot be made clear in retrospect.

From Potsdam in July 1945 through the London Conference of Foreign
Ministers in September to the similar Moscow meeting in December, more
issues arose to challenge the harmony of the Allies than were resolved
around the conference table. The arrest of prominent Poles when they
returned to Warsaw (they were put on trial in July), the consolidation of
one-party police-state government in Hungary, Bulgaria, and Rumania,
made a mockery of the Yalta Agreement that had promised democratic
self-government to liberated Eastern Europe. The Soviets for their part
protested Churchill's intervention in the Greek civil war in December
1944 (though Stalin adhered to his October 1944 "percentages" deal with
Churchill that had left Greece to Britain's sphere). With many in the West,
the Soviets called for an internationalization of atomic energy, essentially
demanding that the United States and Great Britain share with them their
knowledge of nuclear weapons. Churchill was defeated at the polls in the
midst of the Potsdam conference and came home from there to hand over
the seals of office to Clement Attlee and the new foreign secretary, Ernest
Bevin. Like Truman and Byrnes—who became secretary of state in June—
they had spent most of their careers dealing with domestic politics and
most of the war ignorant of the inner secrets of Allied diplomacy, the
development of the atomic bomb, and planning for the postwar world.

At the beginning of 1946 all four men were still in search of a principle
to guide the postwar world. Each sought a way to preserve either the
wartime coalition or unilateral relations with each of the other allies. Both
the United States and Great Britain were convinced that each other *and*
the Soviets were being unreasonably aggressive, even imperialist in their

self-interested diplomacy of demand and counter-demand. There was an implied moral equivalence in this that led to expressions like Bevin's after the London conference. He called down "a plague on both houses" of Russia and the United States for wanting to divide the world into spheres of influence. That his own Foreign Office was using the same language hardly seemed to register even as an irony to him.

On November 7, 1945, Winston Churchill delivered his second House of Commons speech since the end of the war in Europe. He welcomed Truman's statement that the United States would hold the secrets of the atom bomb as "a sacred trust for humanity" and maintain its strength and involvement in the world. Churchill hoped that Britain would make her own bombs and renew the Anglo-American alliance as the best safeguard for peace; the only hope against "those deep uncontrollable anxieties that another war was preparing" would be "a solemn covenant backed by force." The press—the *Times* of London and the *Manchester Guardian*, particularly—was deeply unimpressed and called, on the contrary, for renewed Anglo-*Soviet* ties.

Ernest Bevin's reply to Churchill's speech and the House of Commons debate was a surprise to the Left in Britain. "Sometimes in these negotiations I make the confession that power politics seemed to me to be naked and unashamed; the next moment you are searching and striving for the other ideal." This is in great contrast to much of the Left such as Clement Davies, the leader of the Liberal Party who was upset at Churchill's realism and said that for his part he hoped there would "be talk only of permanent peace, mutual understanding and mutual aid." Bevin advocated to the contrary: "put the cards on the table face upwards. Our planning, our arrangements in economics and defense must be such that we are ready to stop aggression should the occasion arise." When he had finished what was essentially an endorsement of Churchill's position, Bevin found that the Tories were cheering and that Labour's benches were silent. The *Manchester Guardian* said, "It is not the speech that many Labour members would have liked to hear"; indeed, they "felt chilled" by it.

As Truman and Attlee, Byrnes and Bevin were trying to find their footing the situation in Iran came to a crisis. In 1941 Great Britain, and the Soviets had demanded the expulsion of the thousands of German troops who were in virtual occupation of Teheran. When Iran failed to comply with these demands the Allies invaded and with a minimal loss of life took control of the oil fields and the routes in and out of the Trans-Caucasus. In January 1942, at the urging of the United States, which had been embarrassed by the raw use of imperial power, the Soviet Union, Great Britain, and Iran signed the Tripartite Treaty that guaranteed Iran's independence and domestic authority while dividing the country into spheres of influence. The removal of all troops was to happen six months after the end of the war.

This was the second time in the twentieth century that Iran had, in effect, been partitioned. In 1907 Tsarist Russia and the British Empire signed a convention which partitioned Persia into zones of political and economic influence. The Russians got the north which bordered on Russian Azerbaijan and the British got the southwest which included the oil fields later necessary for the British navy. The Anglo-Russian humiliation of Iran in 1907 helped bring Reza Shah Pahlavi to power. When the second partition came in the forties, the humiliation likewise drove him from the throne in favor of his young son, Mohammad Reza Pahlavi, a tenacious, modernizing nationalist like his father. When the war in Europe ended the son demanded that the Allies adhere to the treaty and depart.

In the period leading up to Yalta, Eden and Churchill saw the future of Iran as, in Churchill's words, "something of a test case." Eden proposed that Allied troops begin withdrawal from Iran before the end of the war as supply routes for lend-lease activity into the Soviet Union and for oil to the West were no longer in military danger. The Soviets refused to discuss the situation.

On May 19, 1945, after the end of the war in Europe the Iranians requested the withdrawal of Allied troops. The entire Northern Tier, as it was called, Greece, Turkey, and Iran, was in dispute. The British had stepped in in December 1944 to stop a civil war between monarchists and the communist-dominated forces of the Left. Although Stalin had agreed to a preponderance of British influence in Greece, he and his foreign minister, Molotov, nonetheless made as much propaganda as they could about that intervention. Against Turkey, the Russians were massing troops, lending support to Kurds and Armenians, and making significant territorial demands on the northeastern border. While also supporting separatist movements of Kurds and Azerbaijanis they accused the British of interfering in the domestic affairs of Greece, Turkey, and Iran.

There were inconclusive discussions about these issues at Potsdam in July and at the London Council of Foreign Ministers in September, but the Americans did not yet know what their position was or indeed if they wanted to have a position outside of their traditional opposition to spheres of influence. And the British were in the midst of a transition from the Conservative to the Labour Party government. And, in any case, it was not yet clear whether the Russians intended to annex, to influence, or to withdraw.

By December 1945 the Soviets had demonstrated their intentions. They had begun the Cold War in Iran. The question was put to Truman and Byrnes and Bevin and Attlee, what kind of men were they: career politicians who would continue to accept the words of bad faith from Stalin and Molotov and Vyshinsky at conference after conference? Would they let Iran go as they had the Poles, the Hungarians, and the Rumanians? Was occupation by Soviet troops tantamount to Soviet conquest?

Harry Truman, who has come down to us as Give 'Em Hell Harry, as the decisive commander who sanctioned the Marshall Plan, gave us the Truman Doctrine and the Berlin Airlift, had yet to decide what he thought about the Soviets or how he would deal with the world. He needed a shock of recognition. Rhetoric is sometimes seen as the mere pageantry of words. Yet it was Churchill's rhetoric, in the Iron Curtain speech, that turned Truman around, and Bevin, Byrnes, and Attlee as well. It was Churchill's speech that caused Stalin to back down from his attempt to violate the treaties he had signed over Iran. A different but equally deep recognition transformed him—the recognition of Winston Churchill's defiance, of his courage and his sudden power over the West. In the midst of the West's faltering indecisiveness came Churchill's call. And in the image of the world dividing on two sides of an iron curtain, both sides clearly recognized themselves. American and British leaders recognized this picture of the world as true and heard the call to become their better selves.

Disappearances of political leaders, expropriation of landowners, the rising tide of nationalist propaganda began to look like a familiar pattern, that of Eastern Europe. In addition to the Communist Tudeh Party itself, a man named Ja'afar Pishevari had founded the Democratic Party of Azerbaijan. Pishevari had served the Soviets before as minister of the interior in the short-lived Republic of Gilan in 1921, a product of the Soviet invasion of Iran, and as a representative of the Comintern in the thirties and into the forties. The purpose of the party was to take advantage of the noncommunist opposition to the Shah and his centralizing, modernizing government in Teheran. The Soviet occupation forces distributed arms in Azerbaijan and in Iranian Kurdistan.

The Soviet army turned back troops sent by the Shah from Teheran to quell the disturbances. Border posts between the Soviet Union and Iran were taken down. On December 15, independence movements were declared in both Tabriz, the capital of Azerbaijan, and Mahabad, the capital of the Iranian Kurds. The Iranian army chief of staff asked British Ambassador Bullard if he would fulfill the treaty obligations of the Allies and defend Iran's independence. "We are not going to declare war on Russia for that" was his crushing reply.

At the same time, Molotov, Bevin, and Byrnes, the three Allied foreign ministers, were meeting at the second postwar conference of foreign ministers. Like Potsdam, and the London conference, this meeting displayed the strategic incoherence of the British and Americans. While their own troops were leaving Iran and the Soviets were pushing the familiar scenario (familiar from Poland, Bulgaria, Rumania, Hungary, and the Baltic States) of encouraging subversion of the established government, bringing armed force to bear, and putting out propaganda about their support for democratic and popular movements, the United States and Great Britain made representations to the Soviets and sent protest notes but continued to withdraw and demobilize.

In Moscow on December 15, the same day that Soviet-sponsored governments were thrust on Tabriz and Mahabad, both Byrnes and Bevin had interviews with Stalin. They presented protests over the continuing occupation of northern Iran. Stalin stated his intentions to be peaceful, to honor obligations, and to continue to cooperate with the British and the Americans. But in each conversation he left open a series of loopholes: he talked in traditional Russian great power terms about the defense of the oil fields of Baku (implying a need for buffer zones inside Azerbaijani Iran), he continued to allude to the 1921 Soviet-Persian Treaty with its implied spheres of influence, concessions, and right of Soviet intervention. Stalin and Molotov attacked British involvement in Greece and continued to press for bases in the Straits between the Black Sea and the Mediterranean, and bases in the Mediterranean itself, implying a series of quid pro quos. Bevin, still new and innocent of Stalin's way of negotiating, proposed a three-power commission to work things out (he had apparently not learned that lesson from the Balkans yet). Byrnes, sensing Soviet intransigence and like the old war horse politician he was, bent on achieving consensus, abandoned the subject altogether when he realized the unlikelihood of reaching an agreement. When he returned to the United States on December 27, he used a national radio broadcast—without the approval of President Truman—to announce Allied unity at the conference on all major issues. One of the great moments of wishful thinking in the history of diplomacy, this was the beginning of the end for Byrnes with Harry Truman.

Truman himself was unclear about what to do, though he had encouraged Ambassador Harriman's strong posture in Moscow and wrote a memorandum to Byrnes upon his return from the December conference whose key sentences were "I do not think we should play compromise any longer. . . . I'm tired babying the Soviets." His pre–Iron Curtain desire to please and ability to empathize was so great, Dean Acheson would later write, "I have never heard him say, or heard of him saying a harsh, bitter, or sarcastic word to anyone whatever the offense or failure." Henry Wallace, his secretary of commerce, had also said, "He so likes to agree with whoever is with him at the moment." Truman's reputation for toughness would be earned over the next few months, not only in his dealings with Stalin, but also with his Cabinet. We shall see this at work in Fulton and after. Time, Stalin, and Churchill helped focus United States policy.

The confusion of the West was resolved by two speeches. On February 9, Stalin gave his election address to the Supreme Soviet. This was the first Soviet election since 1937 and, as such, a moment of high philosophical comedy: the Russian voter was presented with a single list of Party-endorsed candidates, including a substantial number of Secret Police (in 1937 twenty-six out of thirty-three provincial police chiefs). The results were encouraging: in 1937 the Party list had received 98.6 percent of the votes, and in 1946 it received 99.18 percent.

"Comrades," he said, "our Soviet system has won." The wartime identification with the great Russian past of Peter and Alexander was abandoned in the moment of triumph. The heroic sacrifices of the Allies and his fellow Russians were not credited with victory but the Soviet state, "a form of organization superior to all others," and its victory were, like the war itself, "the inevitable result of the development of world economic and political forces on the basis of modern monopoly capitalism."

"The development of world capitalism takes place, not as a smooth and even advance, but through crisis and war." Fascism, the careful reader of Stalin knew, was simply one of the last crisis stages of monopoly capitalism. The "superior organization" would not only overtake but "surpass the achievements of science beyond the boundaries of our country." The speech was a celebration of the "material possibilities" of the nation as utilized by the Communist Party in the collectivization of land, the production of steel, iron, and coal, the production of guns, tanks, and aircraft, and the construction of scientific institutes. Stalin concluded on an ominous note: "Our Party intends to organize a powerful new upsurge of the national economy. . . . Only under such conditions can we regard ourselves as guaranteed against any eventualities."

It is possible to read this speech in several ways. Truman himself said that "we all have to demagogue a little sometimes." Secretary of Commerce Henry Wallace thought Stalin was "merely taking up the challenge" of the American military (an American military halfway to the most dramatic demobilization in history). Byrnes thought the speech "a shock" and Secretary of the Navy Forrestal was convinced that "there is no way in which Democracy and Communism can live together."

There were those at the time, and historians since, who have seen the speech variously as boilerplate, as a realistic Great Russian program for defense, and as the declaration of the Cold War. Le Monde in Paris said it was a "great speech which . . . will inspire all who desire to participate in the speedy advance to Socialism."

Socialism in our time is so begrimed by the bureaucratic parodies of the police states collapsed or collapsing around us that it is difficult to remember how bedazzling the advance of socialism seemed at the end of the war. Czeslaw Milosz has perhaps best described it in his *The Captive Mind*. The inevitability of what Stalin called in his speech "the material possibilities" took on an almost apocalyptic finality. Churchill in a conversation with the Canadian Prime Minister Mackenzie-King in October 1945 described it as "Jesuits without Jesus . . . any means to gain an end. That end being the end of Christianity, of Christian purposes. They were realists in the extreme." This was true, he said, because "Communism is a religion," the religion of "the realist lizards."

Churchill embarked for the United States on January 7. While on board ship he finished the section of the history of the English-speaking peoples that dealt with the Hundred Years' War. While the wartime speeches echoed the great speeches at Harfleur and Agincourt of Shakespeare's *Henry V,* Churchill's real sympathy was with the great opponent of the English, Joan of Arc. Far from the "hollow empire" of Henry V with its wasteful search for military glory was her noble simplicity, from which "the whole conception of France seems to have sprung and radiated. . . . She embodied the natural goodness and valor of the human race in an unexampled perfection. Unconquerable courage, infinite compassion, the virtue of the simple, the wisdom of the just shone forth in her. She glorifies as she freed the soil from which she sprang. All soldiers should read her story and ponder on the words and deeds of the true warrior."

When Winston Churchill arrived in Washington on February 10, after a visit in Florida, there was need of these qualities. The dispatches from Tabriz of the new Vice-consul Robert Rossow made for unpleasant reading. Pishevari had declared, on the same day as Stalin's election speech, that he was creating an army through conscription and would ask Muslim leaders to embark on a Holy War against the government in Teheran. A speech by Lavrenti Beria, Stalin's police chief, on February 6, implying a plot to attack the Soviet Union in the Trans-Caucasus combined with Stalin's February 9 vision of the inevitable clash of capitalism and the Soviet state, set an ominous background for what Robert Rossow saw in Tabriz. Russian troops, equipped with offensive weapons such as tanks and artillery, newly captained by Marshal Bagramian, one of the most successful and toughest of Stalin's generals, were moving toward Teheran.

Meanwhile the Shah and his staunch representative in the United States Hassan Ala and his representative at the UN Sayid Hassan Taqizadeh were requesting action against Soviet violation of Iranian sovereignty in the Security Council. This was done over the initial objections of the British and with only lukewarm support of former secretary of state and U.S. delegate Edward R. Stettinius Jr. at the UN and Byrnes in Washington. The new Prime Minister of Iran, the elderly Ahmad Qavam, hitherto thought to be an appeaser and perhaps subject to venal interests, sacked the pro-British Chief of the Iranian general staff and pushed Taqizadeh to continue to seek Security Counsel intervention.

Into the middle of this cauldron Churchill dropped the first draft of the Iron Curtain speech. Mimeographs of the speech were read by Admiral Leahy, Truman's chief of staff and chief military adviser, by Secretary Byrnes himself, and by Lord Halifax, the British Ambassador. Halifax unsuccessfully sought to tone down the aggressiveness of Churchill's speech. Byrnes and Leahy, on the other hand, found the description of the world more realistic.

What specifically galvanized which actor is difficult now to tell, but it is the case that Bevin, now in New York, went on the attack at the UN and Byrnes turned his shock at Stalin's speech into a positive statement of the necessity for the United States to act as a great power "in order to preserve the peace of the world" if "force or the threat of force is used contrary to the purposes and principles" of the United Nations.

Byrnes said this on February 28, after reading not only Churchill's draft of the Iron Curtain speech but also George Kennan's Long Telegram (February 22), which predicted the consequences of Russian paranoia, Communist ideology, and military success to be a constant series of challenges to the West which must be met with a "much more positive and constructive picture of the world which we would like to see." The United States Joint Chiefs had issued on February 27 a paper which called the "consolidation and development of the power of Russia . . . the greatest threat to the United States" and further stated, with remarkable directness, that "the greatest single military factor in the security of the world is the absolute military security of the United States." In the West and in the Near East, spines were stiffening.

Stalin was not backing down either. In Moscow in his first interview with Qavam and the Shah's sister, the Princess Ashraf, he demanded oil concessions, the right to station troops in Iran, and the recognition of Azerbaijani and Kurd autonomy under the Soviet puppet regimes. To Qavam's insistence that the Allies would object, Stalin said "we don't care what the United States and Great Britain think and we are not afraid of them."

Leahy and Byrnes saw a new draft of Churchill's Fulton address on the night of March 3, and they informed Churchill, who informed Attlee and Bevin, that they were sending a strong note to the Soviets over the crisis in Iran and dispatching the battleship *Missouri* with a task force to the Straits, bearing home the body of the late Turkish Ambassador.

Also on March 3, Vice Consul Rossow reported that 450 Russian trucks loaded with ammunition had left Tabriz on the road to Teheran. The next day the Tudeh Party took to the streets in Teheran, surrounded the Iranian Parliament, the Majlis, and prevented it from meeting. The next day members of the Majlis were beaten as they tried to enter.

On March 4, having read Winston Churchill's draft, Byrnes and Truman discussed the situation. Byrnes had had an earlier meeting with Loy Henderson, the head of the Near Eastern section of the State Department, who reiterated the position he had taken since at least August that the United States must be firm—whereas Benjamin Cohen, Byrnes's personal adviser, urged the steady State Department position of moderation, of essentially taking no position. Byrnes for once took the stronger course. With Truman in wholehearted agreement the most powerful statement of opposition to Soviet expansion so far was sent to Moscow. The message stated that the situation of Soviet troops in Iran beyond the treaty limits was one to which the United States could "not remain indifferent," diplomatic code for the strongest possible reaction.

The stage was set for the trip to Fulton. Churchill, Leahy, Truman, and an entourage boarded the train on March 4 in Washington and traveled overnight to Jefferson City. On board, Churchill drank heavily with little impairment of his skills. He won a substantial sum off of Truman and others at poker. They stayed up late and Truman read the speech, pronouncing himself enthusiastic and telling Churchill he thought "it would do a lot of good."

The next day after lunch, a short procession to the gymnasium, and a shorter introduction from President Truman, Churchill spoke to the Westminster community and the world.

The Iron Curtain speech is built on three simple ideas. The first is that despite victory, war and tyranny, "the two marauders," still haunt the earth. Indeed because of the power of the atomic bomb they are potentially even more inimical to the future well being of the planet. Second, though the ideals of the world organization of the United Nations must be supported and disseminated, the power in the world capable of stopping tyranny is the fraternal organization of the English-speaking peoples. The strategic concept that Churchill bumps up against but does not flatly state is a continuation of the U.S.-British wartime alliance. But his most important point was about the strength of the Allies and the English-speaking peoples. That is its greatest point because of the "moral force" behind it. This moral force is found in the "joint inheritance of the English speaking world." These are "the great principles of freedom and the rights of man," to be found in "Magna Carta, the Bill of Rights, the Habeas Corpus, trial by jury and the English common law," and finally in their greatest expression, the American Declaration of Independence.

The speech is a grand contrast between the police-state tyranny descending like an Iron Curtain "from Stettin in the Baltic to Trieste in the Adriatic" and its challenger "Christian civilization." Implicitly the United Nations, indeed any world organization with plural voices, will be helpless faced with the will of the sophisticated tyranny like that of the Communist International. Hence the necessity for the "special relationship" and the "fraternal association of the English-speaking peoples with their kindred systems of society" and "common study of potential dangers."

Five times in the speech Churchill refers to the "humble folk" and their "cottage homes." Dialectically, they are what the English-speaking peoples are fighting for, and because of the strength of the common inheritance of the rule of law, democracy and freedom are the greatest weapons in that fight.

Material force is necessary too—the "overall strategic concept" as Churchill calls it—victory over tyranny will be impossible without the "sinews of peace": "intimate" Anglo-American military relationship, control of nuclear energy, and weight of the forces of the United States and the British Empire and Commonwealth. But above all else, faith in a "common purpose" and a "sense of duty" with "an awe inspiring accountability to the future."

As a piece of rhetoric the speech is a classic: the cottage home in danger; the fraternal association making its defense possible; the comprehensiveness of the assault of tyranny; the awfulness of modern war; the common purposes and material strengths that make the future possible; it is all a great coming together of an unblinkingly real description of the tragic suffering of the world with her brightest hopes shining through. What is most impressive is the vision of civilization and its defense which Churchill offers.

> If the population of the English speaking commonwealths be added to that of the United States with all that such cooperation implies in the air, on the sea all over the globe and in science and in industry, and in moral force, there will be no quivering, precarious balance of power to offer its temptation to ambition or adventure. On the contrary, there will be an overwhelming assurance of security. If we adhere faithfully to the Charter of the United Nations and walk forward in sedate and sober strength seeking no one's land or treasure, seeking to lay no arbitrary control upon the thoughts of men; if all British moral and material forces and convictions are joined with your own in fraternal association, the high-roads of the future will be clear, not only for us but for all, not only for our time, but for a century to come.

Truman had read and approved the speech. He clapped and smiled and nodded approvingly during its delivery. And when the thunderstorm broke Harry S. Truman was remarkably, for him, disingenuous. The reaction to the speech was swift, strong, and chaotic. American isolationist newspapers and those of the Left as well denounced it. The *Chicago Sun Times* rejected "its poisonous doctrines." Senator Capper of Kansas and the *Boston Globe* saw a plot of imperialist Britain to enlist American support for the "collapsing colonialism" of the British Empire. Senator Robert Taft thought the analysis correct but the proposed alliance, as he saw it, went too far. The *Times* of London felt that Western democracy and communism "have much to learn from each other." There was too much moral equivalence to so strongly contrast the two systems as Churchill did. While the Soviets could learn about individual rights from the West, the democracies could learn about "the development of the economic and social planning" from the Communists. Truman, for once less than honest, faced with a fire storm, told a press conference on March 8 that he hadn't read the speech in advance. Attlee similarly said it was just a private opinion but avoided a vote on a motion of censure tabled by ninety-three irate Labour MP's. The most reverberating reaction came from Moscow. On March 11, the same day as the Labour protest, *Pravda* printed a full-page denunciation of Churchill's proposals for an "anglo-american alliance," words Churchill had not used, and therefore being a clear indication of the Soviet Union's deepest fear. And the charge they most resented, that of Soviet expansionism, was the charge most true. Qavam had come home from Moscow on March 10 with no agreement for withdrawal of Soviet troops. Indeed on March 11 the Soviet Chargé in Teheran told him that if he persisted in bringing the case to the Security Council the Soviet Union would consider it "an unfriendly and hostile act that would have unfortunate results."

In Moscow on March 14 Stalin, most extraordinarily, gave an interview to *Pravda* attacking Churchill as a war monger, fascist, a dealer in racial theory that only those whose mother tongue was German could be considered a full-blooded nation. He compared Churchill to Hitler. He asserted that the governments in Poland, Rumania, Hungary, Bulgaria, and Yugoslavia were more democratic than the English Parliament for they had representatives of many parties where in Britain the government came of only one party. And finally he said, "the growth of influence of the Communists is not just a chance happening, it is a perfectly natural happening." As Brooks Atkinson, the *New York Times* correspondent in Moscow, put it, the Russians had become "hysterical." *Izvestia* was violent while *Pravda*'s article took special notice of Truman's lack of commitment at his press conference. Khruschev in his memoirs said "it was largely because of Churchill's speech that Stalin exaggerated our enemies' strength and their intention to unleash war on us."

On March 15, in a speech at the Waldorf Astoria, Churchill, referring to Fulton, said, "I do not wish to withdraw or modify a single word." The ideals of the United Nations had the "overwhelming assent of the peoples of the world," which gave them an "ever-growing moral authority." The success of the United Nations would come to pass only with the "persistent, faithful and above all fearless exertions of the British and American systems of society . . . [of those] who love freedom and are foes of tyranny." There was never "a greater misunderstanding" than Stalin's assertion that Britain was not a democracy while Poland, Rumania, and Bulgaria were. In his peroration, Churchill called the United States to the duties of *the* great imperial power, a power unseen since Rome, power which in fraternal association with the British would lead to ever-greater opportunities and ever-greater responsibilities.

The same day there were Russian troop movements toward Teheran. Qavam continued to instruct his ambassador to the United Nations to push the Security Council. On March 16 Byrnes called for extension of the Selective Service Act, on March 18 Ambassador Ala laid the matter formally before the Security Council, and on March 20 Winston Churchill gave an interview to his son Randolph for the *United Press* stating that the United Nations reaction to Soviet troop movements was "a very important test," of the legitimacy of the world organization.

On March 22 Stalin gave another interview, also to the *United Press,* that began a Soviet stand-down that would culminate in a joint Soviet-Iranian communiqué finished and released on the early morning of April 5. While the Iranian and Soviet negotiators were working on it Stalin had another late-night interview, this time with General Walter Bedell Smith, the new American Ambassador and former chief of staff to Dwight Eisenhower. Smith went to the meeting with only the sketchiest of instructions from Truman on Iran.

Stalin wanted to talk about Churchill. After Smith had opened the discussion by asking Stalin "how far will Russia go" and detailing the questions that the United States had about Soviet policy (and definitely questions, not objections, at this stage) Stalin replied by attacking the Iron Curtain speech. As the discussion went along Stalin erupted once again with an attack not only on the Iron Curtain speech but on Churchill's entire career going back to his support for the White Russian armies in 1919, twenty-seven years earlier. The key moment in the conversation came after Bedell Smith's recitation of a rather weak review of the U.S. policy of nonintervention with other nations and support for the United Nations. Stalin began a lengthy tirade attacking the United States for supporting Iran at the UN. Asserting the vulnerability of Baku and the oil fields, he called the Iron Curtain speech an unfriendly act. Bedell Smith asked Stalin if he believed in a U.S.-British alliance, to which Stalin replied, emphatically, yes. Bedell Smith then stated that Churchill's speech, for which "I have no brief," nonetheless reflects an apprehension common to both the United States and Britain" and will justify the support given by both to Iran in their votes at the United Nations. Once again Bedell Smith came back to his initial question, how much farther would Stalin go and Stalin answered this time, "not much further." The interview ended shortly after this. The negotiators from Iran and the Soviet Union, having received the blessing of Stalin, were able to reach an agreement that guaranteed the withdrawal of Soviet troops from Iran—the only Soviet retreat from occupied territory under the threat of force until the withdrawal from Afghanistan in the 1980s.

So this tale of two speeches ends: Stalin's "material possibilities" and "superior systems of the Soviet state" versus the "moral force" of the English-speaking peoples backed by the material force of the "special relationship." Some historians believe that it is a mystery why Stalin chose to withdraw from Iran. I do not. Churchill had alerted the world to the totalitarian menace of Communism as he had that of Nazism. His true passion for civilization, for what he called "freedom, comfort and culture" in his address at Bristol shines through as something worth fighting for, perhaps even dying for. In the dark night of the forties he had said the cause of freedom among the English-speaking peoples was so worth fighting for that "it was equally good to live or to die." If fortune be with us, no tyranny can overcome a love so deep as this.

In a time of moral and strategic incoherence Churchill had brought the English-speaking peoples back to their better selves. He recognized the common danger because he saw the destruction of the common inheritance. His words were so fleet and so true, the horses of the chariot flying so nobly, that even the Devil withdrew.

The Churchill Memorial, the Crosby Kemper Lectures on Churchill, and this book derived therefrom—all remind us of our better selves.

MARTIN GILBERT is the author of the official multivolume biography of Sir Winston Churchill, as well as numerous other books in British and European history. He has lectured at many universities in Britain and the United States and served as history correspondent for the *London Sunday Times*.

1

❧

The Origins of the "Iron Curtain" Speech

Martin Gilbert

I have tried to piece together the story of Churchill's experience of Soviet Communism—and of his reactions to that experience—in the thirty years leading up to his "Iron Curtain Speech" at Westminster College. Many thousands of miles to the East, across the Atlantic Ocean and across the wide democratic zone of Western Europe, the Iron Curtain is still there. I crossed it myself, only three weeks ago, on the Austria-Czechoslovak border, just halfway between Stettin and Trieste. For twenty minutes the train, with its one through-carriage from Rome to Moscow, stopped astride the Iron Curtain: it is a fierce curtain of tall fences, vigilant watchtowers, barbed wire, and electronic eyes.

Here in Fulton, Missouri, during an extremely pleasant reception, I was told two things about Churchill: first that he was spoilt and selfish, and second that he was cantankerous and quarrelsome. But surely here, of all places, here on this delightful campus, where you have built and are still building such a superb and living memorial to Churchill, something should also be known of the superb and living quality of his thoughts and understanding of world affairs. *His* quarrel was with tyranny.

Here at Westminster College—at the age of seventy-one—with fifty years of public life behind him, Churchill spoke with foreboding of the behavior and intentions of Soviet Russia and outlined a course of common democratic unity, led by Britain and the United States. Churchill's knowledge of Russia stretched back more than twenty years before the communist revolution of November 1917. Indeed, the actual occasion on which his parents first met was at a ball onboard the yacht of the Tsarevich, later Tsar Nicholas II. Churchill's own memories of the Russian Empire centered on three facets of czarist imperial rule, each of which was greatly to influence his attitude to the Soviets:

First, his hatred of the official, government-sponsored anti-Semitism of czarist Russia, as shown in the anti-Jewish violence, or pogroms, in the first decade of this century. In 1906 Churchill had been the main speaker at a mass rally in Manchester to protest against official czarist connivance in these anti-Jewish attacks.

Second, his dislike of the czarist treatment of the Poles and his belief that the twentieth century must eventually see what Churchill himself was to call (in 1918), "the harmonious disposition" of Europe among its inhabitants—his belief in and sympathy for an independent Poland, freed from Russian tutelage, was instinct in Churchill's early thought: he admired enormously the Polish courage, hopeless though it had proved, in the uprisings against czarist Russia in the 1830s and 1860s.

And third—and we come now to the most complex and ultimately most vexed questions in Soviet relations with the outside world—the right of Russia, if she were to join in the defeat of Germany (whether in 1914 or 1941), to territorial recompense and reward, to the return of "lost" territories, and to secure, defensible borders.

In 1914 Churchill accepted that if Russia were to remain in the war, and to contribute to the Allied victory over Germany, then she would be able to expand her territorial control to Constantinople, the Straits, and the warm waters of the Mediterranean. It was to enable Russia to remain at war, in 1915, that Churchill and Kitchener had launched the Gallipoli expedition—when Russia looked on the verge of surrender, pressed back by German forces in the West and Turkish forces in the East.

It was the Russian Bolshevik decision to leave the war in March 1918 that made Churchill feel that this, the first international act of the Bolsheviks, and their enduring legacy, was to cut Russia off, as an ally which had fought for two and one-half years, from the benefits of victory when it came.

As a result of this antiwar decision by Lenin and Trotsky, Churchill realized from the onset of communist rule, when at its weakest, that Russia would seek, when once again strong, to regain those areas she regarded as hers and had only lost as a result of the political decision to leave the war.

Henceforth, from 1917 until today, one question was to emerge—and reemerge—in almost each decade: how far west would Russia wish to go—or be allowed to go.

At the time of the Bolshevik revolution, in November 1917, Churchill was Minister of Munitions in David Lloyd George's wartime coalition, and, for the first five years of the Bolshevik triumph in Russia, Churchill remained an influential member of British policymaking at the center: first as Minister of Munitions, then as Secretary of State for War and Air, and finally as Secretary of State for the Colonies.

In these three posts, and over these five years, he was an avid and careful reader of all the information reaching Britain—public and secret—about the nature of Bolshevik rule.

And it was as a result of Churchill's detailed knowledge of the actual behavior of the Bolsheviks inside Russia, and of their plans to spread revolution outside, that he urged Lloyd George to strengthen the democratic forces in Weimar Germany. Indeed, as early as November 1918, on the day before the armistice with Germany, Churchill had told the British War Cabinet: "We might have to build up the German Army, as it was important to get Germany on her legs again, for fear of the spread of Bolshevism."

In Churchill's mind, Bolshevism was an evil system, totally destructive of all the freedoms, and all the human values, in which he believed. Already, by 1917, an enemy of tyranny for more than twenty years, for him Bolshevism was the supreme tyranny, crushing all of the liberties he prized. Even in Bolshevism's early days, when sailors of the Red Fleet had shot down and murdered Captain Cromie, the British Naval Attache, inside the Petrograd Embassy, Churchill had been outraged, telling the War Cabinet on September 4, 1918: "The exertions which a nation is prepared to make to protect its individual representatives or citizens from outrage is one of the truest measures of its greatness as an organised State."

Every subsequent piece of information which reached Churchill confirmed his view that Bolshevism was totally destructive of individual liberty. At first he hoped that it would, as he told his colleagues at the Imperial War Cabinet on December 31, 1918, "be exposed and swept away by a General Election," held if necessary under "Allied auspices." Later he sought to strengthen the existing Allied support for each of the anti-Bolshevik Russian armies pressing in at different times upon Moscow and Petrograd.

Churchill's main task in 1919 and 1920, a task imposed upon him by Lloyd George, and carried out with reluctance, was actually to withdraw the British troops that Lloyd George himself had sent a year earlier to help the Russian anti-Bolsheviks.

Yet Churchill was convinced that unless Bolshevism were overthrown, Western democracy and civilization would be threatened, and might even be destroyed. As he wrote of Lenin, Trotsky, and the other Bolshevik leaders in a public article on June 22, 1919:

> Theirs is a war against civilised society which can never end. They seek as the first condition of their being the overthrow and destruction of all existing institutions and of every State and Government now standing in the world. They too aim at a worldwide and international league, but a league of the failures, the criminals, the unfit, the mutinous, the morbid, the deranged, and the distraught in every land; and between them and such order of civilisation as we have been able to build up since the dawn of history there can, as Lenin rightly proclaims, be neither truce nor pact.

It was the tyrannical aspect of Lenin's regime that most roused Churchill's fury. Writing in January 1920 he declared:

> A tyrant is one who allows the fancies of his mind to count for more in deciding action than the needs, feelings, hopes, lives and physical well-being of the people over whom he has obtained control. A tyrant is one who wrecks the lives of millions for the satisfaction of his own

conceptions. So far as possible in this world no man should have such power, whether under an imperialist, republican, militarist, socialist or soviet form of Government.

On May 1, 1920, Churchill set out his view of Bolshevik tyranny in a cabinet memorandum. The Bolsheviks, he wrote, have "committed, and are committing unspeakable atrocities, and are maintaining themselves in power by a terrorism on an unprecedented scale, and by the denial of the most elementary rights of citizenship and freedom."

Churchill's hatred of Bolshevism sprang from his belief that the ultimate aim of the communist philosophy was the complete destruction of parliamentary democracy, personal liberty, and free speech. He had of course followed the events of postrevolutionary Russia closely: the suppression by Lenin of the Constituent Assembly—with its already predominantly proletarian franchise—Trotsky's brutal suppression of the Kronstadt revolt, the closing of churches, and the killing of priests.

To an audience at Sunderland, Churchill set out, on January 1, 1920, the points of difference as he saw them, telling his audience, about all communist and socialist systems:

> We believe in Parliamentary Government exercised in accordance with the will of the majority of the electors constitutionally and freely ascertained. They seek to overthrow Parliament by direct action or other violent means . . . and then to rule the mass of the nation in accordance with their theories, which have never yet been applied successfully, and through the agency of self-elected or sham-elected caucuses of their own. They seek to destroy capital. We seek to control monopolies. They seek to eradicate the idea of individual possession. We seek to use the great mainspring of human endeavour as a means of increasing the volume of production on every side and of sharing the fruits far more broadly and evenly among millions of individual homes. We defend Freedom of conscience and religious equality. They seek to exterminate every form of religious belief that has given comfort and inspiration to the soul of man.

In August 1920 the Red Army advanced into Poland, approaching within a few miles of Warsaw. Even Lloyd George was so horrified that he delivered an ultimatum to the Bolsheviks to halt their forces. In the event, it was a Polish victory, the so-called Miracle of the Vistula, not the British ultimatum, which saved Polish independence.

At the very moment when the Red Army seemed poised for victory, Churchill had written an article in the *Evening News:*

> It is easy for those who live a long way from the Russian Bolshevists,— especially those who are protected by a good strip of salt water, and who stand on the firm rock of an active political democracy— to adopt a cool and airy view of their Communist doctrines and machinations. But a new, weak, impoverished, famishing State like Poland, itself quaking internally, is placed in hourly jeopardy by close and continuous contact with such neighbours. The Bolshevik aim of the world revolution can be pursued equally in peace or war. In fact, a Bolshevist peace is only another form of war. If they do not for the moment overwhelm with armies, they can undermine with propaganda. Not a shot may be fired along the whole front, not a bayonet may be fixed, not a battalion may move, and yet invasion may be proceeding swiftly and relentlessly. The peasants are roused against the landlords, the workmen against their employers, the railways and public service are induced to strike, the soldiers are incited to mutiny and kill their officers, the mob are raised against the middle classes to murder them, to plunder their houses, to steal their belongings, to debauch their wives and carry off their children; an elaborate network of secret societies entangles honest political action; the Press is bought wherever possible. This was what Poland dreaded and will now have reason to dread still more; and this was the cause, even more than the gathering of the Russian armies on the Polish front, continuous for nearly a year, that led the Poles to make that desperate military sally or counter-stroke which English Liberal opinion has so largely misunderstood, and which Socialist opinion has so successfully misrepresented.

Recall for a moment that phrase in Churchill's article of 1920: "Not a shot may be fired," and Churchill's realization that, even without a shot being fired, Poland could be subjugated: and then come forward twenty-six years, here to Westminster College, and listen to the same clear echo, reinforced by nearly three decades of further experience: "I do not believe that Soviet Russia desires war. What they desire is the fruits of war and the indefinite expansion of their power and doctrines."

Churchill's detestation of communism was complete. Yet the center of his political philosophy was the survival of parliamentary democracy. And to ensure this survival, he was prepared to consider any expedient. Twice in his lifetime this included the expedient of working with Communist Russia as an active ally. The first occasion was in the summer of 1918 after the German breakthrough on the Western Front: a breakthrough only made possible because the Russia of Lenin and Trotsky had made its peace with Germany, thus liberating millions of German soldiers for active service in the Western Front. To halt the German advance, Churchill proposed a deal with the Bolsheviks: if they would reopen the eastern front against Germany, Britain (and America) would jointly guarantee the survival of the Bolshevik revolution. "Let us never forget," he wrote in a memorandum for the cabinet of April 7, 1918, "that Lenin and Trotsky are fighting with ropes round their necks. Show them any real chance of consolidating their power, of getting some kind of protection against the vengeance of a counter-revolution, and they would be non-human not to embrace it."

Churchill proposed sending some senior Allied statesman, such as Theodore Roosevelt, to Russia, to be at Trotsky's side when war was again declared by Russia on Germany, and to act as "a rallying point" sufficiently prominent for all patriotic Russians to fix their gaze on it. Theodore Roosevelt would become the commissar of the Allies, with the full authority and power of Britain and America combined, to ensure—as Churchill put it—"safeguarding the permanent fruits of the revolution."

Twenty years later, when Hitler's dominance of Europe was almost complete, Churchill again argued in favor of an alliance with the Soviet Union. When, in June 1941, Hitler attacked the Soviet Union, Churchill immediately offered Russia all the military and economic assistance that

Britain could provide (and did provide, at considerable cost): "The Nazi regime," he said then, in a broadcast on June 22, 1941, "is indistinguishable from the worst features of communism. It is devoid of all theme and principle except appetite and racial domination. It excels all forms of human wickedness in the efficiency of its cruelty and ferocious aggression."

Churchill's broadcast continued: "No one has been a more consistent opponent of communism than I have for the last twenty-five years. I will unsay no word that I have spoken about it. But all this fades away before the spectacle which is now unfolding. The past with its crimes, its follies and its tragedies, flashes away."

"We have," Churchill went on, "but one aim and one single, irrevocable purpose. We are resolved to destroy Hitler and every vestige of the Nazi regime. From this nothing will turn us—nothing. That is our policy and that is our declaration. It follows, therefore, that we shall give whatever help we can to Russia and to the Russian people. We shall appeal to all our friends and allies in every part of the world to take the same course and pursue it, as we shall, faithfully and steadfastly to the end."

Twenty years before this decisive broadcast—by the end of 1920—one can already find three interwoven strands in Churchill's political philosophy: "the appeasement of class bitterness" at home; "the appeasement of the fearful hatreds and antagonisms abroad"; and the defense of parliamentary democracy and democratic values in Britain, in Western Europe, and in the territories under British rule or control. Wherever possible, Churchill believed that the method to be used must be conciliation, the route to be chosen was the middle way, the path of moderation. But where force alone could preserve the libertarian values, force would have to be used. It could only be a last resort—the horrors of war, and the very nature of democracy, ensured that—but in the last resort, it might be necessary to defend those values by force of arms.

By 1921 these three strands, and all of their ramifications, were clear in Churchill's mind. He was forty-four years old, and he could look back on twenty years of public life, including four wartime years, through almost all of which he had been an active participant at the center of policymaking, arguing his points with men of experience and expertise, testing his ideas amid the daily practical problems of departmental business, and reflecting, with each year, on the evolution of the world scene and the nature of man.

Churchill believed at all times in speaking the truth as he saw it—as he said here at Westminster College—to have "full liberty to give my true and faithful counsel in these anxious and baffling times."

These reflections were sometimes somber. As Churchill told his own constituents on November 11, 1922, six years after the armistice (and twenty-six years before Fulton):

> What a disappointment the Twentieth Century has been.
> How terrible & how melancholy
>   is long series of disastrous events
>   wh have darkened its first 20 years.
> We have seen in ev country a dissolution,
>   a weakening of those bonds,
>   a challenge to those principles
>   a decay of faith
>   an abridgement of hope
>   on wh structure & ultimate existence
>   of civilised society depends.
> We have seen in ev part of globe
>   one gt country after another
>   wh had erected an orderly, a peaceful
>   a prosperous structure of civilised society,
>   relapsing in hideous succession
>   into bankruptcy, barbarism or anarchy.

Churchill then spoke of each of the areas which were in turmoil: China and Mexico "sunk into confusion"; Russia, where "that little set of Communist criminals . . . have exhausted millions of the Russian people"; Ireland, scene of an "enormous retrogression of civilisation & Christianity"; Egypt and India, where "we see among millions of people hitherto shielded by superior science & superior law a desire to shatter the structure by which they live & to return blindly & heedlessly to primordial chaos." He then went on to warn of the future:

> Can you doubt, my faithful friends
>> as you survey this sombre panorama,
>>> that mankind is passing through a period marked
>>>> not only by an enormous destruction
>>>>> & abridgement of human species,
>>>>>> not only by a vast impoverishment
>>>>>>> & reduction in means of existence
>>>> but also that destructive tendencies
>>>>> have not yet run their course?
>> And only intense, concerted & prolonged efforts
>>> among all nations
>>>> can avert further & perhaps even greater calamities.

Speaking in Paris fourteen years later, on September 24, 1936, after the rise of Hitler, Churchill stressed the need to maintain parliamentary democracy, and liberal civilization. He also explained why the democracies could never submit to Nazi or communist rule, asking his audience:

> How could we bear, nursed as we have been in a free atmosphere, to be gagged and muzzled; to have spies, eavesdroppers and delators at every corner; to have even private conversation caught up and used against us by the Secret Police and all their agents and creatures; to be arrested and interned without trial; or to be tried by political or Party courts for crimes hitherto unknown to civil law. How could we bear to be treated like schoolboys when we are grown-up men; to be turned out on parade by tens of thousands to march and cheer for this slogan or for that; to see philosophers, teachers and authors bullied and toiled to death in concentration camps; to be forced every hour to conceal the natural workings of the human intellect and the pulsations of the human heart? Why, I say that rather than submit to such oppression, there is no length we would not go to.

There were still some people, Churchill continued, who believed that the only choice for Europe was between "two violent extremes." This was not his view. "Between the doctrines of Comrade Trotsky and those of Dr. Goebbels," he said, "there ought to be room for you and me, and a few others, to cultivate opinions of our own." No aggression, he warned, from wherever it came, could be condoned. All aggressive action must be judged, not from the standpoint of Right and Left, but, as he put it, of "right or wrong."

Politically, Churchill was very much alone at this time; but slowly, in the trade unions, in business circles, among the economists of the LSE, even in the Labour Party, his support for a middle way between fascism and communism was gaining ground. It was from this standpoint that Churchill looked on the Spanish Civil War. "I refuse to become the partisan of either side," he told the House of Commons on April 14, 1937. As to communism and Nazism, he added: "I hope not to be called upon to survive in the world under a Government of either of these dispensations. I cannot feel any enthusiasm for these rival creeds. I feel unbounded sorrow and sympathy for the victims."

Throughout Churchill's so-called Wilderness Years, the decade from 1929 to 1939 when he was out of office, Churchill continued to publish articles drawing attention to the Nazi terror and Soviet tyranny. In Oxford, on May 22, 1937, he told the assembled students: "It is sometimes said that Communism and Fascism are poles apart," he said. "Perhaps they are. But what difference is there between life at the North Pole and life at the South Pole. Perhaps as one crawls out of one's igloo there may be a few more penguins at the one or polar bears at the other. At both, life is miserable. For my part I propose to remain in the Temperate Zone."

Churchill's concept of democracy involved the linked factors of democratic leadership and of democratic example. In opposing Neville Chamberlain's search for a compromise with Hitler, he warned the House of Commons, on December 21, 1938, after the return of Lord Halifax from a visit to Hitler: "If it were thought that we were making terms for ourselves at the expense either of small nations or of large conceptions which are dear, not only to many nations, but to millions of people in every nation, a knoll of despair would resound through many parts of Europe."

Churchill always rejected any policy that might lead to confusion or division among the democracies, or in democratic behavior: as he was to say nine years later, here at Westminster College: "It is necessary that constancy of mind, persistency of purpose, and the grand simplicity of decision shall guide and rule the conduct of the English-speaking peoples"; but in 1937 he saw no such constancy, persistency or simplicity in British policy: only weakness, confusion—and even duplicity. As for America: isolation was still the order of the day, and the mass of American opinion, as Churchill phrased it, "remote and indifferent."

I have spoken of Churchill's innermost concern for the survival of Western democracy—on both sides of the Atlantic—and of how, to ensure the survival of democracy, he was prepared to enlist any help that could be found.

From 1937 to 1939 this included help from the Soviet Union. On April 13, 1939, he told the House of Commons in one of several speeches urging Anglo-Soviet talks:

> The other day I tried to show the House the deep interest that Russia had against the further eastward extension of the Nazi power. It is upon that deep, natural, legitimate interest that we must rely, and I am sure we shall hear from the Government that the steps they are taking are those which will enable us to receive the fullest possible co-operation from Russia, and that no prejudices on the part of England or France will be allowed to interfere with the closest co-operation between the two countries, thus securing to our harassed and anxious combinations the unmeasured, if somewhat uncertain, but enormous aid of the Russian power.

These hopes were in vain. The British government of the day—led by Neville Chamberlain—was reluctant to embark on the course which Churchill advised, and Stalin deemed his immediate interest to lie in a pact with Hitler: not to defend Poland, but to partition her.

Churchill's other hope lay in the United States. But here too he was disappointed. Of course he understood the strength of noninterventionist feeling, but he also hoped to be able himself to influence American opinion toward a greater involvement in helping to preserve the European democracies; for he believed at the core of his being that the only way to preserve any one democracy was for all the democratic states to act in clear, open, and declared unison.

On August 8, 1939, Churchill set out his thoughts on dictatorship and democracy in a direct broadcast to the United States: "One thing has struck me as very strange," he said, "and that is the resurgence of the one-man power after all these centuries of experience and progress. It is curious how the English-speaking peoples have always had this horror of one-man power. They are quite ready to follow a leader for a time, as long as he is serviceable to them; but the idea of handing themselves over, lock, stock and barrel, body and soul, to one man, and worshiping him as if he were an idol—that has always been odious to the whole theme and nature of our civilisation."

Churchill's broadcast continued:

> The architects of the American Constitution were as careful as those who shaped the British Constitution to guard against the whole life and fortunes, and all the laws and freedoms of the nation, being placed in the hands of a tyrant. Checks and counterchecks in the body politic, large devolutions of State government, instruments and process of free debate, frequent recurrence to first principles, the right of opposition to the most powerful governments, and above all ceaseless vigilance, have preserved, and will preserve, the broad characteristics of British and American institutions. But in Germany, on a mountain peak, there sits one man who in a single day can release the world from the fear which now oppresses it; or in a single day can plunge all that we have and are into a volcano of smoke and flame.

"If Herr Hitler does not make war," Churchill added, "there will be no war."

Four weeks later Hitler invaded Poland, and on September 3, 1939, both Britain and France declared war on Germany. "This is no war," Churchill said that day, "of domination or imperial aggrandisement or material gain;

no war to shut any country out of its sunlight and means of progress. It is a war, viewed in its inherent quality, to establish, on impregnable rocks, the rights of the individual, and it is a war to establish and revive the stature of man."

As we have seen again and again, Churchill believed that if the government gave an honest lead, the public would follow. But it was essential, as he saw it, to face difficulties straight on; and it was because of this belief that he was able, throughout the thirties, his so-called Wilderness Years, to read the warning signs as they occurred, and without any self-delusion as to what they meant.

Nor was his assertion in 1939 that handing over power to a single man was "odious" to Anglo-Saxon civilization a mere oratorical flourish. Although it was heartbreaking for him personally to relinquish power in 1945—believing that he had so much still to give to the peacemaking process, by means of his enormous personal authority, knowledge of past errors, goodwill of so many of the world statesmen (including Harry Truman) and understanding of current and emerging problems—it was nevertheless the British people's good fortune that he was such a profound democrat, relinquishing power within hours of electoral defeat. Indeed, as he himself later recalled: "The verdict of the electors had been so overwhelmingly expressed that I did not wish to remain even for an hour responsible for their affairs." That same evening, July 27, 1945, Churchill issued a statement to the press which included the sentence: "Immense responsibilities abroad and at home fall upon the new Government, and we must all hope that they will be successful in bearing them."

"Civilization," Churchill wrote in his novel *Savrola* at the turn of the century, was "a state of society where moral forces begin to escape from the tyranny of physical forces." But since the end of the First World War he had seen those moral forces themselves being challenged, not by any physical enemy but by immoral forces of man's own making. To George Bernard Shaw he wrote, on September 2, 1928, of men and women in general:

"Everything they try will fail—owing to their deplorable characteristics, and their liking for these very characteristics. The only world fit for them is a Hugger Mugger world. Ants and Bees would be worthy of better things."

Yet Churchill believed in the ability of man to improve his situation, and to defend what had already been achieved: the ability of man in general, not simply of individual leaders. Since 1940 he himself has come to epitomize the war leader, the man of the hour, the indispensable hero. But all his life, he regarded such a person as having no independent existence. "Do you think I am what I am," his fictional hero, Savrola, asked at the turn of the century, "because I have changed all those minds, or because I best express their views? Am I their master or their slave? Believe me I have no illusions." And on his eightieth birthday, at a ceremony in Westminster Hall, London, he declared—looking back over the war years: "It was a nation and race dwelling all around the globe that had the lion's heart. I had the luck to be called upon to give the roar."

To outsiders, Churchill could sometimes seem insensitive and harsh, cynical and brusque. His outbursts of temper, recorded by colleagues at times of incredible national stress and wartime danger, were interpreted by some—and have been echoed recently by several historians and television programs—as a sign of an underlying tyrannical nature. But to those who worked closest with him, whether as cabinet colleagues or civil servants, the quality of his mind was clear, as indeed was his overriding gentleness of character, his humor and sense of fun, as well as his deep understanding of human nature, history, and public affairs.

One civil servant, Eric Seal, who was Churchill's principal private secretary throughout the testing time of 1940, but who never became a close personal friend, wrote, in retrospect, of Churchill's motive force:

> The key word in any understanding of Winston Churchill is the simple word "Liberty." Throughout his life, through many changes and vicissitudes, Winston Churchill stood for liberty. He intensely

disliked, and reacted violently against, all attempts to regiment and dictate opinion. In this attitude, he was consistent throughout his political life. He believed profoundly in the freedom of the spirit, and the liberty of man to work out his own salvation, and to be himself in his own way. His defense of the British Government in India is not at variance with this idea; he defended British rule in India because he thought that it brought individual freedom in its train. He demanded for himself freedom to follow his own star, and he stood out for a like liberty for all men. All organized attempts to dictate to men what or how they should think, whether by the Nazis in Germany, or by the Communists in Russia, incurred his passionate hatred and fell under his anathema. In the last resort, this was the mainspring of his action.

This was a private opinion, not written for publication. But in August 1944 Churchill himself sent a public message to the Italian people which contained, in seven questions, a compact summary of his own philosophy. The message contained seven "quite simple, practical tests," as Churchill called them, by which freedom could be recognized in the modern world:

1. Is there the right to free expression of opinion and of opposition and criticism of the Government of the day?

2. Have the people the right to turn out a Government of which they disapprove, and are constitutional means provided by which they can make their will apparent?

3. Are their courts of justice free from violence by the Executive and from threats of mob violence, and free of all association with particular political parties?

4. Will these courts administer open and well-established laws which are associated in the human mind with the broad principles of decency and justice?

5. Will there be fair play for poor as well as for rich, for private persons as well as Government officials?

6. Will the rights of the individual, subject to his duties to the State, be maintained and asserted and exalted?

7. Is the ordinary peasant or workman who is earning a living by daily toil and striving to bring up a family free from the fear that

some grim police organisation under the control of a single party, like the Gestapo, started by the Nazi and Fascist parties, will tap him on the shoulder and pack him off without fair or open trial to bondage or ill-treatment?

Even as Churchill asked these questions his beliefs were about to be put to their most terrible test: the struggle between Stalin and the West over the future of Poland, a struggle which the West lost, and the lessons of which were to be the culminating theme of his Fulton speech—lessons which are still with us, alas, today.

In the aftermath of the First World War, Churchill had been a determined supporter of Polish independence—and an admirer of Poland's brilliant defense of its own sovereignty against the Red Army in 1920. Thirteen years later, in 1933, he was scandalized when British politicians began to emulate Hitler in denouncing the newly independent states of Europe and in belittling them as unreal or unstable creatures. Czechoslovakia and Poland were particularly singled out for abuse—both by Hitler, and by the British ministers: Ramsay MacDonald, the prime minister of the National, All Party Government, called them "ghosts."

On April 13, 1933, Churchill told the House of Commons:

> The Prime Minister last year, in a speech at Geneva, used a very striking phrase when he described Europe as a house inhabited by ghosts. That is to misinterpret the situation. Europe is a house inhabited by fierce, strong, living entities. Poland is not a ghost: Poland is a reincarnation. I think it a wonderful thing that Polish unity should have re-emerged from long hideous eclipse and bondage, when the Poles were divided between three empires and made to fight one another in all the wars that took place.

Churchill added:

> I rejoice that Poland has been reconstituted. I cannot think of any event arising out of the Great War which can be considered to be a more thoroughly righteous result of the struggle than the reunion of this people, who have preserved their national soul through all the

years of oppression and division and whose reconstitution of their
nationhood is one of the most striking facts in European history. Do
not let us be led, because there are many aspects of Polish policy that
we do not like or agree with, into dwelling upon the small points of
disagreement, and forget what a very great work has been achieved,
a work of liberation and of justice, in the reconstitution of Poland.
I trust she will live long to enjoy the freedom of the lands which
belong to her, a freedom which was gained by the swords of the
victorious Allies.

On September 25, 1939, as a result of the Nazi-Soviet Pact, Hitler and
Stalin ordered the partition of Poland between Russia and Germany. Poland
was once more enslaved. Yet Churchill also realized that in the end, Hitler
and Nazism could only be destroyed if Stalin joined the Allies.

Here then was the terrible dilemma of the Second World War in which
Churchill too was soon to be caught up. The Nazi-Soviet partition of
Poland distressed Churchill enormously. But he knew that the line of the
partition gave Russia those areas which, in 1920, Britain had also wanted to
give Russia—where Poles were in a minority. He therefore told the House
of Commons, on October 1, 1939: "Poland has been again overrun by
two of the great Powers which held her in bondage for 150 years, but
were unable to quench the spirit of the Polish nation. The heroic defense
of Warsaw shows that the soul of Poland is indestructible, and that she
will rise again like a rock, which may for a spell be submerged by a tidal
wave, but which remains a rock." Churchill's speech continued: "Russia
has pursued a cold policy of self-interest. We could have wished that the
Russian armies should be standing on their present line as the friends and
allies of Poland instead of as invaders. But that the Russian armies should
stand on this line was clearly necessary for the safety of Russia against the
Nazi menace." Churchill ended his remarks with a profound reflection:
"I cannot forecast to you," he said, "the action of Russia. It is a riddle
wrapped in a mystery inside an enigma; but perhaps there is a key. That
key is Russian national interest. It cannot be in accordance with the interest
or the safety of Russia that Germany should plant itself upon the shores
of the Black Sea, or that it should overrun the Balkan States and subjugate

the Slavonic peoples of southeastern Europe. That would be contrary to the historic life-interests of Russia."

In June 1941 Hitler invaded the Soviet Union and Churchill made his unilateral offer to Russia of alliance and aid. But still the Polish question cast its shadow on the new and vital alliance. In April 1943 the Soviet murders at Katyn were revealed: more than 10,000 Polish officers killed in cold blood by the Russians.

But it was in August 1944 with the Warsaw uprising, and with Stalin's refusal to help the Polish insurgents, that Churchill's sense of anger and disillusion were heightened—and unassuaged. The uprising had begun on August 1, 1944, when Soviet forces, having crossed the Vistula to the Warsaw side of the river, were less than ten miles from the city. On August 4, 1944, Churchill appealed to Stalin on behalf of the Poles to send aid. On the following day Stalin refused.

British planes and Polish volunteers flew nearly 1,400 miles from Italy and back to drop aid: but Stalin refused even a 100-mile flight or use of his airports by the Allies, or any further military advance. "Can you not give them some further help," Churchill telegraphed Stalin on August 12, "as the distance from Italy is so very great." But still Stalin refused. Nor would two further appeals from Churchill persuade him to help the Poles in their agony.

The Warsaw uprising was crushed. Stalin now prepared his new Polish plan, and on January 5, 1945, against the wishes of both Churchill and Roosevelt, Stalin recognized his own communist nominees, the Lublin Committee, as the provisional government of Poland. Twelve days later Soviet forces entered Warsaw, and with them—Stalin's puppet government. The future of Poland—to be discussed in vain at Yalta a month later—had already been decided by force of arms: Soviet arms.

At Yalta, though much was tried, nothing could be done to move Stalin from his determination to create a Communist Poland, under a Soviet military power that was already in place; and Poland, as Churchill later recalled, "was to prove the first of the great causes which led to the breakdown of the grand alliance." Bluntly, Churchill told Stalin at Yalta: "I want the Poles to be able to live freely, and live their own lives in their own way."

Roosevelt supported Churchill in this plea. But the Britain and American hopes of democratic elections in Poland had been challenged at Yalta, and were dashed after Yalta. On April 29, 1945, Churchill wrote to Stalin that the British "would never feel that this war will have ended rightly, unless Poland has a fair deal in the full sense of sovereignty, independence, and freedom." Churchill added that the pledge, which he and Roosevelt had given at Yalta, "for a sovereign, free and independent Poland, with a Government fully and adequately representing all the democratic elements among Poles, is for us a matter of honour and duty."

Churchill's letter to Stalin continued (it was just a year before he came here to Westminster College):

> There is not much comfort in looking into a future when you and the countries you dominate . . . are all drawn up on one side, and those who rally to the English-speaking nations . . . are on the other. It is quite obvious that their quarrel would tear the world to pieces and that all of us leading men on either side who had anything to do with that, would be shamed before history. Even embarking on a long period of suspicions, of abuse and counter-abuse, and of opposing policies, would be a disaster, hampering the great developments of world prosperity for the masses.

Churchill's letter ended: "Do not, I beg you, my friend Stalin underrate the divergences which are opening about matters which you may think are small to us, but which are symbolic of the way the English-speaking democracies look at life."

Stalin, of course, made no concessions—and in a letter to Anthony Eden on May 4, 1945, Churchill warned Eden of the new situation with Soviet forces in effective control from the Baltic to the Adriatic (the very same line that he was to describe here at Fulton ten months later as the "Iron Curtain").

In his letter to Eden, Churchill pointed out how, as a result of the continuing Soviet advances, the territory of Poland would be, as he put it, "completely engulfed and buried, deep in Russian-occupied lands." And that Poland would (I quote) "sink with many other States into the vast zone of Russian-controlled Europe . . . police-government."

The Second World War had ended. As Churchill had seen, retrogression—the flight from justice, the lapse into anarchy, the return to totalitarianism—constituted the main dangers confronting the development of the twentieth century. He had expressed that view clearly in 1928 in relation to the First World War: "Think of all these people—" he wrote, "decent, educated, the past laid out before them—what to avoid, what to do etc—patriotic, loyal, clean, trying their utmost—what a ghastly muddle they made of it! Unteachable from infancy to tomb—there is the first and main characteristic of mankind." And yet, as Churchill wrote on May 21, 1938, at the height of the Munich crisis: "It is a crime to despair. We must learn from misfortune the means of future strength."

And in his address here at Westminster College eight years later, in 1946, he set out yet again, as he had decade after decade for more than fifty years, the beliefs he still held, and the vision he still cherished, for mankind's future. As Churchill declared: "When I stand here this quiet afternoon I shudder to visualise what is actually happening to millions now and what is going to happen in this period when famine stalks the earth. None can compute what has been called 'the unestimated sum of human pain.' Our supreme task and duty is to guard the homes of the common people from the horrors and miseries of another war."

In his speech here, Churchill went on to give as his studied opinion:

> The people of any country have the right, and should have the power by constitutional action, by free unfettered elections, with secret ballot, to choose or change the character or form of government under which they dwell; that freedom of speech and thought should reign; that courts of justice, independent of the executive, unbiased by any party, should administer laws which have received the broad assent of large majorities or are consecrated by time and custom. Here are the title deeds of freedom which should lie in every cottage home.

During the course of his speech here at Westminster College, Churchill had also set out, as you know, the steps he believed should be taken:

above all what he called (I quote) "the fraternal association of the English-speaking peoples . . . not only the growing friendship and mutual understanding between our two vast but kindred systems of society, but the continuance of the intimate relationship between our military advisers, leading to common study of potential dangers."

Churchill was emphatic, here at Westminster, on the need for Anglo-American cooperation based on the eventual post-war recovery of Britain and on a strengthening of Anglo-American bonds. As he said (of Britain)

> Do not suppose that we shall not come through the glorious years of agony, or that half a century from now, you will not see 70 or 80 millions of Britons spread about the world and united in defense of our traditions, our way of life, and of the world causes which you and we espouse. If the population of the English-speaking Commonwealths be added to that of the United States with all that such cooperation implies in the air, on the sea, all over the globe and in science and in industry, and in moral force, there will be no quivering, precarious balance of power to offer its temptation to ambition or adventure. On the contrary, there will be an overwhelming assurance of security.

These concepts, which Churchill set out so clearly here at Westminster College, have not been entirely forgotten. May I quote, briefly, from a recent example:

> We are moving already beyond exchanges of views toward common strategic perceptions and concrete acts. We and our allies are taking common steps to restrain Soviet aggression and to restore our strength. On Poland, we have collectively sent a firm signal to the Soviet Union. The Soviets are now well aware that intervention would bring severe and lasting consequences. Indeed, the restraint we have seen offers some evidence of the benefits of alliance, cohesion and resolve.

These words were spoken only two days ago in Washington by Secretary of State Alexander Haig, and they reminded me forcibly of two of Churchill's remarks in his speech here.

The first: "The United States stands at this time, at the pinnacle of world power. It is a solemn moment, for the American democracy. For with primacy in power, is also joined an awe-inspiring accountability to the future."

The second remark made here in 1946, and which is as relevant today as it was then: "This," Churchill said, speaking of Poland, Hungary, Rumania, and Bulgaria subjected to Soviet rule, "is certainly not the Liberated Europe we fought to build up."

I should like to end, if I may, and surely no place is more suitable to end this than here at Westminster College, with the central theme of Churchill's Fulton speech, in which he drew both on his knowledge of past Soviet behavior and on his own experience of warning in vain against the Nazi danger in the 1930s.

As Churchill said (and with this quotation I shall end),

What we have to consider here today, while time remains, is the permanent prevention of war and the establishment of conditions of freedom and democracy as rapidly as possible in all countries. Our difficulties and dangers will not be removed by closing our eyes to them. They will not be removed by mere waiting to see what happens; nor will they be removed by a policy of appeasement. What is needed is a settlement, and the longer this is delayed, the more difficult it will be and the greater our dangers will become.

From what I have seen of our Russian friends and Allies during the war, I am convinced that there is nothing they admire so much as strength and there is nothing for which they have less respect than for weakness, especially military weakness. For that reason the old doctrine of a balance of power is unsound. We cannot afford, if we can help it, to work on narrow margins, offering temptations, to a trial of strength. If the Western Democracies stand together in strict adherence to the principles of the United Nations Charter, their influence for furthering those principles will be immense and no one is likely to molest them. If however they become divided or falter in their duty and if these all- important years are allowed to slip away then indeed catastrophe may overwhelm us all.

Last time I saw it all coming and cried aloud to my own fellow-countrymen and to the world, but no one paid any attention. Up till the year 1933 or even 1935, Germany might have been saved from the awful fate which has overtaken her and we might all have been spared the miseries Hitler let loose upon mankind. There never was a war in all history easier to prevent by timely action than the one which has just desolated such great areas of the globe. It could have been prevented in my belief without the firing of a single shot, and Germany might be powerful, prosperous and honoured today; but no one would listen and one by one we were all sucked into the awful whirlpool. We surely must not let that happen again.

Epilogue

Historical research is never ended; and on my return to England, after delivering the above lecture, I naturally continued with my Churchill researches. Indeed, even while preparing the lecture itself for publication, I came across material bearing directly on Churchill and the Fulton speech. From this material one sees how Churchill closely followed from day-to-day events in those regions of Europe controlled by Russia since the end of the Second World War. Thus, on October 15, 1945, he wrote to a friend: "I shudder to read the accounts that come to me of the Russian maltreatment of Vienna and the paralysis of Allied assistance."

One of the most fascinating documents to emerge during my research since my return is a letter which Churchill wrote to the Labour prime minister, Clement Attlee, and to his foreign secretary, Ernest Bevin, only two days after speaking to you at Westminster College. His letter, dated March 7, 1946, read in full:

> The President told me, as we started on our journey from Washington to Fulton, Missouri, that the United States is sending the body of the Turkish Ambassador, who died here some days ago, back to Turkey in the American battleship MISSOURI, which is the vessel on which the Japanese surrender was signed and is probably the strongest battleship

afloat. He added that the MISSOURI would be accompanied by a strong task force which would remain in the Marmara for an unspecified period. Admiral Leahy told me that the task force would consist of another battleship of the greatest power, two of the latest and strongest aircraft carriers, several cruisers and about a dozen destroyers, with the necessary ancillary ships. Both mentioned the fact that the MISSOURI class carry over 140 anti-aircraft guns. I asked about the secrecy of this movement and was told that it was known that the body of the late Ambassador was being returned in a warship but that the details of the task force would not become known before March 15. I feel it my duty to report these facts to you, though it is quite possible you may have already been informed through other channels. At any rate, please on no account make use of the information until you have received it from channels, other than my personal contact with the President.

The above strikes me as a very important act of state and one calculated to make Russia understand that she must come to reasonable terms of discussion with the Western Democracies. From our point of view, I am sure that the arrival and stay of such a powerful American Fleet in the Straits must be entirely beneficial, both as reassuring Turkey and Greece and as placing a demurrer on what Bevin called cutting our life-line through the Mediterranean by the establishment of a Russian naval base at Tripoli.

I did not consult the President on the exact text of my speech at Fulton before I finished it, but he read a mimeographed reproduction which was made on the train in its final form, several hours before I delivered it. He told me he thought it was admirable and would do nothing but good, though it would make a stir. He seemed equally pleased during and after. I also showed it to Mr. Byrnes the night before leaving Washington, making it clear that this was quite private and informal. He was excited about it and did not suggest any alterations. Admiral Leahy, to whom I showed it first of all, was enthusiastic. Naturally I take complete and sole personal responsibility for what I said, for I altered nothing as the result of my contacts with these high American authorities. I think you ought to know exactly what the position is and hope you will observe the very strong and precise terms in which I disclaim any official mission or status of any kind and that I spoke only for myself. If necessary these words of mine could be quoted.

Having spent nearly three days in most intimate, friendly contact with the President and his immediate circle, and also having had a long talk with Mr. Byrnes, I have no doubt that the Executive forces here are deeply distressed by the way they are being treated by Russia and that they do not intend to put up with treaty breaches in Persia or encroachments in Manchuria and Korea, or pressure for the Russian expansion at the expense of Turkey or in the Mediterranean. I am convinced that some show of strength and resisting power is necessary to a good settlement with Russia. I predict that this will be the prevailing opinion in the United States in the near future.

Following his return to England from Fulton, Churchill continued to study Soviet behavior, and saw no reason to change the views which he had expressed in his speech at Westminster College, or in the letter quoted above. Seven months after returning to England, Churchill wrote again to Clement Attlee, in a letter charged with irony and vision: "It is clear to me that only two reasons prevent the westward movement of the Russian armies to the United States and the Atlantic. The first is their virtue and self-restraint. The second, the possession by the United States of the Atomic bomb."

SIR JOHN H. PLUMB, a Fellow of the British Academy, was knighted by Queen Elizabeth II in 1982. He is Master of Christ's College, Cambridge, and has served as visiting lecturer at several universities in America.

2

The Dominion of History

Sir John H. Plumb

My theme—"The Dominion of History"—is appropriate, I think, for a lecture in honor of Sir Winston Churchill, who, after all, was, if anyone, the master general of that dominion.

The British reaction to the Falklands crisis astonished many Americans, astonished all Germans, and indeed most all Europeans except the French whose historical experience is also concerned with the struggle for liberty. Many feared that Mrs. Thatcher's furious belligerence would be inflamed in the future by similar threats to Hong Kong or Gibraltar. Such reactions betrayed a lack of historical judgment and complete ignorance of the role that history has played in Britain's sense of itself. A similar lack of historical empathy has bedeviled understanding of the French by any American president since the war. None of them could respond with warmth to De Gaulle, Pompidou, Giscard d'Estang, and now Mitterand: the French, like the British, are gripped by their past. Churchill, of course, would have understood instinctively why the overwhelming majority, left or right, supported Mrs. Thatcher, just as he found it easy to understand why French men and women acclaimed De Gaulle—even though he, himself, found him unbearable. Or why so much of Mitterand's policy has his nation's, as well as his party's, support.

The reason, of course, lies in the dominion of history. The British people are still entangled in their past, far less maybe than they were, but still very deeply. And so are the French. Memories of French greatness still influence Mitterand just as they did De Gaulle: hence their common attitude both to NATO and the independent nuclear deterrent. Any past, however, is multifaceted: at times liberating, at times dangerous. In Ireland, William III and Oliver Cromwell are real presences, bloodying the present in the most tragic and desperate way. And even in the Falklands crisis the legality of the past was endlessly and uselessly argued about. Whether John Smith first sighted the islands seemed to matter to some English intellectuals far more than the fact that an entirely British community had lived there for generations, displacing no one.

That history should matter comes as no surprise to most Britons, nor, it would seem, to most Argentinians, although the majority of the world's governments were bewildered. No historian, however, commented with much sense on the historical dimension of the Falkland crisis. Those who did largely confined themselves to a legalistic investigation of the nature of territorial sovereignty. Mrs. Thatcher had a much firmer grasp—and history told her that the British stood for the liberty of free Britons and the rule of law. For her, as for Churchill, that was what British history had been about, especially English history, from Magna Carta to the defeat of Hitler. In this crisis of the Falklands the latter mattered more than the former, particularly to anyone over fifty. But undoubtedly there was a very real sense of the past which Mrs. Thatcher rightly sensed and used.

Of course that essentially simple belief that British history had witnessed the slow unfolding of parliamentary democracy which protected not only property but also the liberties of the individual—free speech, free trial, free assembly—is no longer held by any, or scarcely any, professional historian. Indeed by scarcely any popular historian either. Its greatest popular exponent today is Sir Arthur Bryant, but his books belonged to a previous age—to the age of Churchill for whom the British past was a part of his daily life. There is a myth, which I myself held for a time, that Churchill only found the delights and the truths of history as a young subaltern in India when he spent long afternoons in his hammock reading Gibbon, Macaulay, and ancient volumes of the *Annual Register*, living again the grim parliamentary battles of his father's day. But this is not true. He was far from being a model schoolboy—he was idle, willful, self-involved, and quite stupid about mathematics or Latin but he was well ahead of his class at Harrow in history and top of the examination in history for the examination of Sandhurst every time that he took it: he failed of course, many times, but never in history. So his reading in history in India strengthened and furthered attitudes that were already burgeoning in childhood and adolescence.

History, for Churchill, was not a subject like geography or mathematics, it was a part of his temperament, as much a part of his being as his social class and, indeed, closely allied to it. It became a part of his politics, his diplomacy, his strategy and tactics: I think that it is extremely difficult for anyone not born into Churchill's world or time to realize what a dominance the past had over all of his thinking and action. And one should recall that for Churchill the past was very personal. Think, merely, of Blenheim Palace where he was born, which is not so much a house as the greatest war memorial ever built, by a grateful nation for his ancestor, indeed, to proclaim Marlborough's victories over Louis XIV. And the extent of his personal commitment to his family's, as well as his country's, past can be measured by his refusal to acknowledge Marlborough's greed, his vaunting ambition, his capacity for duplicity, even his treachery. In Churchill's *Life of Marlborough*, he certainly becomes *sans peur* and almost *sans reproche*. And what was true of Churchill was true of so many of his political colleagues: some (like the Salisburys) to a greater, some (like the Chamberlains) to a lesser degree. The former could claim the great age of Elizabeth, the latter merely Birmingham in the nineteenth century. A man like Churchill with an intensely creative mind, a natural capacity for the resplendent phrase and a huge need for money was drawn to the writing of history like a lover. His success, as we know, was prodigious. He certainly sold more books on history than any historian in this century and perhaps any century. And yet I am sure that these books could not be written today as they were written, even by a Churchill; I doubt whether, if submitted, any publisher would accept today—were it by an unknown author—*A History of the English-Speaking Peoples.*

Let us turn for a moment to two other British historians whose books, at times, rivaled those of Churchill and both of whom wrote histories of England comparable to that of Churchill—Sir Arthur Bryant and

G. M. Trevelyan. Bryant had something of a reputation before the war, but he really burgeoned during the World War II years when he wrote *The Years of Endurance* and *The Years of Victory,* which dealt with Britain's struggle against Napoleon. The narrative was heroic, beautifully orchestrated, and the prose dripped with rose-tinted sentiment—the roses around the simple cottage's door, the canary's cage hanging on the wall, the simple patriotism of simple men, Napoleon Bonaparte looming over it all like a Hitler in fancy dress. (Yet those were the terrible years, the 1790s when Britain came nearest to famine and when it had its worst naval mutiny, hardly mentioned at all by Bryant.) Nevertheless, the public loved his books. They were curiously readable and they were far, of course, from being entirely untrue but the patriotic glow dissolved what historical critical faculties Bryant possessed. It was followed after the war by a *History of England* which was even more patriotic, pulsating with Britain's manifest destiny, a paean to the long struggle fought by Britain for the sake of liberty and liberties: nowhere here will you find much on the exploitation of Ireland or Scotland, or the butcheries by the British in India or Africa, or a denunciation of its use of opium to rattle the decaying fabric of Imperial China; nothing here about the vile slums of the East End of London or the grinding poverty of so much of rural England that drove men and women here into what was your wilderness, which to them was a wilderness with hope. And yet to tens of thousands of British men and women, these books of Bryant bore witness to the truth that they felt in the very marrow of their bones. And not merely to Tories or to long-established families; Bryant was, after all, Sir Harold Wilson's (the Labour Party's prime minister) favorite historian and Wilson showered him with well-merited honors, for Bryant had, in a sense, become the voice of the Englishman's past.

Now, scarcely anyone reads Bryant. And this is not purely due to the passage of time or because others have taken his place. They have not. Fewer and fewer and fewer can read Bryant with any belief. And, alas, the same is true of a far greater, far wiser historian and writer of far greater genius—G. M. Trevelyan.

Trevelyan was Britain's most distinguished historian of the twentieth century, the most widely known and, after Churchill, the most widely read. All of his books remained in print throughout his lifetime, from

The Age of Wycliffe, published in 1899, to his *Autobiography* that came out fifty years later. All honors came to him—the Regius Chair of History at Cambridge; the Order of Merit; honorary degrees at Oxford, Harvard, and Yale. He refused a knighthood. He achieved far greater eminence than any academic historian of his age, and far greater sales of his books. He was, like Churchill whom he greatly admired, an aristocrat. His family went straight back to thirteenth-century Cornwall. His attachment to the British past had the same personal quality as Churchill's. He was denied the use of the Marlborough papers at Blenheim because Churchill was working on the life of his ancestor, although Trevelyan was at the height of his fame and needed them for his great portrayal of England in the reign of Queen Anne. When I commiserated with him, he looked at me somewhat baffled and barked, "But they're Winston's papers, aren't they?" Proprietorial regard for England's past could go no further. Like Churchill, too, he greatly admired Bryant whose career he helped considerably.

But Trevelyan was more scholarly, more sensitive than either Bryant or Churchill and a better historian. Like them, he was committed to a sense of England's manifest destiny, as guardian of personal liberty and liberties. But he was aware, far more acutely than the others, of how that story was clouded with ambiguity—a Roundhead by sympathy and intellectual commitment, he felt deeply the horror and tragedy of Charles I's execution and wrote some of his finest prose about it. He was even more acutely aware of the disastrous side of both the Industrial Revolution and the growth of British Imperialism, which appalled him. He loved "Old England"—and saw the eighteenth century as its golden age. And yet he had no doubts of Britain's greatness, of the miracle of her power and history, and believed that at their best the British stood for the decencies not only of human life but of behavior between peoples. The fact that they sinned, time and time again in India, in Ireland, and as they did in his sad old age at Suez did not weight the scales for him against them. They had ended, after all, the autocracy of Philip II of Spain and its Inquisition, opposed the megalomaniac ambitions of Louis XIV and Napoleon Bonaparte; above all, they had been steadfast against the monstrosity of Hitler. He is the only man I have ever known who paid his colossal taxes cheerfully, believing that these taxes were just when spent in stopping Nazi Germany. (Out of

£45,000 earned at the first publication of his *Social History,* he paid £42,500 in tax, and with glee. A rare man!) He believed to his dying day that history had to be a part of a nation's literature; otherwise that nation would lose not only the sense of its heritage but also of its destiny. Today in professional academic circles, he has no reputation any more than Bryant or Churchill. I doubt whether any young professional, except a historiographer, would deliberately read a work of his. He is, however, read by others and most of his books are in print, but his audience is now largely composed of civil servants and scientists and other professional men who stumble on his books partly by chance. Another decade, and he will be as dead as Froude or Freeman, or, in your terms, Bancroft. A man such as Trevelyan could not now be considered for an academic chair: even in his own day he was something of an anomaly. All of his major appointments and honors were gifts of friends or from the Crown, never from his academic colleagues, or rarely.

However, no matter how coolly or disdainfully academic historians received the works of Churchill, Bryant, or Trevelyan, they were not only rapturously received by the general public but they were used widely in schools and often plundered by writers of school textbooks for all grades. And this was at a time when the teaching of history was regarded in British education as central to its purpose and a large number of teaching hours devoted to it. My radical friends would regard this as a not very sophisticated piece of social control, for the version of history being taught was essentially that of the Establishment—that curious English mixture of professions, the City of London, the Church, and the land-owning aristocracy. Its major aim was to teach constitutional history, that is the struggle between Parliament and the Crown to secure the liberties that Englishmen of means enjoyed. It should be noted that little economic history figures in the Establishment's version of the English past. There was analysis of political change, but not of social change. And in Trevelyan and Bryant and indeed Churchill there was an anti-industrial bias, particularly so in the work of Trevelyan who was the most influential in schools; for him the golden age of England came before, not after, the Industrial Revolution. Schoolboys and schoolgirls were taught a dislike of industry and a dislike of the modern word, much to our present cost.

That such social control—largely unconscious—should be practiced should dismay no one; after all, in an age of nationalism it is not surprising that nations should glory in their past. For a Briton in 1920, a young Briton like myself, the extent of his empire bordered on the miraculous and he felt, perhaps rightly, that that cannot all have been due to chance, but to some virtue in his ancestors and their society.

And one further point must be stressed. This interpretation of the British past, which we might call the Churchillian past, which took root in the attitude of the ruling classes in Victorian England, was spread throughout the land in the early twentieth century by the growth of secondary and grammar school education. The history syllabus of the new civic universities, which provided so much of the teaching profession, adopted the syllabuses of Oxford and Cambridge in which the constitutional conflict between Crown and Parliament and the growth of personal liberties was central. The same attitude toward industry which colors the work of Trevelyan and Bryant and Churchill was also taught. The indifference of so many ordinary Englishmen toward the failure of their economy or to the shortcomings of their industrial production partly stems from this historical attitude; just as much as their quick, instinctive, patriotic response to the Falklands crisis.

Unless one comprehends this instinctive attitude to the past held by most Englishmen, one cannot understand the astonishing dialogue which Churchill held with his people throughout the war. Nor, of course, is Britain the only European country with such intense preoccupation with its own past. In the middle decades of this century it was true of most European countries. But, because of Hitler, Germany and other countries have now become dislocated from their past: indeed, have become schizophrenic about it. Indeed in Germany, in Hesse, history is no longer taught in schools: in no German university can you major in history and nothing else. Even professional history in Germany is still hesitant, tentative, and the number of professional historians comparatively small for so large a population. I speak, of course, of West Germany, not of the East.

The sense of the past, has, of course, weakened in all other Western countries. Churchill's view of Britain's past now seems archaic, not only to the professional historian in Britain but to a very large segment of the nation under fifty years of age. This is due to a variety of reasons, too many to explore in detail today. But some I do want to explore, especially those aspects of the problem that are common to Western societies, and especially to this country.

In the nineteenth century American historians were almost to a man New Englanders. From the eighteenth century onward an Anglo-Saxon past was forged—a sense of special American destiny, a land of liberty, free from the corruptions and tyrannies of Europe; indeed, as Washington Irving stated it, America was the tribunal before which, and I quote, "the whole world is to be summoned, its history to be revised and rewritten, and the judgement of past ages to be cancelled or confirmed." What confidence, what arrogance at a time when slavery was still a fact of American life. Indeed, in their coarser expressions, these concepts of the past were easy to destroy, and of course they were by the growth of professional history.

It is commonplace to remark on the almost unbelievable growth of science in the last century—the proliferation of journals, institutions, academies, and university faculties or indeed universities devoted to science and technology and little else. The spread in schools of science is equally remarkable. Children are now more numerate than they have ever been throughout the course of human history. Even five-year-olds can play with their computers. What is less remarked upon is that a similar growth has taken place in history at university level, but NOT in primary and secondary schools; there, tragically, the number of lessons devoted to history has steadily declined since World War I throughout the Western world or been subsumed into social or civic studies. But not at the university level. Throughout the middle decades of this century and particularly in the fifties, sixties, and seventies, the number of professional historians has grown prodigiously and if, as we should, we link with them the historians of literature, of science, of medicine, of art, etc., then the number becomes even more amazing. Let me give one example—eighteenth-century studies of European history. There are now well over six thousand men and women who teach it, write it, or lecture about it, and all derive their livelihood from it. An international conference in eighteenth-century studies will draw hundreds of scholars. At the fifth international conference on eighteenth-century studies, *thirty-five scholars* read major papers on "The portrayal and condition of women in eighteenth-century literature," and, of course, the number of participating scholars in those sessions was infinitely larger. The transactions of the conference, which lasted about five days, ran to 2,040 pages. What is true of the eighteenth century is true of other centuries or eras: the Renaissance, the Reformation, the Age of Discovery. They all have thousands of scholars working on them. Add every other variety of history and you will realize that the Western world's historians would populate a very large city indeed if, God forbid, they were all brought together. And remember that one hundred years ago there were only a handful of professional university historians. I doubt whether, throughout the world, they would have numbered a thousand.

A part of the growth has been due to the development of new areas of historical investigation which is a response to our own social worries, bafflements, or problems—the growth of Black history, women's history, the history of childhood or of death; investigations of popular culture or social protest; all of these (and there are many more—food, clothes, toys, etc., etc.) have added new dimensions to history—to its research, and, as we shall see, more dangerously to its teaching. But what has been created, and this is very important, is a professional world and a professional audience with all that implies. There is a professional world in which a historian must succeed by writing specialized monographs or ever more specialized papers and journals for other historians. He must go to specialized conferences and participate in ever more specialized seminars. There is a professional audience there and an important one not only for historians but also for publishers; behind scholars stand libraries and all the supportive paraphernalia of research. Indeed, historical scholarship in Europe and America is now an industry upon which billions of dollars are spent every year. An industry that sets its own standards, makes its own criticisms, and, very largely, its own appointments.

It becomes increasingly difficult for the historian to know what is happening in fields adjacent to his own. It is quite impossible even for an eighteenth-century historian to know all that is published every year about the eighteenth century. There are, of course, works of synthesis, and often good ones, but these are largely, if not entirely, directed at specialized professional audiences. And one further point, professional audiences do not have to be beguiled; they will read avidly in their subject for facts and ideas no matter how pedestrian the prose. Winning readership is not a preoccupation of the professional historian.

Research, of course, influences teaching, particularly in universities. And the influence has been far from benign. There has been a steady decline in most countries in the number of men and women who major in history at universities; in some countries this decline has been precipitate—in five years in the seventies enrollment in western Canada declined by over thirty percent. At my own university numbers for many years remained static but this gave an illusory impression of stability, for at the same time the number of undergraduate students at Cambridge had increased by nearly forty percent. However, there is an even greater decline in the number of university students who become teachers of history in schools. Before the war, about fifty percent of all undergraduates reading history became schoolmasters; now it is less than ten percent. This, of course, is due to the decline of the amount of teaching of history in schools. Up to 1950 history in schools was a major subject as central as mathematics or English. Now in almost all secondary schools in Britain it is optional or subsumed in social studies. In very few schools indeed is history taught as Churchill learned it or I did. Nothing is taught simply and directly. Instead of teaching the history of the nation, in Britain or in America, nowadays it is thought to be too nationalistic, too chauvinistic, too Eurocentric, and so what is taught is themes. Indeed, one of the themes offered for teaching in the New York schools is "The Position of Women in Imperialist Africa," which I think must be rather baffling to the most clever and expert twelve-year-old.

In my lifetime the teaching of history in universities has changed dramatically both in Britain and in America, as well as Europe. It has fragmented. In all British universities, the core of the history syllabus in the old days was the history of Britain, mainly political and constitutional history but with the addition of a little economic history. Major papers were compulsory, and there was a certain amount of choice between political history or the history of the United States. In most universities proficiencies in languages were also required. That, of course, was thought to be too elitist and has been abolished. This syllabus has been attacked constantly during my lifetime and has become so fragmented now that the situation, I think, borders not only on the ludicrous but also on the scandalous. Now it is possible to leave Cambridge without knowing anything about the Reformation or the civil war in Britain or America's struggle for independence. One need know nothing of the Renaissance or the French Revolution, nothing of the Industrial Revolution or of the Enlightenment. One can spend half of one's assignment for one's last year as a history student on the history of Ruanda-Burundi. I assure you that is true. There are other subjects almost equally as obscure being offered to the undergraduates. The fragmentation goes on and on so that teaching reflects little more than the research interests of those who teach. The fragmentation of research is paralleled by a fragmentation of teaching. Only specialists can teach on such narrow subjects. The entire process is directed to professional ends and interests, with no real interest in the undergraduate at all.

This process is little different from what has happened here in America. One has only to point to the sharp decline in Western civilization courses, the addition of Black studies, of the history of women, even gay studies, or of the history of family structure, the growth of courses in urban and local history, etc., etc. Here, as well as in Britain, the concept of narrative history, of society, in all its aspects, not merely one aspect of it, developing over time has been broken and dislocated.

This fragmentation, or if one wishes to use a more neutral phrase, this growth of specialization, is not peculiar to the study of history; it is true of literary studies, of the classics, and of philosophy. It is also, of course, a natural development amongst the sciences. And it is true, too, of the scholarship relating to the visual arts and music. Unlike the Marxist world, the culture of the West is not held in an ideological framework.

For history itself and for history's social role, this fragmentation has had some very unfortunate effects. For one thing, it has created a chasm between professional and popular history which does not exist, for example, in any Marxist country—there the full force of scholarship pervades what the public is given. In the Western world during the twentieth century there have been a number of writers who have attempted universal history and historical explanations of mankind—Spengler, Wells, Toynbee: not one commands any respect from professional historians who, with one or two honorable exceptions, refuse to attempt it themselves. Mankind itself hungers for historical explanation. Below the level of universal history it is much the same story—historical books which reach the bestseller list— the Barbara Tuchmans, the Longfords, the Antonia Frasers—are often beautifully written, shrewd about human behavior, but weak and shallow on historical context. They are not concerned with primary problems so much as surface texture. They do not explain; they describe. There are one or two professionals who stand out like pyramids in a desert— men such as William McNeill, Carlo Cipolla and a few others who take a vast theme stretching over millennia, who sell amply and do convey the excitement of historical analysis over the long time. They try to offer an explanation of why all societies are as they are but often they are somewhat maverick and get obsessed by unilateral explanations. One should regard them as rope bridges crossing the vast canyon that now divides public and professional history.

If we turn for a moment to Russia or to the committed Marxist societies, the picture is totally different. There a coherent framework of historical explanation is imposed on history in schools, on history in universities, on history for the public, and most certainly on historical research. Furthermore, history is not ignored in these countries. In primary school, in secondary school, in the universities, all disciplines have to learn some history and are taught some history. We know, of course, that this framework can have sudden and arbitrary changes in detail—Stalin can be writ large or very small; others who once loomed, like Khrushchev, can vanish like a shadow—but the grand design, the fundamental analysis remains: that human history is a dialectical process, a conflict of classes for the control of the means of production that inevitably leads to the dictatorship of the proletariat. What they are being taught is that history is an unfinished process, that the West and the Third World are in earlier stages of development than the Marxist countries and must inevitably collapse or become Marxist, whether pushed by Marxist countries or not. The historical past, therefore, not only justifies the Marxist present but predicates an inevitably Marxist future. That is to say that Marxist statesmen and Marxist revolutionaries, wherever they may be, possess a profound historical certainty as deep and as all embracing as any historical belief can be. Just as profound, just as instinctive as Winston Churchill's or Mrs. Thatcher's. But whereas Marxist statesmen reflect the historical commitment of their societies, no one can say that Mrs. Thatcher reflects a historical attitude that embraces her entire society. She reflects an attitude that has weakened immeasurably, particularly amongst the intelligentsia, if not among the working classes where her major support was over the Falklands, and whatever strength it has certainly belongs to the years of 1940–1942 when Britain stood out in its defiance of Hitler which as it were, through Churchill, reinvigorated its sense of historical destiny. Even though Britain and the West are not entirely without a sense of historical destiny, no one, I think, can deny that history is a most formidable weapon in the hands of Marxists and an intolerably weak one in the hands of the West.

At this point, doubtless, my critics would raise the question that Marxist history contains a great deal of falsehood whereas Western historians pursue the truth. Of course, I would agree that Marxist history is often false.

Distortion, Orwellian language of unbelievable hypocrisy are surely part and parcel of the Marxist version of the past. But if untruth works so well, should not truth work better? Can the West present a version of history based on accurate fact and true analysis that is easy to grasp, that works at all levels from simple primary history to sophisticated levels of professional scholarship? The short answer, of course, is "No." Western society, rightly, is too critical and also knows that professional history, like science, steadily refines and modifies generalizations through research. To accept rigid interpretation would be folly.

The communist solution is not possible; no free government can dictate what history should be studied, written, and perhaps taught—in schools certainly some control is possible even in democratic societies and perhaps should be exercised.

The problem that I have outlined today—the collapse of Western societies' sense of historical destiny, the constant fragmentation of history by professionals, the chasm between historical research, and the writing of popular history are problems fortunately exercising a growing number of historians. There is a growing sense of a crisis in history which derives from the steady decline in the number of student historians and the diminishing time spent on history in schools. Many teachers realize that no society will tolerate the huge expenditure on this minor but considerable industry without some decent return. The professional bodies are themselves stirring and tentatively looking for new or old methods to win back its central place in our culture. And these attempts must be encouraged. The pages of The American Historical Association's house journal, *AHA Perspectives,* contain nostrums to resuscitate the interest of students and the public in history in every issue that is published—some trying quite desperate means to encourage people to read history in their universities.

One exotic experiment is taking place in Illinois where, terrified by declining student interest, a bold professor introduced a course on the history of American sport, using it as far as one can tell to drag in a number of social problems as well as technological developments. At least he attracted the support of about fifty students and so probably kept his job going for a year or two. But this does illustrate a certain sense of despair. I am not against, far from it, the history of sport. I regard it as an admirable leisure activity: but I cannot see it changing the present climate of historical studies or giving America at large a sense of confidence about its historic past.

More important is a larger experiment in the University of Southern California. The reason again was the same; during the seventies the number of history majors at USC had fallen by fifty-two percent. But instead of trying to pump up the number of majors, Professor E. Bradford Burns went for a new audience—life scientists, engineers, physical scientists, social scientists, students of literature. A course, "The United States since 1945," filled the classroom to overflowing; another broad course on Latin America had an enrollment of nearly 150, most of them not historians. As Professor Burns rightly points out, the hunger to know about the past is there. And he rightly points out so is the ignorance due to the endless fragmentation of historical teaching. As he writes trenchantly, "Countless studies reinforce what we know from classroom experience. The majority of history students cannot identify Socrates, confuse the Enlightenment with the name of a rock band and draw a blank when McCarthy, Kennedy, or Vietnam are mentioned." These young men and women are not more stupid than their parents, nor do they have weaker memories. They are badly taught: so badly taught that their ignorance endangers the health of

American society; ignorance cannot breed confidence, only bewilderment. Nor is this an American disease; I could quote equally alarming ignorance from Britain and Western Europe. There is a battle with the Soviets for men's intellectual development as well as in nuclear parity.

Professor Burns is, I am sure, on the right road even though he hasn't found the turnpike. Historians should be concerned about teaching all students, not merely history students. Teaching just history majors, I think, should be a minor part of their work.

In our free society, the government cannot, of course, direct the history that shall be taught; but men in public affairs at the local and state level can certainly exert a benign influence and would do so were they to be lobbied by concerned historians (who should also be more active in the general culture of their universities). And this is the only way to change the climate which needs to be changed.

As a foreigner, but also as a lover of America and one who has believed all of his life, and still does, that this country is the hope of mankind, I am deeply unhappy about the level of self-confidence that Americans now seem to possess and a part of that lack of self-confidence stems from a sense of America's past failures and past injustices—Vietnam and slavery and civil rights hang like a curse across America. Of course, societies as well as men, no matter how free or well-intentioned, make dreadful mistakes and run into almost intolerable disasters. And I do not deny the value of social criticism or the recognition of evil in politics: of course, they must be a part of the teaching of history. But it can be overdone; it can become a sort of sickness in itself. Against the disasters, the follies, the crimes which all societies have committed, there is another side and one where America reigns supreme—namely, achievement.

I would like to see a course taught in every school in this land and in every university on American achievement not only of its sciences, of its technology, of its commerce but also in creating a free and, what Americans seem curiously frightened of admitting, a continuously revolutionary society. Let me explain what I mean. Compare the frozen nature of communist society which is almost insanely conservative in social habits as well as ideas with your own: ideas, minority groups, experiments in work, experiments in living and leisure are given free expression here, whereas in Russia they would lead to imprisonment or death. By its very nature capitalism must welcome experiment, change, the creation of new markets. And it leads, again by its very nature, to a self-critical society, unlike the communist world. Can environmentalists protest in Russia and where do you find Russians having a campaign to stop whales or young seals from being slaughtered? Not possible. Gulag would be the answer. And it is this quality of life in America—its freedom created by generations of Americans that the ordinary people in the communist world long for. The achievements of America are very real and need to be taught as much as those achievements of European civilization in which Americans are rooted.

The true dominion of history, unless we are to lose the battle for the world's freedom and liberty, must be reestablished at the heart of America's education, and, indeed, at the heart of Britain's education. One would wish all Americans in high office and especially those in the highest to have the same historical confidence in their society as Winston Churchill possessed in his. Without that confidence, so nobly expressed, and to which his nation responded, the forces of Hitler might never have been defeated. If we are to win the battle for the future, our statesmen must bring back a proper sense of our destiny: and that can only be done through knowledge of our past, of what history has committed us to. And that knowledge will only come through a proper teaching, a sensible direct teaching of the basic historical values of our two societies.

SIR WILLIAM DEAKIN, D.S.O., literary assistant to Sir Winston Churchill, was knighted by Queen Elizabeth II in 1975. Among his several book publications are *The Brutal Friendship: Mussolini, Hitler, and the Fall of Italian Fascism* and *The Six Hundred Days of Mussolini.*

3

Churchill and Europe in 1944

SIR WILLIAM DEAKIN

I have chosen to address the subject of Churchill and Europe in 1944, hoping to present an image of the man at a particular moment in time when he was faced with the supreme crisis in the conduct of the closing war in Europe, and the as yet unresolved debates within the Grand Alliance on the shore of peace still beyond the horizon—before the chips were down.

The balance of power on the Continent—a traditional concern of Great Britain, one of whose central purposes in going to war in 1939 was to reestablish—was in the last stages of disintegration. The military liquidation of Germany would, in a matter of months, leave a central desert and empty space. A revolutionary adjustment of power in Europe would follow, its form molded by the relative interests and strengths of the United States, Great Britain, and the Soviet Union.

The culminating military strategy of the Grand Alliance was, in reality, worked out on two isolated fronts: in the West and the East. At no point was there a combined great operation accepted by the Three Great Powers. Indeed, two separate wars were being fought against Germany: the only common denominators being her total destruction.

The last stages of the conduct of the war in the West by the United States and Great Britain brought into the open frustrating strategic controversies, which have since bedeviled historians and led to the emergence—and at times demolition—of myths and legends on both sides.

The outcome was inevitably a compromise. The year 1944 led to strains in the "special relationship" between us.

The debate over the launching of "Overlord" and the opening of the Second Front is both too complex and familiar for me to venture into this well-trampled arena.

My own study of the British records—of many talks with Churchill himself and British leaders of the day—lead me to what he would call certain "recorded truths."

To Churchill the strategic concept of the Second Front was never in doubt, and would be *the* decisive Anglo-American operation in the European war—an irreversible and unrepeatable assault on Germany from the West—which could only be carried out once, and with an absolute margin of safety.

The nagging center of argument between the American and British leaderships was essentially one of timing and coordination with the subordinate Mediterranean theater in which your president and chiefs of staff had become reluctantly involved in 1942.

At the Teheran Conference in November 1943, Roosevelt, without prior consultation with Churchill, announced to Stalin that the expedition across the Channel was fixed to take place on May 1, 1944.

Churchill then spoke: "It has long been agreed with the United States that we should invade North or North-West France across the Channel . . . (and) we were resolved to do it in 1944. The President and I had always regarded Mediterranean operations as stepping-stones to the decisive cross-Channel operation." But he continued: "I wish to place on record that I could not, in any circumstance, agree to sacrifice the activities of the armies in the Mediterranean in order merely to keep the exact date of May 1 for 'Overlord.'"

In the event, this tremendous combined operation was launched on June 5, 1944.

Churchill's consistent caution about timing has been so perceptively analyzed by one of your leading military historians, Professor Kent Roberts Greenfield, that I feel that I should quote his sentences as a model of commentary:

The British had a grave reason for caution as they counted what it would cost them in basic strength as a World Power. In the course of 1943 their economy and military manpower were mobilized to the limit of endurance. They had far more to lose than the Americans. "Overlord" on a big scale would be their last shot. Even if it succeeded they would be unable to replace the losses it would inflict. The strength of their nation would decline not only relatively to that of the United States, but absolutely, leaving Great Britain a second or third rate power in world affairs. Failure of the invasion would mean, if not ruin, a prolongation of the war beyond their power to sustain.

Churchill did not fully comprehend what seemed to him the rigidity and obsession with fixed schedules in your military analysis—what he once called "the American clear-cut logical large scale mass production style of thought."

The Americans organized from strength for a crushing and decisive operation, and behind their thinking was a fear of an attritional and peripheral war against Germany which would strain the ultimate limits of American manpower and damage the conclusive campaign against Japan.

As General Marshall put it: "A democracy cannot fight a seven years' war." You were, with every reason, in a hurry. So were we.

The exploitation of "Overlord" and the stage of the penultimate phase of hostilities in the West engendered the real, fierce controversy between the American and British leadership, centering on the best use to be made of the secondary Mediterranean theater.

On June 4, 1944, two days before the Normandy landings, Anglo-American forces entered Rome.

The British had reluctantly agreed in principle to an American operation—code name "Anvil"—to land ten divisions in southern France to link up with Eisenhower's armies, after their invasion in the north and to strengthen the decisive assault across the Rhine.

The exchanges between the American and British chiefs of staff ended in rigid deadlock. As Churchill put it: "The first important divergence on high strategy between ourselves and our American friends." It was to be the last.

This could only be resolved directly between the two leaders. On June 28, 1944, Churchill cabled to Roosevelt:

The deadlock between our Chiefs of Staff raises most serious
issues. Our first wish is to help General Eisenhower in the most speedy
and effective manner. But we do not think this necessarily involves
the complete ruin of all our great affairs in the Mediterranean and we
take it hard that this should be demanded of us. . . . I think the tone
of the American Chiefs of Staff is arbitrary, and certainly I see no
prospect of agreement on the present lines. What is to happen then?

Although Churchill did not mention specifically the Balkans, Roosevelt
replied:

My interest and hopes center on defeating the Germans in front of
Eisenhower, and driving on into Germany rather than limiting this
action for the purpose of staging a full major effort in Italy. . . . I
cannot agree to the employment of United States Troops into the
Balkans. For purely political considerations here, I should never
survive even a slight set-back to "Overlord" if it were known that
fairly large forces had been diverted to the Balkans.

Churchill answered on July 1, 1944, in a message which he did not print
in his memoirs:

We are deeply grieved by your telegram. . . . The splitting up of
the two operations (Anvil and the advance to the Po Valley to contain
the German forces in Italy) neither of which can do anything decisive
is . . . the first major strategic and political error for which we two
are responsible.

At Teheran you emphasized to me the possibilities of a move east-
ward when Italy was conquered. No one involved in these discussions
has ever thought of moving armies into the Balkans; but Istria and
Trieste in Italy are strategic and political positions, which as you
saw yourself, very clearly might exercise profound and widespread
reactions, especially now after the Russian advances.

If you still press upon us the directive of your Chiefs of Staff to
withdraw so many of your forces from the Italian campaign and leave
all our hopes there dashed to the ground, His Majesty's Government,
on the advice of their Chiefs of Staff, must enter a solemn protest.

I need scarcely say that we shall do our best to make a success of anything that is undertaken.

On the day following this message, July 2, the President gave instructions to proceed with "Anvil," and on August 15 General Wilson, as British commander in the Mediterranean, received final orders for the assault.

Roosevelt conveyed this—in effect—unilateral decision to Churchill on that day: "I always think," he wrote, "of my early geometry—a straight line is the shortest distance between two points."

This presidential decision confirmed the overwhelming military predominance of the United States in Europe in relation to Great Britain, and the limits of British influence on summit strategic decisions as from the summer of 1944.

The depleted but hard core of an Anglo-American army under British command remained in Italy and its employment, further reduced by the assaults on southern France, remained for marginal debate between the two leaderships.

Discussions were transferred to Quebec in September—the last Anglo-American summit meeting of the war.

The American leadership could now afford to grant to Churchill a Pyrrhic but significant concession: The Italian front should be held in its present diminished form with a view to possible operations in the directions of Vienna if the war lasted until 1945—a last remnant of peripheral strategy.

Churchill's warning at Quebec of "the rapid encroachment of the Russians into the Balkans and the consequent dangerous spread of Russian influence in the area" met with no comment or response on the American side. The minutes of the conference made laconic reference: "Balkans: Operations of our air forces and commando-type operations continue."

Arising out of the breakdown of the Grand Alliance after 1945 a postwar strategic theory was evolved by historians and publicists, mainly here in the United States, to explain that events might have taken a different course and changed the whole outcome of the Second World War if only the strategy of a major Second Front in the Balkans had been evolved.

The basic assumptions of such a theory were—and still are—that an Allied landing in southeast Europe was an integral and central element in British planning after 1942, and consistent with the historical traditions of the British conduct of war on the European Continent: the "Eccentric" operations of the Napoleonic wars; the Dardanelles and Salonika in the First World War; the horror of the Western Front and the nightmare of another trench warfare; and the continuing aim to preserve British imperial interests in the Mediterranean.

This alleged Balkan operation—so the theory runs—was thus deliberately conceived by Churchill and the British chiefs of staff as the alternative to "Overlord." It had also a longer-term political motivation to beat the Russians into Central Europe, and limit the Soviet drive into the Balkans and the spread of communist influence westward: in other words, to reconstruct the Sanitary Cordon of the 1920s and forestall the creation of an Iron Curtain.

The protagonists of this theory were, in the main, critics of President Roosevelt. Churchill, as its architect, was right in the event, and Roosevelt, in his opposition, wrong.

This Balkan legend has taken firm root in the postwar interpretation of the conduct of the last war. As one American historian has written: "It is virtually accepted as a self-evident truth."

I learned recently that the story also appears in the curriculum of some Canadian schools.

As early as 1944 Churchill was intuitively aware that such a legend would emerge.

In that summer he addressed a conference of the Dominion prime ministers in London:

> There had never been any question of major action in the Balkans. . . . Due priorities must prevail in the application of resources. . . . The Americans all along said that we were leading them up the garden path in the Mediterranean. His reply had been that, in return, we had provided them in the garden with nourishing vegetables and fruits. Nevertheless, the Americans had remained very suspicious.

I think, myself, that American suspicions, particularly among the chiefs of staff, had deep historical roots, which mark their approach to the Grand Strategy of the European war.

The landings in North Africa were anathema to the American military leaders—part of an ill-conceived doctrine of encirclement—and, as one of them put it, "scatterization." They had felt lured into the Mediterranean at the Casablanca Conference in January 1943, not only because they had to admit that the build-up for a decisive landing in northern France was far from completion, but that Mediterranean operations were essentially designed to further exclusively British interests—to preserve and control from Mediterranean bases the imperial route to Asia and the Far East.

The liquidation of Italy as the main Axis partner was all very well, but this operation also might imply the use of Italian territory as a base for further operations across the Adriatic.

As viewed from Washington, the British leadership under Churchill followed two war aims: firstly, the destruction of German military power; and secondly, the preservation of the British Empire and the recovery of Malaysia and Singapore.

In pursuit of the latter, control of the Mediterranean routes and both shores was essential to British thinking.

As seen from London, the first aim concluded, with the unanswerable argument of the overwhelming military and economic power of the United States by 1944, on absolute agreement on "Overlord."

I have often wondered why, in the personal talks and correspondence between Roosevelt and Churchill, scant attention was given to the momentous problem of how to deal with Russians, not only in terms of seeking to work out a combined military strategy, but on issues of common concern for the future balance of power in Europe as the Soviet armies reached and crossed the eastern frontiers of the European Continent.

The first test of our future relations with the Soviet Union was to be the fate of Poland.

The formal cause of Great Britain's declaration of war against Germany was to honor her guarantee to Warsaw against Nazi aggression. Immediate military aid was geographically impossible and beyond our straitened resources.

Our gesture had been a symbolic defiance of spreading German hegemony throughout Europe, and of its early result, the fourth partition of Poland and her extinction as an independent state (by division between Germany and the Soviet Union).

Britain had undertaken a moral obligation to bring about the restoration of Poland. She accepted and recognized a provisional government-in-exile in London, and the creation of a Polish army and air force under British command.

The German attack on the Soviet Union in June 1941, and the abrupt and unexpected acquisition by Britain of Russia as an ally, opened at once the whole issue of Poland within the frame of Anglo-Russian relations in a climate of mutual suspicion which was never dissipated. The Russians made it clear at once that their major war aim was to secure a tenable defensive western frontier as already sketched in the Nazi-Soviet pact which had achieved all the key positions of their historical claims to such a line.

The major link in this chain was the Polish territories already occupied by the Soviet Union in 1939 in eastern Poland.

The acceptance by Britain of this mutilation of prewar Poland became a grim test of the Anglo-Soviet alliance as a whole.

The United States was bound by no such obligations and the Polish "problem" did not early reach summit level, and then, fleetingly, until the Teheran Conference in December 1943.

In the meantime, the British government struggled to maintain, on a diplomatic level, the bare formal recognition by Stalin of the Polish provisional government in London until the nightmare of the Katyn massacre, when Churchill was obliged personally to force the Poles to suppress any public reference to Soviet guilt. He took the same action with the Foreign Office and British censorship.

At Teheran, Churchill first raised with Stalin a common policy of the Three Great Powers.

A vague frame was set for further discussion. Stalin proposed compensating a future Polish state in the West along the line of the Oder, while retaining the eastern territories already under Soviet occupation. He would not recognize the provisional Polish government in London—with whom he had severed relations over Katyn. This tragedy was not mentioned.

As to the future western Russian-Polish frontier, Stalin was prepared to consider the proposed and unadopted Curzon Line of 1920, and there was much confused study of maps.

Churchill undertook to advise the London Poles to accept this line as the basis of future negotiations and in the hope of ultimate agreement on an agreed and reconstructed Polish government.

There the matter rested. No formal statement was agreed. A tacit assumption seemed to have been accepted that all parties favored, in principle, the Curzon Line.

In conclusion, the minutes read: "The Prime Minister demonstrated with the help of three matches his idea of moving Poland westward, which pleased Marshal Stalin."

Throughout the following months, the advance led armies toward the frontiers of Poland, and sealed her political fate.

The tragedy of the Warsaw rising at the end of July 1944—a story still unresolved in calm historical terms—marked the end of any effective and agreed solution of a genuine or independent Poland.

Stalin could now realistically count on the ultimate acceptance by America and Britain of certain territorial concessions from Finland, the Soviet annexation of the Baltic states, and the Curzon Line in Poland.

The assault of the Soviet armies along the frontier of Romania and Yugoslavia raised urgently the whole future of Central Europe and the Balkans and of Soviet military and political intentions throughout these regions of Europe—as yet to be defined.

The lessons of Teheran had shown the confused limitations of three-power conferences.

Churchill was always skeptical of unprepared tripartite talks.

The competitive bids for Stalin's ear seemed a novel procedure in the conduct of business. As Churchill put it, "I would rather put up with Stalin's bad manners than be deprived of the means of carrying on the war effectively by consultation between Great Britain and the United States."

But the lack of any contact or even joint discussions between Washington, London, and Moscow on future arrangements in the Balkans prompted Churchill to make a direct approach to Stalin.

On May 31, 1944, he cabled to the president:

> There have been recently disquieting signs of a possible divergence of policy between ourselves and the Russians in regard to the Balkan countries and in particular Greece. We therefore suggest to the Soviet Ambassador here that we should agree between ourselves as a practical matter that the Soviet government would take the lead in Roumanian affairs, and ourselves in Greece.
>
> I hope that you would give this proposal your blessing. We do not, of course, wish to carve up the Balkans into spheres of influence, and in agreeing to such an agreement we should make it clear that it applied only to war conditions. . . . We feel, however, that the arrangement now proposed would be a useful device for preventing any divergence of policy between ourselves and them in the Balkans.

Roosevelt replied (on June 11) in the negative. He felt that the British proposal would "result in the persistence of differences between you and the Soviets." He thought it better "to establish consultative machinery and restrain the tendency towards the development of exclusive spheres."

On July 29 the Polish Home Army rose against the German garrison in Warsaw. This tragic episode is familiar to you: The refusal of Moscow to allow more than a token Anglo-American airlift and the abrupt halt of their armies in the suburbs of the Polish capital could logically only lead to the ultimate Soviet decision to support a satellite administration trained in Russia.

Both the British and Americans were now reduced to maneuvering with no cards in their hands, except the supposed general goodwill of Stalin, to seek an agreed coalition government—part Soviet and part Anglo-American backed.

On August 23, 1944, King Michael of Romania and his close advisers organized an anti-German coup d'état in Bucharest. The Romanian armies followed their king against the German occupier. This whole front was thrown open to the southern Soviet armies.

After Poland, the fate of Romania was secured before any proposed summit meeting would be held.

One country alone in southeast Europe seemed to provide an approximate model for a realistic understanding within the Grand Alliance. That was Yugoslavia. It had been agreed at Teheran to recognize Tito as a military ally. Churchill undertook, as a British "operation," to initiate negotiations between Tito and the Yugoslav king to form a provisional coalition government until the end of hostilities. He had met Tito in Italy in August 1944 and talks were in slow progress between Tito and the king's representative.

Soviet forces had reached the borders of Hungary. Envoys from Budapest and Bucharest were already in Moscow seeking an armistice.

Bulgaria, technically "neutral" as to the Soviet Union but at war with Britain and the United States, was suing for an armistice with them and negotiating with Moscow for a Soviet occupation.

On September 7, 1944, the Soviet armies entered Bulgaria and a fragile coalition government was set up. Bulgarian forces were cleaned up and put under Soviet command.

The British were at once alarmed at the possibility of Bulgaria-Russian forces moving into Greece and supporting the Greek communist guerrillas.

The Balkan situation which Churchill had proposed to discuss with Stalin in June 1944 had then been relatively fluid. By September the Russians were already firmly in charge in Romania and Bulgaria, Hungary was about to fall into their hands, Tito was in Moscow later in the month to negotiate joint military operations against Belgrade (his political intentions were unknown to the British and Americans). The main British interest—Greece—seemed under threat.

Against this background Stalin could afford to receive Churchill.

On September 29 Churchill cabled Roosevelt, reporting that he and Eden proposed to fly to Moscow.

Stalin accepted warmly the British visit: "We shall have to consider military and other questions which are of great importance."

Roosevelt was invited to join this Moscow Conference but felt unable to leave during the presidential campaign.

Unknown to Churchill, he had cabled to Moscow: "It is important that I retain complete freedom of action after the conference is over."

When I was studying the papers of the prime minster's office, which for the first time in our history were kept and filed separately from the archives of government departments and were housed after 1945 in the basement of the then Ministry of Defense, I found a scrap of paper. When I showed it to Churchill, he seemed to have forgotten its existence.

On the first night of the Moscow Conference the British official minutes record the essence of the talks between the two leaders. Stalin was "ready to discuss anything."

He began skillfully by stating that "it was a serious matter for Britain when the Mediterranean route was not in her hands. . . . He agreed that Britain should have the first say in Greece," but did not immediately comment on Churchill's remark that "he was not worrying much about Romania": "The British Prime Minister then reviewed the question of the interests of the two Governments in the various Balkan countries."

At the end of their first discussion Churchill leaned across the table and handed to Stalin the half-sheet of paper which I have just mentioned.

This incident is not recorded in the official British record, but, for the first time, in Churchill's war memoirs.

The paper contained a list of countries and against each a suggested proportion of respective British and Russian interests:

Romania	Russia 90%: The others 10%
Greece	Great Britain 90% (in accord with the United States): Russia 10%
Yugoslavia	50–50%
Hungary	50–50%
Bulgaria	Russia 75%: The others 25%

Stalin made no comment and handed back the document with a large tick in blue pencil against Romania.

Neither Churchill nor Stalin regarded this eccentric form of procedure as of any significance in itself.

At his first encounter with Stalin in 1942 in Moscow, Churchill had drawn a sketch of a crocodile with a soft underbelly to explain the strategic importance of attacking the Axis animal from the south.

At Teheran, as I have mentioned, he played with three matches to illustrate compensation from Poland at the expense of Germany.

Mr. Averell Harriman, the American ambassador to Moscow, who was not present at this meeting, has recorded later that he learned from Churchill in bits and pieces the story of the percentages. He seems, however, at the time merely to have reported to Roosevelt that the British and Russians were trying to work out some sort of respective spheres of influence.

The public revelation of this episode first appeared in Churchill's war memoirs, and caused a furor in the world press and subsequent memoirs and studies.

Whatever the real and lasting significance of this scrap of paper, the convenient and rough concept of percentages remained in the mind, both of Churchill *and* Stalin.

They had already been discussed in detail between Eden and Molotov.

In the event, Stalin decided, and probably much earlier than at this Moscow Conference, to give the British a free hand in Greece in return for control of Romania.

These Moscow talks, intended by Churchill to provoke Stalin to reveal his political and military intentions in southeastern Europe, were very badly received in Washington and created suspicions of the British conception of spheres of influence, which might be dangerously applied elsewhere in Europe and, indeed, the Far East.

The very secret military talks between the British and Russian delegations to which Churchill does not refer in his memoirs were of some modest moment.

Stalin mentioned that "The Russians did not propose to advance further west in Yugoslavia than Belgrade. They preferred to join hands with General Alexander's forces in Austria." The immediate task of the Red Armies was to eliminate Hungary and the German forces in the Baltic area, prior to the main operation—the invasion of Germany. He added politely that "a break-through in the West would decide the war."

Spreading military victory in the West gave rise to latent political issues between Washington and London which had a grave bearing on the future of Western Europe.

Churchill was never a planner of policies and deliberately avoided facing any irrevocable decisions regarding the restoration and shape of power in those countries in the course of the liberation and occupation of the states in the West.

He hoped for a minimum of change and firmly believed in restoration of legitimate governments, and, when relevant, monarchies.

It was also Churchill's profound guiding conviction that the British concept of democratic parliamentary government was indissolubly bound up with the preservation of the monarchy itself and that this was our essential contribution and model for others.

The first issue arose over the provisional political government of Italy.

The armistice negotiations had been exclusively handled by Eisenhower and his staff; the temporary administration was confined to Marshal Badoglio, and the king, Victor Emmanuel, continued nominally to reign.

Beneath a thin and complacent facade of cobelligerency presided over by Marshal Badoglio, after February 1944, there were the restless conclaves of the old political parties disintegrated by the advent of Mussolini in 1922.

The phenomenon of fascism was beyond the range of Churchill's direct experience and it was not in his character to speculate on alien ideologies. He was merely concerned that no irreversible decision, indeed interference, should complicate the ultimate political settlement of Italy until hostilities had ceased and genuine democratic elections could be held.

In the summer of 1944, after the liberation of Rome and without the knowledge of London or Washington, the king abdicated abruptly and nominated his son as regent: Badoglio withdrew, and a ragged antifascist administration under the prefascist socialist leader, Bonomi, was installed.

Churchill exploded in furious astonishment in a cable to the president on June 11, 1944:

> I think it a great disaster that Badoglio should be replaced by this group of aged and hungry politicians. . . . Instead, we are confronted with this absolutely unrepresentative collection. I was not aware . . . that we had conceded to the Italians . . . the power to form any government they chose without reference to the victorious powers, and without the slightest pretense of a popular mandate.

American attitudes to Italy, however, were marked by a powerful antifascist lobby of both American citizens of Italian origin and the main group of Italian exiles from the regime of Mussolini. These mobilized round the former Italian foreign minister before the advent of Mussolini, Count Sforza, who was now convinced that he be the head of any immediate administration which Washington and London would accept.

Without prior consultation between us, Sforza had returned to Italy in late 1943 and found his way into the new Bonomi government.

In view of the forthcoming presidential elections, in which the 600,000 Americans of Italian descent possessed a significant vote, Churchill refrained from using his personal line to the president; but he instructed the British ambassador in Washington, Lord Halifax, on December 3, 1944, to "hold the following language with the State Department" after having made clear in Rome that he had no trust or confidence in Sforza as a candidate for leadership:

> We feel ourselves fully entitled to make the Italian government aware of our view . . . because, as we have been accorded the command in the Mediterranean, as the Americans have been in France, and therefore we have a certain special position and responsibility.
>
> In short, if I were compelled, which I should regret, to state my objections to Count Sforza . . . I should also be forced to disclose the fact that I consider him . . . an intriguer and mischief-maker of the first order . . . He has no mandate or democratic authority of any sort or kind. . . .
>
> You should remind our friends, as I shall, if necessary, remind the President, of the great trouble I have taken to secure mitigations of the Italian position.

In the event, Churchill did not take private issue with Roosevelt on Italian affairs—nor did he publish these records in his memoirs.

In response to this official British demarche, the State Department issued, on the night of December 5–6, 1944, a statement that, in the American view: "The composition of the Italian government was purely an Italian affair and the U.S. government had not declared themselves opposed to Count Sforza, and expected the Italians to work out their problems of government on democratic lines without interference from outside. This policy would apply to an even more pronounced degree with regard to the Governments of the United Nations in their liberated territories."

This last sentence was, by direct implication, a censure on the British handling of that moment of affairs in Greece.

Developments in German-occupied Greece from 1941 to 1944 defy coherent study.

In the spring of 1941 the British *had* thoughts of a Balkan operation against the Axis.

The British Commonwealth expedition to Greece landed at the request of her king (prior to extending a front into the Balkans).

The catastrophe of this Greek campaign left the British leadership with an emotional and moral obligation to conduct the liberation of Greece and to secure the return of the king.

The American leadership did admit that Britain had a "special relationship" in regard to Greece, and left her advisers to cope with the alternative strategy of building up resistance within the country under the cover of special operations. It was understood as an ideal that, under the leadership and control of British officers, politically opposed groups would be brought together and, with the king and Greek government-in-exile, would prepare their return to Greece and, hopefully, of King George himself.

But the problem of Greece bedeviled relations within the Grand Alliance—a microcosm of controversial issues arising elsewhere.

As Churchill wrote to Field Marshal Smuts later:

> I have had endless trouble about Greece where we have indeed been wounded in the house of our friends.
>
> If, as is likely, the powers of evil prevail in Greece, we must look forward to a quasi-Bolshevised Russian-led Balkan peninsula and this may spread to Hungary and Italy. I therefore see great danger in the world in these quarters, but have not the power, without causing great stresses in the Government and quarreling with the United States, to do anything effective.

At the center lay the issue of facilitating the return of a king and government-in-exile to a country disintegrated by enemy occupation.

The British sought to devise a series of political combinations which would achieve their main objectives—the fulfillment of their initial moral obligation (the return of the King) and avoiding the immediate menace (that of civil war in Greece).

The first crisis in Cairo came just after the Teheran Conference. Churchill was prepared to postpone the issue and agree to the setting up of a provisional regency until conditions were more stable.

When the American and British delegations met in early December 1943 in Cairo and Roosevelt was told of this plan, the president, in private conclave with the king of Greece, informed him that he should be treated squarely and allowed to go back to his country.

Roosevelt wrote to Lincoln McVeagh—his ambassador to the Greek government in Cairo: "My own mind runs to the idea that a tiny spot in the Mediterranean, like Greece, has its reputation enhanced if it has a constitutional monarch."

By the autumn of 1944, Greek affairs were beyond a compromise solution.

There were signs of an imminent German military departure from the country as the start of a major withdrawal northward through the Balkans to a defense line ultimately along the Austrian frontier.

On August 17 Churchill cabled to Roosevelt that in the hiatus left by the German evacuation, the communist extremists would seize Athens and crush all other forms of Greek expression but their own.

Churchill therefore suggested that a British force should be formed to occupy Athens "when the time is ripe."

Roosevelt replied: "I have no objections to your making preparations to have in readiness a sufficient British force to preserve order in Greece when the German forces evacuate the country."

As the Germans pulled out, British troops moved in with the Greek government and attempted to disarm those communist forces in the capital and surrounding areas. Fighting broke out in the streets of the capital and moral indignation was roused by the Allied press, particularly American. The British were accused of suppressing Greek liberties in the form of EAM, a coalition of resistance movements dominated by the communists, and forcing a reactionary and royal Greek administration on the people.

The threat or not of a communist Greece disguised as liberal republicanism became the theme of a concerted attack on the British.

Only Stalin offered no comment.

On December 13 Roosevelt cabled to Churchill that he would like to help but limits were set by "the traditional policies of the U.S. . . . No one will understand better than yourself that I, both personally and as Head of State, am necessarily responsive to the state of public feeling. It is for these reasons that it has not been possible to take a stand along with you. I don't need to tell you how much I dislike this state of affairs as between you and me."

Churchill replied: "I have felt it much that you were unable to give a word of explanation for our action, but I understand your difficulties."

The original solution of a regency, which the British had raised in December 1943, King George of Greece refused to accept.

In the event, Churchill was obliged to travel to Athens on Christmas Day 1944 and impose, as the urgent solution, the creation of a regency.

He was after to take this grave step, knowing that the Greek communist leaders were not—at least ostensibly—backed by Stalin. Therefore, the present crisis in Athens would be limited to Greece.

He was also obliged to impose a political solution in order to release the British troops involved for the final stages of the Italian campaign.

Addressing you in this place in March 1946, Sir Winston Churchill said, "One cannot imagine a regenerated Europe without a strong France. All my life I have worked for a strong France, and I never lost faith in her destiny, even in the darkest hours. I will not lose faith now."

There remained throughout the war a deep variance of opinions between the United States and Great Britain as to where authority and power should ultimately lie in Axis-occupied France.

Washington was convinced that the Vichy Regime of Petain represented the continuous legitimacy of the French Republic and had the support of the majority of Frenchmen. In the final event of Allied liberation this view would be proven one way or another.

The overwhelming might of American military power implied a decisive voice in recommending the lines on which the political future of France would take shape.

By 1944 Churchill had accepted General de Gaulle whom he knew and respected, as the probable leader of French resistance and as the most likely figure to rally the majority of Frenchmen as the symbol of Free France.

The alien reactions of the Americans to de Gaulle, were at moments shared by the British, and in the confusion of a search for an agreed policy toward France there was a tacit understanding between Churchill and Roosevelt to avoid extensive measures of disagreement.

The eventual solution came with liberation. Evidence accumulated as the French resistance came into the open of massive support by the population for de Gaulle.

The British had already taken a risk in recognizing the French provisional government set up in Algiers—a step which would be tested when "Overlord" had been launched.

As Churchill wrote to Roosevelt as late as September 1944: "After all they are the French provisional government and it is fully admitted in the Boniface series (intelligence intercepts from the "Ultra" decodings) that they represent all France."

The final American decision to accord recognition to de Gaulle was quaint.

While Churchill was in Moscow in October 1944 he pressed Roosevelt to take this step and received the reply that the president would rather wait.

Eisenhower had, on his own, come to an agreement with de Gaulle's committee to hand over control of the zone of the interior (that considerable part of France now liberated) to their control.

Eisenhower sent a secret message to Stalin on October 23, 1944, informing him of the American intention to grant recognition: "In this event you may wish to take some similar action." No copy was sent to Churchill. An urgent message in this sense was sent by the State Department to London where Churchill learned the news on returning from Moscow.

A scuffle of diplomatic interchanges between Washington, Moscow, and London assured that the timing of the announcement by the three governments would be simultaneous.

In such a "technical" fashion, France under de Gaulle was readmitted as a main member of the war coalition.

It remained to agree on her allotted role. De Gaulle was long determined to take part in the ultimate occupation of Germany and employ the French army, now created largely by American logistical support, under separate command.

Churchill, on his triumphant visits to Paris, had, on Armistice Day, November 11, 1944, told de Gaulle that the British would favor a French occupation of as much of Germany as their capacity allowed, and cabled Roosevelt of this proposal: "One must always realize that before five years are out the French army must take on the main task of holding down Germany."

The President answered: "I, of course, sympathize with the French point of view and hope that we may all be able to help her meet post-war responsibilities. You know, of course, that, after Germany's collapse, I must bring American troops home as rapidly as transportation exists."

Churchill was alarmed. The French postwar army was not equipped or trained: "How would it be possible to hold down Western Germany beyond the present Russian line? We certainly could not undertake the task without your aid. . . . All would therefore rapidly disintegrate as it did last time."

The grim reminder of 1918 seemed to appear on the scene as an immense and alarming repetition.

Roosevelt replied that perhaps the French could be supplied out of the defeated German army. He did not yet "have the authority to equip any post-war foreign army" and the "prospect of getting it out of Congress was not good."

The final decisions over the postwar role and strength of France were to come up at the Yalta Conference in February 1945.

The building up of a strong France, which Churchill stressed to you here in 1946, was one of his last achievements as the British member of the Grand Alliance.

The attitude of Churchill toward the Germany of Hitler clarifies certain vital aspects of his character.

He was incapable of a sustained passion of vengeance. To him, the central, and indeed exclusive, aim of the war was the total destruction of the cardinal danger—Prussian militarism, as he termed it—and the German general staff.

As in the case of Italian fascism, he expressed little curiosity in the subtleties of Nazism or totalitarianism (in a sense to him a military term) as ideologies.

Hitler was a personal foe: "We keep to bear the life and soul out of Hitler and Hitlerism. That alone, all the time, to the end."

Churchill had an instinctive and total repulsion to the Nazi regime and its leaders, but no precise thoughts of the form of apocalyptic retribution might take, or of the responsibility of the Germans for their leaders. Already in 1941 he said that he did not believe in pariah nations and he saw no alternative to the acceptance of Germany as part of the family of nations.

As Churchill said among the ruins of Berlin in 1945: "My hate died with their surrender."

But the defeat of Germany must be total.

At the Casablanca Conference on January 24, 1943, the president announced in a press conference: "The elimination of German, Italian and Japanese war power means unconditional surrender."

In his memoirs Churchill wrote that he heard this phrase with some feeling of surprise, but of course "supported the President in what he said."

As to the future shape of defeated Germany, Churchill displayed obstinate caution. After the Teheran Conference, when Stalin and Roosevelt first raised the subject and speculated on finally dividing Germany into a number of separate states, in a discussion at the British War Cabinet, Churchill confirmed this talk and added: "I did not commit HMG beyond the isolation of Prussia," and later he stated that both Roosevelt and Stalin "wished to cut Germany into smaller pieces than I had in mind."

Basic decisions about the future structure of the Reich were taken after Churchill had left office the following year.

The partition of Germany involved, in Churchill's mind, many unforeseen situations: the ultimate battle lines drawn between the three great allies; the revelation of American and Russian intentions in regard to zones; the presence of the French.

The ultimate partition symbolized and confirmed the emergence of Russia as a superpower. Germany could never recover and hold the central balance of power in Europe.

Throughout the war Churchill displayed little interest in encouraging or contacting opposition groups inside Germany with a view to a coup d'état and the physical elimination of Hitler.

The British were singularly ill-informed about the activities of interlocking conspiracies within the German army and certain right circles.

When the July Plot exploded on July 21, 1944, the news was received in London with indifference. Churchill devotes one paragraph to the episode in the whole of his memoirs.

There was a central objection in Churchill's mind that any slight gesture by secret agents to contact political or military opposition elements in Germany would smell of a move toward a separate peace behind the backs of the other members of the Grand Alliance.

Stalin remained constantly suspicious of such adventures on the part of his allies.

Churchill's only comment of the July Plot was a laconic statement in the House of Commons on August 2, 1944: "The highest personalities in the German Reich are murdering each other, or trying to, while the avenging armies of the Allies close upon the doomed and ever narrowing circle of their power."

He was, for a moment, shocked by Eisenhower and his staff toying with the propaganda weapon of high-level appeals to the German people and schemes of undermining German morale.

On November 24, 1944, Churchill cabled to Roosevelt (a telegram not published in his memoirs): "I do not see any alternative to the General Grant attitude "to fight it out on this line if it takes all summer. . . . But to make the Great Governments responsible for anything that would look like appeasement now would worsen our chances, confess our errors, and stiffen the enemy resistance . . . Meanwhile I remain set where you put me on unconditional surrender."

Conclusion

When I chose as the title of my talk to you this afternoon "Churchill and Europe in 1944," it was my hope to convey to you his thoughts, visions, and disappointments as to the conduct of the war in the penultimate year of hostilities.

Churchill could not conceive of Europe in 1944 as an independent region of the universe. The continent with which he had been familiar had ceased to exist. There was no point—to him—in early speculation on forms of future European federation.

During his visits to Moscow in October he was faced with the realities and implications of the invasion of half the continent by the Russians.

As he told the War Cabinet on his return: once a World organization had perhaps been set up, "there was nothing against a special European group."

When Sir Winston Churchill addressed you here, he mentioned only on one occasion the phrase "liberated Europe." He was both cautious and pessimistic.

In his view, postwar Europe could only be organized by the triumvirate of the Big Three: Roosevelt, Stalin, and himself.

His lack of confidence in the abstract debates being held on new world organizations grew as the months passed.

Churchill shocked Sir Alexander Cadogan—the number two in the Foreign Office—at a War Cabinet meeting in August 1944: "There now, in 25 minutes we have settled the future of the world. Who can say that we aren't efficient?"

He conveyed his thoughts best—as after in a letter to Field Marshal Smuts in December 1944:

> I have done my best to prevent vain attempts to settle the future of the world before we even won the war. However, it was felt in the ruling circles at Washington that the spectacle of the United States assembling great conferences attended by all nations was one which would be helpful in the recent election. What is really needed is a three-power meeting, but I see no possible hope of this for several months. . . .
>
> Meanwhile, there approaches the shadow of the (British) General Election which, before many months have passed, will certainly break up the most capable Government England has had or is likely to have. Generally we have a jolly year before us.

By the end of 1944 Churchill was fully aware that Great Britain had ceased to be a first-class power in Europe.

Never again would she have the strength to intervene with her armed forces in European affairs. The elite Eighth Army in Italy, composed of British and Commonwealth troops, would be the last presence on the Continent.

In opening the first session of the Quebec Conference in September 1944 Churchill drew attention to the fact that "In the Italian theatre there was the most representative British Empire army there had ever been" (sixteen divisions).

He made one final effort to employ this symbol of British military power in the concluding operations of the war. The lightning advance in the spring of 1945 of the Eighth Army, supported by the American Fifth Army, under British command, reached Vienna in time to prevent a total Russian occupation and made possible an independent Austria. The Russians forestalled and prohibited a similar move by Eisenhower to Prague.

The effective frontiers of Europe were fixed along the Elbe and down the Adriatic.

The Grand Alliance marginally held together for a few months longer.

Most important of all, however, and I trust that I have put it before you with due clarity and emphasis at the heart of my talk, was that the "special relationship" between our two countries held firmly throughout the greatest crisis months of the last war.

Great Britain could not have survived without the massive and generous support—moral or material—of the United States, crowned by the close if undefinable relationship of intuitive understanding between Churchill and Roosevelt. Their ability to take personal summit decisions—often to the frustration of their respective staffs and advisers—must be unique in the history of the conduct of a world war.

This bond did not imply a consistent identity of view. Both men were capable of impulses and whims, which terrified their counsellors: both men, at times, listened to their staffs; but above all, both leaders operated in isolation at the summit of power.

Churchill and Roosevelt had, among other attributes in common, a sense of loneliness. They seldom sought advice from their personal advisers or, indeed, government ministers of civil servants.

Great issues would be tried out between the two leaders, usually within the confining frame of telegrams and occasionally at talks before or during major conferences.

Both Churchill and Roosevelt were skeptical of the confusion of contradictory advice put up to them at home, as, for example, Churchill and the issues arising with the French.

Both made up their minds on their own on matters of high policy and intent. They then argued their case with their staff. Each was permanent chairman of a kind of debating society, and always, hopefully, with the casting vote.

They were experienced politicians and sensitive to the moods of their respective Parliaments and Senate or Congress—and to tides of public opinion.

As president, Roosevelt could afford to be more aloof to such pressures than Churchill—with the weighty exceptions during times of presidential elections, while Churchill's personality, with his immense prestige as a war leader, dominated the British parliamentary scene throughout the lifetime of a House of Commons.

Churchill accepted—with courageous resignation—the exhaustion and economic decline of Great Britain as the main cost of victory and survival.

But he viewed with trust and confidence the emergence of the United States as the greatest military and economic power in the New World.

I feel that, in conclusion, I must quote a telegram which he sent to Roosevelt on November 28, 1944 (which is not in his memoirs):

> You will have the greatest Navy in the world. You will have, I hope, the greatest air force. You will have the greatest trade. You have all the gold. But these things do not oppress my mind with fear because I am sure the American people under your re-acclaimed leadership will not give themselves over to vain-glorious ambitions, and that justice and fair-play will be the lights that guide them.

I have often tried to put into words a sum of impressions of the man. I am defeated.

Perhaps the main secret of his personality was its total integration.

Sir Winston Churchill was no different at his own dinner table than he appeared in the House of Commons, at the election hustings, or in international conference. He lived publicly and privately by a simple code of behavior: upright, generous, subtly aware of everyone and everything around him, intolerant only of smugness and falsehood. He was a total human being with a total lack of inconsistency in his character, and as such must be accepted as a whole. He made political enemies and bitter opponents, but their survivors wept at his passing.

At the hour of his death, Sir Harold Wilson, then prime minister, spoke on the BBC: "Tonight our nation pays tribute to the greatest man any of us have known. He was never a superman, but a man. He was the most human of all human beings."

One cannot do better than that.

As one of those who was privileged to know him closely as a private person, I would only add that, having been at times in his company over nearly thirty years, he made me feel better than I was—and am.

Thank you for your special kindness in giving me this opportunity to talk to you about him this evening.

SIR JOHN ROBERT COLVILLE, C.B., C.V.O., served under three British prime ministers—Neville Chamberlain, Clement Attlee, and Sir Winston Churchill. He achieved distinction as an author and historian, a merchant banker, and a Royal Air Force fighter pilot.

4

The Personality of Sir Winston Churchill

SIR JOHN R. COLVILLE

In a great many classrooms and lecture halls, in every country and in each succeeding generation, the question is asked: "To what extent are great men fashioned by circumstances? Does the occasion create the man more often than the man the occasion?" As with most generalized questions, there is no generally valid answer.

If George III and Lord North had been more tactful, would the thirteen colonies have revolted? If the German General Staff had refused to let Lenin return to Petrograd in a sealed train, would there have been a Bolshevik revolution in Russia? If Corporal Hitler had been killed on the Western Front in World War I would there have been another "führer" with a mesmeric hold on the German masses? The "ifs" of history are fascinating, especially when they relate to the influence of individuals, but they are food for fantasy and not for research. What does deserve careful examination are the personal characteristics, the qualities and defects, of those whose decisions did in historic fact mold our destinies; for if the characteristics had been different, the decisions might have been different, too.

In his own country and abroad Winston Churchill had a notable influence on people and on policies for many years, indeed for well over half a century. But it was for a much shorter period, of some eighteen months, from May 1940 till America came into the war, that this influence was truly vital. Under his leadership, his country held the fate of Western civilization in its hand, and it was Churchill's energy, resolution, and example that provided the necessary inspiration. In those eighteen months Churchill and the British stood like King Leonidas and his Spartans in the pass at Thermophylae: they were the sole active opponents of overwhelming military might and of submission to slavery. The Soviet Union, until herself attacked in June 1941, was an ally of Hitler; the government of the United States was as helpful as it could afford to be, but after the isolationist years it was unprepared and disarmed. The European powers were either defeated or cowed into surrender. All this, I am sure you know well, but I think that heroic stories bear repetition.

Churchill did, indeed, have behind him a united and determined people and a vast empire, almost as woefully unprepared for war as the United States, but nevertheless embracing a quarter of the world's population and nearly a third of its territory. What seemed less impressive than the far-flung empire and the fervent goodwill of the United States, but was in the short-term more effective than either of them, was that narrow strip of sea called the English Channel. All the same a British government could quite easily, by bungling and miscalculation, or by faintheartedness, have lost the battle for democracy and condemned us to see Hitler's 1000-Year Reich fill the heads—and destroy the souls—of men and women in every continent for generations to come.

That in 1940 the British Empire was united was, I have no doubt, in part the legacy of the Anglo-French surrender at Munich. In 1938 the British people were split asunder in sentiment. If the British government had decided to go to war for Czechoslovakia there would have been a large peace-party; and New Zealand, alone of the Dominions, was unequivocal in its support. A year later all doubts had vanished: Hitler had proved his naked ambitions and there was no peace-party: Canada, Australia, South Africa, and New Zealand declared war within hours of the mother country. For unity, therefore, Churchill, the outspoken opponent of Munich, cannot claim the credit; but for unfaltering determination and leadership he most certainly can.

We live in days of instant coffee—instant almost everything, including quite a lot of instant politicians. Churchill stood for the reverse of all that. He insisted on quality and he set store by experience. By 1940 he had been forty years in Parliament and had held every major portfolio in the government except the Foreign Office. He had suffered in the hard school of failure and disappointment—his greatest, and perhaps most undeserved failure being Gallipoli in 1915. So he had learned how to face disaster and, in due course, he faced triumph also. Of the two, though triumph be the pleasanter, it can also be the greater test of character. I think Churchill came well out of both tests, and though he was incontestably self-assured, and by no means disinclined to applaud his own efforts, he was not vain. That is something that can seldom be said of politicians, or indeed of successful men in any walk of life. Women are different; the Almighty intends them to be vain of their appearance, though they often underestimate their achievements in other spheres.

Churchill did, of course, have his failings. However great a man may be, it does his memory no service to pretend he was faultless. The finest emeralds have a flaw, and nobody wants 24-carat gold. So before speaking to you of Churchill's qualities, the solid foundation on which his career was built, I will say something of his defects. I would emphasize that those defects were not vices. There was never a less-vicious man.

He was notably self-centered. That did not prevent his being generous, kind-hearted, and affectionate. I am sure, too, that he would have sacrificed his life to save another; but the generosity, the compassion, and the affection were the surplus available, often a large surplus, after his own requirements had been satisfied. There have been, and are, many people like that. In Churchill this characteristic just seemed to loom larger than in others. But then everything about him was writ large.

He was inconsiderate. During the war, provided he himself had seven-hours sleep (one of them in the afternoon), he seldom stopped to think how exhausted others, working perhaps eighteen or nineteen hours a day, might be. He often changed his plans on a sudden whim, careless of the grave inconvenience this might cause. His servants would be kept up to all hours; dining at eight o'clock, he might stay in the dining room till after midnight. Stenographers would have to remain on duty till three or four in the morning in case they were wanted; other people's mealtimes were of no consequence; the presence of ministers or chiefs of staff might be required long after they had gone to bed. Yet none of those who worked for him—

ministers, secretaries, servants—did more than utter a few grumbles. They all loved him, and they all forgave him; for if you give affection, as he did, you receive it in return.

He was impatient. Many a time I was instructed to find the answer to some question and before I had had time to reach my desk and pick up the telephone, he would ring to enquire the answer. He had always been in a position to give orders but seldom to implement them. His understanding of administrative matters was by no means well-developed. In fact, left to himself, he would have been a thoroughly bad administrator. This presented all kinds of problems, but one valuable by-product of his impatience was that speed became an essential feature of the machinery of government. "Action This Day" really did have meaning: delay was not tolerated.

He could be bad-tempered, especially if something to which he saw no immediate solution was worrying him. But though his anger was like a burst of thunder, and was sometimes directed at a guiltless individual, he never let the sun go down without making amends: not indeed by saying he was sorry, but by praising the injured party for a totally different virtue. I remember once when I was the object of his wrath, and he had been particularly disagreeable, just before bedtime he looked at something I had written, and said "What a beautiful hand-writing you have. I have never had a private secretary with such a beautiful handwriting." It was untrue; but it was typical, and I went to bed content.

He was obstinate, though finally open to conviction if the argument marshalled against him were logically and convincingly presented. He might waste hours of busy men's time in pursuing his proposals, but he did not, except on the rarest of occasions, fly in the face of competent and considered professional advice, act without the support of the cabinet (or at least its endorsement), or fail to ask the House of Commons to approve the policies he had adopted.

He did have a failing that his wife constantly deplored—an addiction to luxury, which sometimes prompted him to accept gifts and invitations that, at any rate in Lady Churchill's view, he should have declined. Perhaps it was because having himself always been comparatively poor, but impulsively extravagant, he had moved in circles where champagne flowed and luxury was the accepted way of life—whether for rich dukes, such as Westminster and Marlborough, or for self-made entrepreneurs like Beaverbrook and Rothermere. His friend F. E. Smith once said, "Mr. Churchill is easily satisfied with the best." So he was; and I think that at the end of a long, constructive career he deserved it, however well justified Lady Churchill's strictures had been in former years. Nor can it be said that he ever failed to put the call of duty first—a long way ahead of self-indulgence. And he was always prepared to fight for his convictions without the least regard to his personal popularity or political advantage. In this he was honest to an extent for which, at any rate prior to 1940, he was not given adequate credit.

Let me now make a quite different assessment, one which will, I hope, convince you that the defects I have listed were small and insignificant drops in a far brighter ocean.

Among Churchill's most powerful armaments was simplicity. Simplicity of aim, simplicity of thought, simplicity of expression. There are some benighted, and seldom very impressive, people who think that you must be complicated in order to prove you are intelligent. Churchill had at his side, before and throughout the war, a man who could explain complex scientific and economic problems without recourse to four-syllable words or technical jargon. That man was Professor F. A. Lindemann, later Lord Cherwell. He was a great scientist who revived and inspired the famous Clarendon Laboratory at Oxford, and he was the most brilliant interpreter I have ever known, making the arcane and the diffuse comprehensible to a normally educated layman. The vast power of his intellect was matched by its clarity.

Churchill had different but comparable gifts in making himself admired and understood by the ordinary citizen. He did not seek to dazzle an audience with sophistries. For six years he had, as he said again and again, only one objective: to win the war. And his life was greatly simplified thereby. It was clear what we were fighting for: let those who had any doubts lay down their arms and those doubts would soon be resolved. I must say that in this respect I think both President Reagan and Mrs. Thatcher have a Churchillian touch, with, of course, the added advantage of speaking from material strength rather than from weakness.

Churchill detested obscurity of thought and speech. He rejected "pad-ding"; he believed in going straight to the point; and he was the dedicated enemy of jargon, which is indeed the poison ivy of our times. He was, as we all know, a master of the English language. He mobilized it as a war-winning weapon. Whenever possible he used words of one or two syllables. "Never in the field of human conflict was so much owed by so many to so few": try to express that better or more lucidly. It is one of the tragedies of our generation that, when it comes to language, we are not like Churchill, "easily satisfied with the best." We even find it necessary to tamper with the simple beauty of the King James Version of the Bible. "Because there was no room for them in the Inn": I can well imagine with what scorn Churchill would have regarded some of the modern efforts to improve on that. I have to declare, with whatever lack of tact in this company, that I consider the Americans, though doubtless not those at Westminster College, to be the prime sinners in what Professor Henry Higgins called "the cold-blooded murder of the English tongue"—especially when you apply your pens to industrial, economic, and philosophical matters and compete for the prize of producing long words where the short would suffice. (This is probably where the audience ceases to be a captive one.)

High among Churchill's virtues I rate magnanimity. He was the very reverse of vindictive. Like a pugilist, he enjoyed the fight, but however hard the punches, when all was over he thought no ill of his opponent and wanted to shake hands. In a career replete with political, and sometimes personal, antagonisms he had suffered many bruises and the scars were sometimes deep; but he seemed incapable of bearing a grudge. He often spoke feelingly of those who had helped him: he never spoke ill of the many who, in the years of his unpopularity and isolation, had done all they could to thwart and defeat him. One day during the war he said to me: "I hate nobody except Hitler—and that is professional."

Some years before that he had written: "In place of arguments for coercion, there must be arguments for conciliation." That was the policy he pursued with the Irish Free State in 1922, having previously been a strong supporter of the notorious Black and Tans in their bloody struggle with the equally notorious Sinn Feiners. It was the policy that he successfully advocated for the British treatment of South Africa after the Boer War; it was the policy toward Germany of which he spoke as early as the summer of 1949; and it was the policy he would have liked to adopt toward the Soviet Union after Stalin's death. Of that I shall say more a little later.

Allied to his magnanimity toward opponents, and especially toward the vanquished, were the twin virtues of humanity and compassion. "Tout comprendre est tout pardonner," he used often to say; and indeed there were few things he felt unable to pardon. For cowardice, treachery, and deceit he would make no excuses; but for almost every other form of human weakness, including those which offended his own code of morality, he showed sympathetic understanding, at any rate after the event. He felt deeply for people in distress. Many a time when he was prime minister he would read in the newspaper of some alleged miscarriage of justice, and he would allow government departments no rest until he was satisfied on the issue. He had had no personal contact with poverty and deprivation; but imagination supplied what experience did not.

He was never halfhearted in his pursuit of social justice and improvement in the general standard of living. There was, he argued, no virtue at all in leveling down; egalitarianism was a socialist myth; but the miracles of science should be used to provide a bountiful supply of new measures to improve the lot of all humanity. It was the great Liberal dream of the Victorians; and Churchill had the idealism of both the Liberals and the Victorians. I am sure he would have included what is now called the Third World in that dream, though he used to regard with horror and alarm what he described as the pullulating millions of Asia.

He was sometimes accused of inconsistency. It would have been impossible to be narrowly consistent in a political career which covered more than fifty years of international turmoil and kaleidoscopic change. I think he himself put the matter in a nutshell when he wrote: "The only way a man can remain consistent amid changing circumstances is to change with them, while preserving the same dominating purpose." In other words, consistency should be wedded to flexibility, but there are basic principles that must not be changed.

In this connection it is interesting to trace, over thirty-five years, Churchill's attitude to the Soviet Union. In 1919 he was an eager architect of the unsuccessful allied intervention against the Reds. He understood more clearly than many of his contemporaries the menace of international communism, the virulence of the infection Lenin and Trotsky sought to spread across the world. Throughout the 1920s and 1930s the Comintern was not a threat to be disregarded, though coexistence with the Soviet Union was an unavoidable menace. Churchill did not close his eyes to the ultimate threat. In 1939, the unthinkable happened: Soviet Communism made an alliance with German National Socialism. When the Russians invaded Finland, Britain and France came close to declaring war on them. And at Katyn they murdered in cold blood 14,000 Polish officers they had captured in Poland—a crime unparalleled since the Middle Ages until the Germans turned even more murderous hands against the Jews.

Then on June 22, 1941, the thieves fell out. Hitler invaded Russia and set out to enter Moscow. He would have been wise to listen first to Tchaikovsky's 1812 Overture. As for the British government, we had to put the helm hard over, and sail on the other tack. Churchill who had an uncanny knack for making prophetic statements, had written, nearly ten years before: "A policy is pursued up to a certain point: it becomes evident at last that it can be carried no further. New facts arise which clearly render it obsolete, new difficulties which make it impracticable. A new and possibly the opposite solution presents itself with overwhelming force."

These words were wholly apt on June 22, 1941. As Churchill said to me the previous evening, while we walked together on the lawn at Chequers: "If Hitler were to invade Hell, I would at least make a favourable reference to the devil in the House of Commons."

So it was that for four years you and we gave all we could to Russia; Britain alone sent them five thousand tanks and seven thousand airplanes, accepting the cold misery and sometimes crushing losses of the arctic convoys. You and we received very little in exchange even by way of information; but the Russians certainly fought valiantly.

Then, in August 1944, Stalin halted the Soviet army at the gates of Warsaw so as to give the Germans time to massacre the pro-Western Polish Home Army which, on the strength of a signal given by Moscow radio, had risen to fight the German occupying troops. At once, at any rate to Churchill, who had been ardent in his support of Soviet resistance, a red light which had been flickering for some time began to shine fiercely. He was moved to tears by the message of anguish the women of Warsaw sent to the pope and the pope passed on to us. But it was too late. The Allies, and particularly Roosevelt, put their trust in Stalin's Yalta promises of free and unfettered elections in Poland and Eastern Europe. The Allies won the war; by monolithic obstinacy in negotiation and cynical disregard of promises, the Russians won the peace.

Once again it seemed to Churchill that he must be consistent by himself changing with the changing circumstances. So he came here with President Truman, one of the greatest of American presidents I believe, and made the famous Fulton speech which sent shock waves throughout the free world.

Then, in March 1953, Stalin died. Was there now a chance to bring the increasingly bitter Cold War to an end? It must, of course, depend on the personality of the new men in power at the Kremlin. Churchill believed it was worth a trial, for the issue at stake was so large. His own Foreign Office did not agree, nor did John Foster Dulles and the State Department. Here, they all said, is the arch anti-appeaser, the intransigent opponent of Munich, himself setting out on the dangerous road to appeasement. So his proposals were stymied. Given the personalities in the Kremlin, it must be admitted they would probably have come to nothing in any case. But it was important to discover whether circumstances had changed with Stalin's death; for if they indeed had, it would not have been inconsistent to change with them once again.

I have subjected you to this long digression about Russia, partly because I think it shows the flexibility which Churchill adopted in international politics—indeed in all politics—and partly because it may perhaps have a certain relevance for the 1980s. I will now resume the catalog of what I believe to have been Churchill's more general merits and cardinal virtues.

A statesman must have foresight and if he is to be a great statesman, he must have imagination, too. These are among the gifts that distinguish him from an ordinary politician, just as they distinguish an inspired strategist from a competent tactician. Churchill had both qualities. One example of his foresight was his insistence, despite the doubts of the Foreign Office, and the overt opposition of the American government, on going to Athens at Christmas 1944 and using British troops to crush the communist ELAS rebellion. In so doing he saved Greece from imprisonment behind the Iron

Curtain. He kept the eastern Mediterranean free from Soviet domination. President Truman, unlike Roosevelt, soon saw the wisdom of this policy, and in 1947, with the Truman Doctrine, he took over the torch from our by then exhausted and enfeebled hands.

Churchill combined imagination and a capacity for original thought with independence of judgment. In his political strategy, at home and abroad, he did not rely on other people's initiatives. He saw no special virtue in gathering other men's flowers. If he had an idea he submitted it to his cabinet or to his professional advisers for comment and reflection; but he had to be thoroughly convinced before he dropped it. And it was no use supposing that because he held some friend or colleague in high esteem, that man would necessarily be successful in advocating a particular line of policy. Churchill himself had to be sincerely convinced of its merits. He had in his youth been impetuous, but with age he grew increasingly cautious and reflective. As we see again and again in democratic politics, responsibility is the sovereign remedy for impetuosity. As often as not, he several times said to me, problems can be left to settle themselves. "The trees do not grow up to the sky" was a quotation that came frequently to his lips, though he could not remember whence it came and I have never succeeded in tracing it.

It is often asserted that he interfered too much in detail, especially where military questions were concerned. He was, indeed, interested in detail, but he seldom persisted for long in interference except in relation to broad strategic designs. He wrote that "Those who are charged with the direction of supreme affairs must sit on the mountain tops of control: they must never descend into the valleys of direct physical and personal action." That was a lesson he had learned from his ill-judged personal intervention in the defense of Antwerp when he was first lord of the Admiralty in 1914. He was sometimes tempted; but in the end he seldom did more than urge, inquire, and cajole.

Great as was both his persistence and his determination, he was sometimes obliged to give way by the sheer strength of the opposition. One such case—and I think it is fortunate he was outgunned—was in his opposition to the Government of India Bill in the 1930s when he did his utmost to destroy Mr. Baldwin's liberal move in the direction of giving

India increased self-government. Churchill had a blind spot about India. Another example was, of course, at the time of the abdication of King Edward VIII.

There are, however, other initiatives in which he was thwarted, in my view, unfortunately. One was when in 1944 he strove unavailingly to persuade the American government and chiefs of staff to abandon the fruitless project of a landing in the south of France as a follow-up to the landing in Normandy—Operation Overlord. He wanted the excellent divisions which were removed from General Alexander's command for this enterprise to be used to break through the German defenses in north Italy. He hoped to seize Trieste, cut off eighteen German divisions in Yugoslavia from their supplies, and take Vienna from the East before the Russian armies could forestall us. It was imaginative: it just might have finished the war in the late autumn of 1944 or early winter of 1945; and had it succeeded it would have had an incalculable effect on the postwar history of Europe and the world. For when the Russians reached Vienna they would not even allow the Western Allies into the city until they had installed a communist-controlled government.

A second misfortune was his inability to persuade Eisenhower, in March and April 1945, to take Berlin and Prague and hold them until the Russians had fulfilled their pledges over Poland and accepted the Allied Control Commissions for Berlin and Vienna on the lines previously agreed. Alas, in those two disastrous months, the Roosevelt administration, which had shown such great qualities, was determined to give away everything possible to our Russian allies. They did so with tragic results. I feel sure that Truman would have been more farsighted; but there was a catastrophic hiatus between Roosevelt losing his grip and Truman imposing his. It is, in retrospect, astonishing that in the last months of his rapidly draining life, Roosevelt did not take Truman into his confidence and ensure that he was fully informed of the political and military situation.

Incidentally, in 1952 Churchill told me that he had excised from the final volume of his war history, then on the point of publication, some of the messages on the subject he had sent to Eisenhower. He feared they might be used for political purposes in the 1952 presidential election. If indeed he did so, no doubt Martin Gilbert will publish them in the next volume of his great work. But even those messages he did publish tell a tragic story of missed opportunity.

He had no patience with indecision. Like the Quakers of old he believed that your "yea" should be "yea" and your "nay" should be "nay." I am sure it was that philosophy, so characteristic of the amazing industrial development of this country, that ranked high among the American virtues he admired. He certainly had a fellow-feeling for that clerical poet Father Ronald Knox who, in a parody of Dryden's *Absolem and Achitophel,* wrote: "When suave politeness, tempering bigot zeal, / Corrected 'I believe' to 'One does feel.'" That is a wholesome warning to some modern church-men. It also reflects the distaste with which Winston Churchill viewed those trends in politics which nearly lost us two world wars before they even broke out. And it was not, perhaps, unconnected with the thought behind his Fulton speech.

A gift which captivated even his opponents was his gaiety. He employed it as an art of government, for if ever he was in a tight corner in Parliament he would make the House laugh, and laughter disarms opposition. His wit could be sharp as a rapier; it could also strike home by an unusual turn or phrase, an unexpected adjective, a masterly use of anticlimax. It was spontaneous and it was the same in public as in private. There were not two faces in Churchill: the man in the House of Commons was the same as the man in the family circle. ·

Lord Moran, his doctor, wrote that he suffered from dark depressions which even led one essayist to assert that he was a manic depressive. Nothing could be further from the truth. Of course we all have moments of depression, especially after breakfast. It was then that Moran would sometimes call to take his patient's pulse and hope to make a note of what was happening in the wide world. Churchill, not especially pleased to see any visitor at such an hour, might excuse a certain early-morning surliness by saying "I have got a black dog on my back today." That was an expression much used by old-fashioned English nannies. Mine used to say to me, if I was grumpy, "You have got out of bed the wrong side," or else "You have got a black dog on your back." Doubtless Nanny Everest was accustomed to say the same to young Winston Churchill. But I don't think Lord Moran ever had a nanny and he wrote pages to explain that

Churchill suffered from periodic bouts of acute depression which, with the Churchillian gift for apt expression, he called "black dog." Lady Churchill told me she thought the doctor's theory total rubbish and I am sure she knew more about her husband's moods than did Lord Moran. I wonder how many historic beliefs have been based on equally silly deductions.

Lloyd George, according to Churchill, "could *almost* talk a bird out of a tree." Churchill, for his part, actually could do so—and quite frequently did. Men would go to see him determined not to do what they knew he was going to ask them. In the event they invariably did just that. As I know from personal experience, and as many others discovered to their own astonishment, it was impossible to say "No." Roosevelt had the same persuasive charm, and, indeed, the same gift for expressing himself in simple terms, and so when the two met much depended on which of them happened to be taking the initiative. At the second Quebec Conference I watched each outcharm the other.

Churchill was essentially a romantic, and although he only once wrote a poem—as a boy of fifteen—he was a poet at heart. Describing the scene in 1940, he wrote of "a white glow, overpowering, sublime, which ran through our island from end to end." None but a poet could have written that; and listening as I did, usually in the House of Commons, to all those famous 1940 speeches, I was conscious of an unquenchable fire that burned within him, of a bright flame that gave a blaze to his eloquence.

We live in an age of specialists. Versatility is no longer a gateway to success. A little more than 100 years ago my paternal grandfather was chief whip in the House of Lords when Lord Derby was prime minister. It was a time when Britain was a powerful land power and unquestionably ruled the waves. According to my father, on three successive days the same man saw Lord Derby on the race course at Newmarket judging the finer points of a thoroughbred, in his library at Derby House translating Homer into English verse, and as prime minster standing up in the House of Lords to defend the government's policy. Churchill could have improved even on that, though I don't think he would have been much good at translating Homer. Writer, painter, bricklayer, historian, polo player, orator, and winner of the Nobel Prize for literature, he was perhaps the last of the truly versatile statesmen; and if he did not excel in everything to which he put his hand, he scored a high average. "Let us reconcile ourselves," he once wrote, "to the mysterious rhythm of our destinies." Whether mysterious or not, the rhythm of his destiny was far from the ordinary; and he did succeed in reconciling himself to it.

I will speak briefly of Churchill as a visionary. Like all men of goodwill he greeted with enthusiasm President Wilson's magnificent ideal of a League of Nations. Like everybody else, he then saw, with inescapable disillusionment, the league's decline into impotence. He was in his heart of hearts less enthusiastic about the second attempt at world government, the United Nations, because he doubted if it was conceived on a basis likely to provide enduring authority. How right he was. I first heard him outline his own ideas of a future world organization in August 1940 at Chequers, in the presence of General de Gaulle and several other guests.

I wrote a long account of what he said in my diary and I was particularly impressed because at that time most people were concentrating more on present survival than on future plans. But Churchill, although a dedicated historian, preferred looking forward to looking backward.

This is a brief resume of what he then proposed. He believed there should be regional councils, one for Europe, another for North and Central America, another for South America, and so on. These councils should be responsible for settling their own regional problems—political, military, economic, and financial—and each would send a representative to a small world council of perhaps eight or ten people which would, no doubt, have had specialized organizations, such as the F.A.O. and the I.L.O., dependent on its secretariat. In addition, it would have used its authority to help settle those internal regional disputes on which, say, the council of Europe or the council of Africa might be deadlocked. Ideally, I suppose, the world council's decision would have been binding. Naturally, much would have depended on goodwill and that, alas, is often in short supply; but a small world council would perhaps have stood a better chance of being an acceptable umpire than an undisciplined, and in essence futile, organization such as the assembly of the United Nations, or an almost perpetually deadlocked one such as the Security Council.

Many years later I read in one of Churchill's prewar essays that he had reflected on such a scheme long before I heard him unfold it at Chequers.

He had written of his hope that the representatives of the regional councils "would meet not in an over-crowded Tower of Babel but, as it were, on a mountain top where all was cool and quiet and calm, and from which the wide vision of the world would be presented with all things in their own proportion." What a pity it has never been tried. Perhaps it could even have been made to work without vetoes.

There was no greater admirer of American democracy: of that freedom of action, that breadth of vision, that impatience with governmental and bureaucratic interference, which stem at least as much from your vivid experiences in these western lands as from your inheritance of our own historic liberties. Churchill was thrilled by the romance of America— "Westward look the land is bright" was a line of Arthur Hugh Clough's poem he loved to quote—and he was deeply stirred by the history of the Civil War, which he had studied in detail. I have seen American generals listen openmouthed to his account of Gettysburg, where he had tramped up and down the battlefield; and I saw the unemotional Harry Hopkins actually shed tears when Churchill quoted in full the poem about the old lady draped in the Union flag who told the Confederate troops to "Shoot if you must at this old grey head, but spare your country's flag."

Yet despite all this he was not an unqualified admirer of the American political system. He saw grave disadvantages in the separation of powers, and as regards presidential government he wrote: "The union of both the pomp and the power of the state in a single office exposes a mortal to strains beyond the nature, and to tasks beyond the strength, even of the best and greatest of men."

A man of international stature, he was first and foremost a British patriot (though never a nationalist). He believed in direct ministerial responsibility to Parliament and in a constitutional monarchy. He was sure that what he described as "the peculiar merit and sovereign quality of English national life" resided in the unbroken, golden chain of a constitutional monarchy in which past and present, tradition and progress are united. "A battle is lost, the government falls; a battle is won, crowds cheer the King. What better system could you devise," he once said to me—and doubtless often repeated to others. That was, of course, the recipe for Britain and its empire. He certainly did not visualize a constitutional monarchy for the United States!

Lastly, I want to speak of Churchill's supreme faith in a beneficent union of the English-speaking peoples, the history of whom was his last literary endeavor. His immutable faith and conviction was that a common speech, law and literature, and many centuries of common history bound together the British Commonwealth and the United States across national frontiers in such a way that if we advanced hand in hand no ill could befall. I heard him say that on countless occasions.

He believed in the British Empire, as it was during nearly his whole life, not because he was an imperialist in the modern pejorative sense of the word. On the contrary, he thought that each colony should become self-governing as it reached the stage where it could defend itself and order its own affairs—as Canada, Australia, South Africa, and New Zealand had already done by the beginning of this century. It is legitimate to doubt the wisdom of his somewhat intransigent thoughts on India, but he was always a strong supporter of home rule for Ireland. His hope was that the colonies would remain tied to the mother country by history and the golden link of the Crown. This has in fact happened. What Harold Macmillan called the "Winds of Change" only began to blow at the very end of Churchill's life, but I am sure he would have been proud to know that there are now forty-nine separate members of the Commonwealth, half of them with republican constitutions but all voluntarily recognizing the queen as head of the Commonwealth.

Speaking of constitutions, it is perhaps interesting, though certainly a digression, to point out that the United Kingdom, which has the world's oldest democratic parliamentary system, is also the only country in the world, apart from New Zealand, to have no written constitution. We have found that that has its advantages. Perhaps Churchill had this in mind when he wrote: "In our affairs, as in those of Nature, there are always frayed edges, border-lands, compromises, anomalies. Few lines are drawn that are not smudged."

In his fervent belief in the values of the British Empire, Churchill did not at all see eye to eye with many of his American friends, to whom the British Empire, wrongly I think, represented a repression of freedom. To Roosevelt, Hopkins, Eisenhower and many others the mere term *colony* recalled their early history lessons about the redcoats at Bunker's Hill. To

Churchill and to most of his generation in Britain it seemed that we had, to the lasting benefit of the local inhabitants, provided not only great material benefits—in roads, railways, telecommunications, schools, and hospitals—but had imposed law and order in lands where greed, tyranny, injustice, and tribal warfare had formerly reigned supreme. In India we had created unity out of hundreds of warring states.

However, suspicion of British imperial designs long dominated the White House and did, I believe, play a part in the unfortunate conception, sprouting at Tehran and in full bloom at Yalta, that the future direction of world affairs might be more prudently shared with the Soviet Union, cleansed and purified in the furnace of war, than with old imperialist Britain. I suppose they thought Russia had ceased to be imperialist when the czar fell.

However, it is easy to exaggerate this theme. Churchill was sure, and I hope we all still are, that the affinities of the English-speaking peoples—even if they sometimes speak English, both in England and the United States, a little less gracefully than they might—are a stabilizing influence in an increasingly unstable world. It is right that we should preserve our customs and traditions, as well as our different accents and local peculiarities. Nothing is more depressing and stultifying than uniformity. But I think that if we seek to honor Churchill's memory, as you do so movingly here in Fulton, we must work for ever-increasing understanding—political, economic, and social—between the two countries of both of which Churchill was so proud to be, uniquely, a full citizen.

We live in stormy times. Perhaps it may be appropriate to finish this address with a verse written on the death of William Pitt by George Canning—the man who claimed to have called the New World into existence to redress the balance of the Old. He wrote:

> And oh, if again the rude whirlwind should rise
> The dawning of peace should fresh darkness deform,
> The regrets of the good and the fears of the wise
> Will turn to the pilot who weathered the storm.

ROBERT RHODES JAMES, a Member of Parliament for Cambridge since 1976, is the author of biographies of Churchill, Churchill's father Lord Randolph Churchill, and Robert Boothby, as well as a Fellow of All Souls College.

5

Churchill, the Man

Robert Rhodes James

Introduction

It is especially moving for an Englishman to be honored in this beautiful church, which stands serene and unconquered in the heart of America—a living memorial to the genius of Sir Christopher Wren and those who worked with him to create it. A memorial to the ordeal through which my country passed in war. A memorial to the man who led us in that grim but, indeed, "finest" hour. And an inspiration for future generations.

It was built in London as a labor of love. It was rebuilt in Fulton, Missouri, here in the same spirit. It is cherished by you and, for all this, "We are not ashamed to be grateful."

When Winston Churchill spoke here some forty years ago, he opened with the remark that "the name Westminster is somehow familiar to me. I seem to have heard of it before." I have at least one thing in common with him, that I am also "a child of the House of Commons." I first attended its sessions as a schoolboy; I then became one of its officers in 1955; and then, finally, a member of Parliament. I have been in Opposition and in government. I have seen many changes since the dominant personalities were Churchill, Eden, Attlee, and Bevan. Perhaps not all have been for the better. But there is something special about a human institution—fallible, as all human institutions necessarily are—which has survived in varying form some seven centuries, and has been through so much. It has experienced royal tyranny, against which it rebelled, and civil war; it has passed through terrible national and international crises; but it is still there. So is Britain.

My nation had to achieve survival and prosperity by exports to maintain ourselves in a small island. We have exported food, wool, steel, textiles, coal, chemicals, and all varieties of manufactured goods. But the greatest export of all has been a burning faith in the liberty of the individual. This was our gift to the fledgling United States of America, and, when certain regrettable events occurred in 1776 and thereafter, there were not lacking British members of Parliament who took the side of those Americans who sought, and were prepared to fight for, those liberties. There are few instances in history when eminent men have risked all by taking the side of the enemies of the king. But it happened over the United States, and it happened over India, and these huge democracies, their histories so closely woven with that of my country, constitute a remarkable memorial to those men and women who were the exporters of liberty.

This was what Churchill was referring to when he coined the phrase "the special relationship" forty years ago, and spoke of the English-speaking peoples and their links that go far beyond a common language and a common history. It is indeed special. As Louis Botha said to Lady Randolph Churchill of her son, "He and I have been out in all weathers together." We can apply that phrase to Britain and America.

It took a man who was himself half-American to describe, in unforgettable language, how that destiny merged and how, in the most terrible of all wars at the most terrible of all times, when England stood alone and, in the words of Dorothy L. Sayers, "Europe clanged shut, like a prison door. And men who loved us not yet looked to us for liberty." And when young Americans, in defiance of your Constitution, came to Britain to form the Eagle Squadron in 1940 or, like the late Stewart Alsop, joined the British Army, they did so because our cause was theirs as well.

Just outside my constituency of Cambridge is the American air force cemetery and memorial. The land was given by the grateful people of Cambridge to the people of the United States forever, and every year we meet in memory of those who did not return, and those who did.

But they, and so many tens of millions of others, served and suffered because so few had listened to the warnings of Winston Churchill after 1933 about the monstrous evil of Hitler and the Nazis. When there were ugly reports of the treatment of Jews, these were discounted. When Mussolini brutally invaded Abyssinia, there was moral outrage but no action. When Hitler tore up Versailles and Locarno and marched into the Rhineland, he was "only going into his own backyard." When he rearmed at terrifying speed and scale, this was none of our business. When he marched into Austria, this was, of course, regrettable; when he laid his hands upon Czechoslovakia, we had Munich and "peace in our time." The appeasers in Britain and the isolationists—and worse—in the United States persuaded him that he had nothing to fear. Why should he listen to a derided and aging British politician in the wilderness, or an unknown American senator? When Churchill and Truman met at Potsdam, it was on the wreckage of a once-proud and fine nation.

There are, obviously, perils in the study of history. There are few cases when circumstances exactly repeat themselves. When Churchill in 1945, privately to President Truman and then here in his presence in 1946, warned of "the Iron Curtain" that had fallen across Europe, he was careful not to put the Stalin tyranny into the same category as that of the Nazis. Nor did he close the door to understanding and cooperation. He endorsed the United Nations and urged the creation of a Temple of Peace. He spoke of the horror of global starvation. Contrary to the critics of his speech in Britain, he did not make a belligerent speech. He opened a window on the world as it really was.

When Churchill spoke here in 1946, large areas of Europe were in ruins, its economy no less than its cities and towns utterly devastated. Millions of forlorn and tragic displaced persons, as these wretched refugees were called, were barely surviving; the psychological wounds were almost as deep as the real ones. The United States and Britain had brought their men back home; the Russians had not. Europeans who had suffered so terribly under the Nazis now had to endure another dictatorial regime. The euphoria of victory had been followed by the profound disillusionment of the aftermath. Britain remained at the head of a vast empire, but now without the means—or even the will—of maintaining it, victorious but exhausted. It was a bleak and desolate scene. It was difficult indeed to foresee that the Western European nations, so recently at war with each other, would cast aside old enmities and unite politically, economically, and militarily—that the United States through the Marshall Plan would be the salvation of Western Europe economically and, through NATO, militarily, nor that the British Empire of which Churchill spoke so proudly here forty years ago would be dismantled so swiftly, and, in the main, bloodlessly. That process began here, in Fulton, on March 5, 1946.

But in 1946 the secrets of the atom bomb were known only to the Americans and the British. That situation was not of long duration. And then came, when Churchill was prime minister again, the horrific hydrogen bomb. Churchill remarked at the time that this was as different from the atomic bomb as from the bow and arrow—a considerable exaggeration, but he had fully grasped the enormity of what mankind had achieved. In 1946 the atomic age had dawned. It will last forever. This is the dominant reality of our time, compared to which our other concerns and preoccupations fade into their proper perspective.

One error, one miscalculation, one act of folly is all that is required for total and almost unimaginable catastrophe. One need not be a pacifist—which Churchill certainly was not—to recognize how dangerous our world is, and how precarious the peace which we have almost taken for granted.

It is natural that people are asking themselves whether it is really necessary, with such fearful power at our disposal already, that we should continue to pile warhead upon warhead, missile upon missile, so that we can destroy each other five times over rather than three times. Churchill firmly believed, as I do, in the nuclear deterrent; again, not through desire but necessity. In his last great speech in the House of Commons, on March 1, 1955, he dwelt upon the paradox that "By a process of sublime irony we have reached a stage in this story where safety will be the sturdy child of terror, and survival the twin brother of annihilation." But, in one of Churchill's favorite sayings, "facts are stubborn things."

In 1946 Churchill, together with millions of others, had hope and faith in the United Nations. He envisaged it having a military arm, and, although this has not happened, we tend to put too little emphasis on the real achievements of the UN peacekeeping forces and the courage and dedication of the men who serve in them. Also, while again excessive optimism has been followed in the West with excessive disillusionment with the world organization, we should be careful. It reflects faithfully—all too faithfully—the political realities of our planet. It is the one global organization. It fights disease, poverty, and hunger. It is the one forum where the five thermonuclear powers meet. When Churchill called his 1946 speech "The Sinews of Peace" he did so as a realist, but also with his eye to the future.

As I said of the House of Commons, no human institution is infallible, and the divides in the world are harsh. But if there is any possibility of at least limiting the pace of the arms race as a prelude to realistic disarmament, this cannot only be done on a bilateral basis between the superpowers. Nor can the scourge of terrorism be met and defeated by the resolution of our two nations alone. Here is an issue in which all nations save the guilty have a direct interest. Russian businessmen and tourists and the Soviet economy are as much at threat as British or American. If we have been slow in waking up to this new menace, that is our fault. Now that we have woken up, and taken decisive action, we must work together. There can be no standers-by in this very real crisis—and I deliberately include those Americans who give money, aid, and arms to the IRA to enable them to continue their war of murder, maiming, and intimidation. And I say to any American who contributes to NORAID, and any American politician who looks the other way, that, literally, "The Buck Stops Here." Spend it on something else.

The spectacle of some Americans providing some of the means for the purpose of killing British soldiers and innocent civilians by terrorism would have appalled the Anglo-American Winston Churchill, honorary citizen of this great republic. It appalls me and my fellow countrymen. I say in all seriousness to you, as a true friend of the United States, that it ought to appall you. As Churchill wrote in the 1930s of the European menace, "Stop it! Stop it! Stop it now!"

If I dwell upon these contemporary issues that haunt us all, it is because I am a politician as well as a scholar, as was Churchill, and I truly believe that he would not want me to use this occasion for a solemn lecture about him. Indeed, a truly solemn lecture about this extraordinary man, with his bubbling humor, intense love of life, and conversation that no Boswell has truly been able to recapture, would be ludicrously inappropriate. To him, life was fun, as full of color as his pictures, "my little daubs" as he modestly called them; he had a detestation of bores, and it was significant that his closest friends—with the notable exceptions of Anthony Eden and Lord Cherwell—had a marked tendency to the buccaneer. His wife strongly disapproved of her husband's enjoyment of the company of men like F. E. Smith, Beaverbrook, Brendan Bracken, and Duff Cooper. One can understand why, but when Harold MacMillan described Churchill as "half English aristocrat and half American gambler" we get very close to the real man.

His entire life was a gamble. He saw, as a child and very young man, his father, the brilliant and mercurial Lord Randolph Churchill, soar rapidly to almost the height of British politics and then crash, dying young, and leaving his widow and two boys with virtually nothing except memories, and in Winston a burning desire to "raise the banner I found on a stricken field." As a young soldier and war correspondent he was eager for action wherever it could be found, whether in Cuba, the northwest frontier of India, or in the Sudan or South Africa. His eagerness, self-esteem, and capacity for pulling strings must have made him a disagreeable companion, as he subsequently admitted. In that masterpiece of autobiography, *My Early Life,* he describes how, as a very young subaltern who had just landed at Bombay, he was invited to dinner by the governor, an old friend of his father:

> His Excellency, after the health of the Queen-Emperor had been drunk and dinner was over, was good enough to ask my opinion upon several matters, and considering the magnificent character of his hospitality, I thought it would be unbecoming in me not to reply fully. I have forgotten the particular points of British and Indian affairs upon which he sought my counsel; all I can remember is

that I responded generously. There were indeed moments when he seemed willing to impart his own views; but I thought it would be ungracious to put him to so much trouble, and he very readily subsided. He kindly sent his aide-de-camp with us to be sure we found our way back to camp all right. On the whole, after forty-eight hours of intensive study, I formed a highly favorable opinion about India. Sometimes, thought I, one sees these things more completely at first sight.

With no money, he launched himself upon intense self-education and into the stormy seas of journalism and politics. As members of Parliament were then unpaid, when he won election at his second attempt in 1900, his writing was essential to him, as it was throughout his active political career. He demanded a high standard of living, and he worked for it, but it was not until 1945 that he was freed from money worries.

Politics was his profession and his life. He was a career politician—highly ambitious, egotistical, and always fascinated by "The Great Game." There is nothing wrong with that, but after he abandoned the conservatives for the liberals and advanced rapidly, the army of detractors remorselessly grew. He failed to understand how much his barbs and sallies were resented and remembered. When disaster struck over the Dardanelles in May 1915, he discovered how few were his friends and how many his enemies. Shattered by events, denounced as "another Lord Randolph," and with the Dardanelles failure cast entirely upon him—not wholly unfairly, it must be admitted—he rejoined the army and served on the Western Front. Only gradually did his political star begin to rise again. And then, in 1922, he lost his seat in Parliament. In the 1923 general election he was defeated again, as a liberal for the last time. In the following spring he tried again, this time as a "Constitutionalist and Anti-Socialist," and lost again. In the autumn of that year he at last found political refuge at Epping, and, to his own amazement, became a conservative chancellor of the Exchequer.

Churchill's character was his career. He had immense application and capacity for work. He was not a natural speaker, with an inability to pronounce the letter *S* but which he turned to advantage. Nor was he really a natural writer—if such a thing exists. It was all hard work. As he once wrote of the Second World War period, he did not begrudge ten hours of his time upon a speech to the House of Commons. Nothing came easily to him. Those glorious speeches and those marvelous books were the result of much toil. This is too often ill-appreciated, but it was a triumph of character in itself.

Then, he was indeed a gambler. He changed his parties twice, and it is fair to say that party was to him a horse of which he was the rider, and he was not too interested in the color. This offended all good party men. When he described himself as "an optimistic Liberal Imperialist" this was as good a description as any. His dislike of the Conservative Party "which treated my father so scurvily" was lifelong, although he was to be its leader and prime minister. He played the party game with gusto—rather too much so for sensitive souls—but he was happiest in coalition, and as a national, rather than a party, leader.

In one sense, he was an innocent. Although he could use fierce words, he had a great capacity for tolerance. As he once remarked, he was always against the pacifists in the fight and against the jingoes at the end. When, in 1919, he was asked to provide some words for a French war memorial, he chose these:

> In War: Resolution
> In Defeat: Defiance
> In Victory: Magnanimity
> In Peace: Good Will

Of course, like so many of his proposals, this was rejected. Magnanimity to the Germans? On a French memorial? Germany was to be punished, nay, ruined; the blood debt must be paid in full. There was to be no magnanimity. Thus the Weimar Republic was born in darkness, and the victors in their folly wrote the script for the rise of Hitler.

Here Churchill was in 1919 on the side of the defeated. When Hitler came, he was virtually the only one who recognized the monster that the Allies had created. But on both occasions no one was listening.

Here was generosity, another central feature of his character, manifested in his political career. In the 1926 General Strike he led the charge against it; when it collapsed it was he who tried to help the miners whose plight had initiated the conflict. Again he lost, but it was typical of his instinctive wisdom and compassion. He had warm blood in his veins, adored animals, and was moved to tears by people in distress.

This led him into many errors. When he was denounced as "impetuous" there was much evidence for this throughout his life. As F. E. Smith once said, "When Winston is right he is very right. But when he is wrong— Oh My God!" Churchill genuinely found this bewildering. What can ever be achieved without taking risks? When admirals were distraught at the loss of warships he asked what were warships for? Of course they get sunk. That is what war is about. Commanders who tried valiantly and failed were far higher in his esteem than the cautious ones, and he had a passion for new ideas and proposals, some of which ended disastrously. Others, like the tank, the proximity fuse, cryptology, and ingenious devices to mislead German bombers, did not. But until 1940 the failures loomed much larger in men's minds than the successes.

Impetuosity led him into a major disaster, his campaign between 1930 and 1935 against the Government of India Act. This drove him into the political wilderness for nine crucial years and so damaged his reputation that when he warned about the situation in Europe no one was listening once again. He had debased the language of alarmism. And, just when people were beginning to listen, he rushed headlong into the abdication crisis, and was literally howled down by the same House of Commons that he was to lead so incomparably throughout the war. His motives were purely those of loyalty to a king he admired; as he later privately conceded, he had been wrong on every count (as on India), but it was truly in character. One would not wish it otherwise.

I do not think he would like contemporary British politics, when we are supposed to be experts on every local subject and to immerse ourselves in an apparently endless march of legislation, regulations, by-laws and ordinances of all kinds, as a kind of "Super-Councillor." As he once impishly remarked to Stewart Alsop, whenever some subject like sewage came up he would ask Eden to take it on, and when Eden protested he would say, "My dear, this is your big chance!" As his whole career demonstrated, he had a real feeling for people and wanted to help them as much as possible. As he once said to his cabinet at the height of the war, "People in high office forget how damnable life can be for the ordinary person." Those words should be on the desk of every politician, in my country and in yours.

For, as Sir Isaiah Berlin has written of Churchill:

> As much as any king conceived by a Renaissance dramatist or by a nineteenth century historian or moralist he thinks it a brave thing to ride in triumph through Persepolis; he knows with an unshakable certainty what he considers to be big, handsome, noble, worthy of pursuit by someone in high station, and what on the contrary he abhors as being dim, grey, thin, likely to lower or destroy the play of colour and movement in the universe.

The fact was that the British people, all for a quiet life, did not relish being cast as players in this splendid but obviously uncomfortable production. Had he died in 1939, he would have been written off as a failure, "another Lord Randolph." But he did not, and the Wilderness Years ended under the most terrible conditions. As he commented to Eden, "Had it not been for Hitler, neither of us would be here" (at Ten Downing Street). And it was true.

Until toward the end, I do not think the British quite lost this distrust. The campaign against him in 1950 that he was a warmonger was disgraceful and untrue, but enough people believed it to be dismally effective. And then the clouds of mistrust lifted, and all was sunshine in that wonderful Indian summer. In another of his favorite phrases, "All had come well." The gallant ship had survived the storms, through the qualities of courage, application, dedication, a sense of destiny, resilience, compassion, and wisdom. If he had indeed, in the wonderful lines of the poet, "Red Hand in the Foray" he also had "Sage Counsel in Cumber," and the lines end: "How Sweet Be Thy Slumber."

That benediction should also apply to his wife. Of their marriage one could very appropriately use another of Churchill's favorite sayings, "Here firm, though all be drifting." I like to think of that phrase also in the context of the Anglo-American alliance.

Thus, we salute this astonishing, brave, fallible, very human man. With a deep and keen sense of history he was always looking to the future. Except for the darkest moments in 1940 when all seemed lost, he awoke every morning with enthusiasm for the day ahead. His energy was prodigious, his achievements extraordinary. He wrote, in his biography of his father, one of the best political histories in the English language. In his twenties he wrote *The River War*, a classic military history. His autobiography stands alone as an unrivaled masterpiece. We marched with him and Marlborough to the Danube and through the First World War in *The World Crisis*. If he had done nothing except write books which any professional historian would envy, he would be remembered. But these were adjuncts, very necessary ones, to the great work of his life. And he did indeed "ride in triumph through Persepolis."

As a very young man he wrote to his mother, "In Politics a man, I take it, gets on not so much by what he does as by what he is." I have tried to demonstrate that the two are inseparable. He would not have achieved what he did had he not been the man he was.

What would he be saying to us today?

I believe that he would look hard at the fact that we not only have an Iron Curtain in Europe but another one in the form of international terrorism and near-anarchy. Having pointed this out, and faced these grim realities, he would not have us despair. He would, I think, remind us of the closing words of his last great Commons speech:

"The day may dawn when fair play, love for one's fellow-men, respect for justice and freedom, will enable tormented generations to march forth serene and triumphant from the hideous epoch in which we have to dwell. Meanwhile, never flinch, never weary, never despair."

And I would reply by saying that the entire life, character, and career of Winston Leonard Spencer Churchill are contained in these words:

IN WAR: RESOLUTION
IN DEFEAT: DEFIANCE
IN VICTORY: MAGNANIMITY
IN PEACE: GOOD WILL

LORD BLAKE, F.B.A., J.P., has served as chairman of the Royal Commission on Historical Manuscripts, trustee of the British Museum, and editor of the *Dictionary of National Biography*. Among his several publications in British history are *The Decline of Power, 1915–1964*, *The Conservative Party from Peel to Thatcher*, and the definitive biography of Benjamin Disraeli.

6

Churchill and the Conservative Party

Lord Blake

C hurchill's relations with the party he came to lead were always ambivalent—more so than is usually appreciated. He was much influenced by his father's political career. Lord Randolph Churchill was a brilliant but flawed Conservative politician who died young— probably from tertiary syphilis or possibly from a tumor on the brain. At the end of his life he became sadly and obviously incapable of thought or speech. But he continued to perform on the parliamentary stage to the embarrassment of all who heard him. Many walked out. Only Gladstone, magnanimous always, treated him with unfailing courtesy.

Lord Randolph, in the famous words of Lord Rosebery, a fleeting Liberal prime minister, "was the chief mourner at his own protracted funeral," but, long before this sad deterioration, he was very bitter about the Conservatives. He wrote in 1891: "No power will make me lift hand, or foot, or voice for the Tories, just as no power would make me join the other side. . . . I expect I have made great mistakes; but there has been no consideration, no indulgence, no memory or gratitude—nothing but spite, malice, and abuse. I am quite tired and dead-sick of it all, and will not continue political life any longer." At about this time he copied out for himself Dryden's lines: "Not Heaven itself over the past hath power / But what has been has been, and I have had my hour."

Lord Randolph was chancellor of the Exchequer for a few months in 1886, resigning before he even produced a budget. Many people believed that he was the morning star of the Tory party, its future leader and prime minister. But the actual prime minister, Robert Cecil, Third Marquess of Salisbury, took a different view. He regarded Lord Randolph as an insufferable colleague. When he offered his resignation on an issue of not great importance with the object of asserting his personal indispensability, Lord Salisbury at once accepted it. Wellwishers tried to reconcile them. Lord Salisbury replied: "Have you ever heard of a man having a carbuncle on his neck wanting it to return?"

Lord Randolph's treatment by the Conservative hierarchy always rankled with Winston. I remember a conversation I had with Lord Salisbury's grandson, the Fifth Marquess, who held high office in various coalition or Conservative governments in the 1940s and 1950s. He told me that he was once dining with Churchill in September 1940 at the height of the Battle of Britain. Churchill, as he sometimes did, sank into a silent and somber reverie. Then he suddenly turned to Lord Salisbury and said apropos of nothing: "I always consider that your grandfather treated my father disgracefully." Lord Salisbury was taken aback. He murmured some emollient comment. The conversation trickled into the sand and the dinner party reverted to the rather more important question of bombers and fighters, and Hitler and Goering.

Winston Churchill was deeply devoted to his father, although he was treated by him in a manner that can only be described as heartless, even cruel. There is a terrible letter from Lord Randolph to his son when the eighteen-year-old boy had been accepted in 1893 for the Royal Military Academy at Sandhurst and had enthusiastically told his father of his—admittedly very marginal—success. "Always behind-hand . . . social wastrel . . . degenerate into a shabby, unhappy and futile existence." It can only be excused because physical and mental deterioration was already clouding Lord Randolph's mind.

The paternal rejection was deeply felt, but Winston did not reject his father. Far from it. Much of his life was motivated by the challenge to make the mark in public life that a hero-worshipped father had never achieved. He found himself at the age of twenty head of the family in precarious financial circumstances. He meant to forge a career, but he felt no great love for the Conservative Party. Its stuffy conformism had destroyed his father—or so he believed. He would not at once abandon the Churchill family tradition. He would begin as a Conservative, but the allegiance lay lightly on him from the start. In 1900 under the Spy cartoon of him in *Vanity Fair* these words appeared: "He is ambitious; he means to get on, and he loves his country. But he can hardly be regarded as the slave of any Party."

He had made enough money by 1900 through lecturing and journalism to risk the career—in those days totally unpaid—of a member of Parliament. In October he was duly elected as Conservative member for Oldham in Lancashire, though by a very narrow margin. He thus commenced on a long love/hate relationship with the Conservative Party. It was reciprocal. Plenty of Conservatives felt as much doubt about him as he did about them. The general election of 1900 was a conclusive Conservative victory, based largely on patriotic emotions generated by the South African War. One could perhaps compare the part played by the Falklands War in the election of 1983. A big majority gave scope for backbenchers to go ahead on their own, make their names by making trouble, and generally behave in an undisciplined manner—easier in those days when party pressure was far weaker than it has become since.

From the start of this parliamentary career Winston Churchill made it clear that he was not a party conformist. His disenchantment with his own nominal party certainly increased when, in the summer of 1902, he began the task of writing his father's biography. Reading many of the documents for the first time he must have become more aware than ever before of the way in which Lord Randolph perceived his treatment at the hands of Lord Salisbury. In that year Salisbury himself had, after a long and electorally very successful seventeen-year period as leader, at last bowed out. But the Cecil ascendancy remained. The new prime minister was Salisbury's nephew, his sister's eldest son, Arthur Balfour. Ostensibly he had been a friend of Lord Randolph; he was a member of the famous "Fourth Party" which stirred up such trouble on the Tory backbenches in the early 1880s. In reality he kept his uncle closely aware of what Lord Randolph was up to. Winston would not have seen their correspondence but he must have

gained an impression from other sources of how matters stood. It cannot
have endeared Balfour to him. One remembers his famous description
in *Great Contemporaries*. The pen portrait is in general favorable, even
flattering, but after describing Balfour's great charm and courtesy he wrote:

> But underneath all this was a cool ruthlessness where public affairs
> were concerned. He rarely allowed political antagonism to be a barrier
> in private life; neither did he, any more than Asquith, let personal
> friendship, however sealed and cemented, hamper his solutions to
> the problems of State. Had his life been cast amid the labyrinthine
> intrigues of the Italian Renaissance, he would not have required to
> study the works of Machiavelli.

Almost from the beginning of his parliamentary career Churchill was
far closer to the right wing of the Liberal Party than to the orthodox
Conservatives. He corresponded much with Rosebery, Grey, and Asquith.
His little coterie of whom the principal member was Lord Hugh Cecil,
a cousin of Balfour but by no means an admirer, were known as the
"Hughligans" and delighted embarrassing the government. Churchill wrote
to Rosebery of his dream of a "Government of the Middle—the party which
shall be free at once from the sordid selfishness and callousness of Toryism
on the one hand and the blind appetites of the Radical masses on the
other." This language in October 1902, well under two years after his entry
into the House as a Conservative, is symptomatic, symbolic, and startling.
But he needed an honorable excuse to change sides.

It came in the spring of 1903 when Joseph Chamberlain, the second
most powerful figure in the government, split the party on the question
of protective tariffs. One section supported him with enthusiasm; another,
deeply attached to traditional free trade, remained firmly hostile, Churchill
being one of them; Balfour and yet another section sought a compromise.
To him Churchill wrote on May 25, 1903: "I am utterly opposed to anything
that will alter the Free Trade character of this country . . . once this policy
[of tariffs] is begun it must lead to the establishment of a complete
Protective system, involving commercial disaster and the Americanisation
of English parties." Churchill, half-American himself, was very far from

being anti-American. But he was aware of the logrolling, the intrigue, the corruption generated by the American tariff system of that time. In the House of Commons three days later he said: "The old Conservative Party with its religious convictions and constitutional principles will disappear, and a new party will arise rich, materialist, and secular whose opinion will turn on tariffs and who will cause the lobbies to be crowded with the touts of protected industries." He now had an issue and a cause. He could break with his and his father's party on a matter of principle. He soon began to distance himself from his old allegiances. In a letter dated October 24, 1903, to Lord Hugh Cecil, which he drafted but did not send, he wrote: "I am an English Liberal. I hate the Tory party, their men, their words, their methods." In March 1904 Balfour, the whole of the Conservative front bench, and the great majority of backbenchers walked out of the House when Churchill rose to speak. In the general election of 1906 he was returned as one of the Liberal members for northwest Manchester. The election was an overwhelming victory for the Liberals throughout the country. Churchill had certainly chosen a good moment to change sides as many people were quick to point out. He was promptly given office as under secretary to the colonies in the new Liberal government.

To cross the floor of the House was by no means an easy thing to do in British politics, even as early as 1904. Party divisions had hardened compared with the fluidity of mid- or even late-Victorian politics. Churchill was sure of a rough ride from his former allies, and he made it all the rougher by his own pugnacity and insensitivity. There can be no doubt that among Conservatives he became, along with Lloyd George, the most bitterly hated figure in the government party. Indeed he was even more hated. Lloyd George had never been anything but a radical Liberal, and he stemmed from a background of Welsh nonconformity in which radicalism was natural, predictable, and expected. Churchill, on the other hand, with his aristocratic and Tory Party connections, appeared as a "traitor to his class."

He sealed his reputation by an extraordinary speech in the House on March 21, 1906. A group of backbench Liberals had put down a motion of censure for illegal practices on Lord Milner who had been high commissioner (i.e., governor) of South Africa from 1897 to 1905—the period of the Boer War, its beginning and its aftermath. He had become a cult figure of the Conservative imperialists, a totem and hero in one, who inspired admiration amounting almost to worship among his followers, and corresponding detestation among his opponents. The government largely at Churchill's instigation put down an amendment deprecating the personal censure while also condemning the illegal practices. Churchill was therefore in a sense trying to shield Milner, but the way he chose to do it was hardly tactful. His line, in effect, was that Milner had now become a figure of such unimportance that he was simply not worth censuring:

> Having exercised great authority he now exercises none. Having held great employment he now has no employment. Having disposed of events which have shaped the course of history he is now unable to deflect in the smallest degree the policy of the day. . . . [He] sees the ideals, the principles, the policies for which he has toiled utterly discredited by the people of Great Britain and [he] knows that many of the arrangements in which he has consumed all the energies of his life are about to be reversed or dissolved. Lord Milner has ceased to be a factor in public events.

These observations and the tone in which they were uttered by a young man of thirty-one, notorious for his bumptiousness and widely regarded as a turncoat, caused enormous resentment from the king himself downward. In some quarters it was never forgiven. The hatred Churchill inspired was only extinguished by the extinction of the haters themselves. He was lucky to live so long. He never seems to have understood the offense he had given.

2.

Churchill's career as a Liberal junior minister and then in the cabinet— board of trade, home secretary, first lord of the admiralty—continued in a blaze of controversy. It was of course a period of great political uproar— the crises first over Lloyd George's famous budget of 1909, then over the powers of the House of Lords, then over Irish home rule and Ulster. In every one of these he was at the forefront, pugnacious and articulate, a master of rhetoric, coiner of unforgettable witticisms and wounding metaphors, a perpetual seeker of the limelight. In the course of these years he was responsible for notable achievements which are familiar in the history books, but he stirred up bitter resentments and intense animosities. Perhaps the episode which caused the strongest feeling was the part he was believed to have played in the Ulster crisis of 1914. He was supposed to have engaged in a plot to provoke the Ulster volunteers into armed resistance which would give the government an excuse to move in troops, smash them, and impose home rule by force for all Ireland. Although there was a good deal of plausible circumstantial evidence for the charge, it seems in fact to have been unjustified. But belief in its truth fueled the flames of anti-Churchill sentiment.

Then came the First World War. Churchill was first lord of the Admiralty and was deeply involved in one of the great fiascos of the war—the Dardanelles expedition of 1915. Reams have been written about this. The blame lies at least as much with Asquith, the prime minister and Lord Kitchener, secretary of war. But Churchill showed an almost quixotic readiness to accept responsibility for a campaign, about which he had expressed many misgivings and which had by no means been conducted as he had planned. It was an honorable attitude but one that did him much unnecessary harm.

The full extent of British defeat did not become apparent till October, but by early May it was clear that things were going badly wrong. At this juncture Admiral Fisher, the eccentric first sea lord, suddenly resigned. He had always had suppressed doubts about the expedition, and when Churchill tampered with some of his instructions he exploded. The ensuing crisis rocked the government. To prevent a breach of the uneasy pact which had kept the Conservatives from overt opposition, Asquith had to form a coalition government. Bonar Law, the Conservative leader, had never liked or trusted Churchill. He insisted as an absolute condition upon his removal from the Admiralty. Churchill departed, under strong protest, took a minor office, resigning when the decision was made in November to withdraw from the Dardanelles and departing to command a regiment on the Western Front. He was soon back in politics, but his conduct from the back benches seemed to many people irresponsible and full of sour grapes. He was now not even trusted by the Liberals. He had no personal following at all.

At the end of 1916 a second cabinet crisis occurred. Asquith was overthrown and Lloyd George replaced him as head of a new coalition even more dependent on Conservative support than its predecessor. To Churchill's immense chagrin, Lloyd George did not take the risk of inviting him to join. Four prominent Conservatives made their entry conditional on his exclusion. But in July 1917 he decided that Churchill "out" was a greater threat than Churchill "in." Without consulting the Conservative leader he appointed him as minister of munitions.

Bonar Law complained bitterly against this fait accompli. The National Unionist (i.e., Conservative) Council carried amidst cheers a motion that it was "an insult to the Navy and the Army." A hundred Conservative MPs signed a resolution condemning him as "a national danger." The *Morning Post* said, "We confidently anticipate that he will continue to make colossal blunders at the expense of the nation." The *Sunday Times* considered his return "a grave danger to the Administration and the Empire as a whole." Lloyd George reckoned rightly on wartime governmental and party unity to ride out the storm. No one resigned, though many came near to it. The waters subsided and Churchill—much disliked, suspected, and even hated—managed to survive.

Let us move on a few years. Churchill's appointment in 1917 was a significant augury for the future. The government he had joined was largely dependent on Conservative support. He had been appointed in spite of Conservative hostility, but he was even less in favor with the Asquithian element in the Liberal Party which now constituted the official opposition to Lloyd George's government. The possibility of that "Center Party" to which he had looked forward in his youth beckoned hopefully. The 1918 election resulted in a crushing defeat for the Asquithians. Lloyd George's Liberals were now far outnumbered by his Conservative supporters. But that support was always conditional upon success. Churchill's position, as the most vigorous and truculent of the Liberal ministers in a largely Conservative cabinet, was precarious. If things went wrong, if the Conservatives withdrew, he would be in trouble.

In 1922 the rank and file of the Conservative Party repudiated Lloyd George and overthrew his government. The ensuing election saw Churchill lose his seat at Dundee and gave the Conservatives under Bonar Law a clear majority. On May 30, 1923, Churchill, asked by a former colleague where he stood politically, replied, "I am what I have always been—a Tory Democrat. Force of circumstances has compelled me to serve with another party, but my views have never changed, and I should be glad to give effect to them by rejoining the Conservatives." On 14 August he had a long conversation with Baldwin, the new prime minister, with a view to joining the party, but no decision was reached. Then in October Baldwin unexpectedly raised the whole question of protective tariffs, which he said were the only cure for unemployment. He called a general election. Churchill now swung back to his old allegiance. He stood as a Liberal for West Leicester mounting a ferocious attack on the government, but he lost yet again, this time to a Labour candidate.

The general election was indecisive. The Conservatives were the biggest single party, but Labour (who came second) and the Liberals (who came third) could in combination outvote them. The Liberals decided to defeat Baldwin. MacDonald, the Labour leader, accordingly took office with Liberal support. For Churchill this was the turning point. Socialism was anathema to him. No one had more vehemently supported the White Russians against the Bolsheviks in 1919–1920. No one had been more distressed when Lloyd George withdrew British support and left the White Russians to their fate. To compare Bolshevism with the British Labour Party may seem absurd. For Churchill, however—and he was not alone— the socialism preached by Ramsay MacDonald was merely a watered-down version of communism. And for communism as practiced in Soviet Russia he had unlimited hatred and contempt. To him it was the embodiment of ruthless terrorism, total tyranny, and destruction of all the values of Western civilization. It would produce grinding poverty, extinguish liberty of thought, belief, speech or the press, and do all in its power to spread its evil doctrines over the rest of the world. And who can say he was wrong? As for Labour, MacDonald was obviously not a Lenin or a Stalin or a Trotsky, but many of his followers saw Russia through rose-colored spectacles, used sympathetic language, and in some cases were clearly fellow travelers. To give such a party the chance to govern Britain, even in a minority and for a short time, seemed to Churchill the height of irresponsibility. In a long letter to the *Times* published on

January 18, 1924, he proclaimed his position and finally broke with the Liberal Party.

In March he tried to get the Conservative nomination for the Abbey division of Westminster, one of the safest seats in the country. Unfortunately, the nephew of the man whose death had caused the by-election was a heavy contributor to party funds. He insisted on standing and, not surprisingly, obtained the official blessing of the local organization. Churchill fought as an independent antisocialist. Never has an election received greater publicity, but Churchill lost by the narrowest of margins—only forty-three votes. It was a brief setback. MacDonald's government did not last long. There was another general election in October 1924. Churchill was adopted as the official Tory candidate for Epping and won easily. He retained the seat for the rest of his political life. Thus, after twenty years he returned to his original party. And he was rewarded to the surprise of most people, including himself, by the office of chancellor of the Exchequer which his father had held thirty-eight years earlier. His account is worth quoting. When Baldwin offered him the post he said, "What about Robert Horne?" who had been chancellor of the Exchequer in 1921–1922. Baldwin said, "No, I offered him that post a year ago when I needed him, and he refused. He will not have it now." There was a pause. Then Baldwin said, "Perhaps you will now tell me your answer to my question. Will you go to the Treasury?" Churchill writes, "I should have liked to have answered 'Will the bloody duck swim?' But as it was a formal and important occasion, I replied 'This fulfills my ambition. I still have my father's robe as Chancellor. I shall be proud to serve you in this splendid office.'"

3.

Churchill's tenure of the chancellorship was not in itself particularly controversial. He followed the orthodox economic policies of the day. Many of them now seem to have been erroneous, especially the return to the gold standard. But, if Churchill erred, he erred in company with almost all the economists, bankers, businessmen, and politicians of the day. Keynes was one of the few exceptions among the economists. What did bring Churchill into hot dispute was his role in the General Strike of 1926 when he planned, edited, and managed an official newspaper called the *British Gazette* which presented the government case against the unions in picturesque and lurid language. A paper whose circulation rose from 230,000 to 2,200,000 between 5 and 12 May can hardly be regarded as unsuccessful, even in the peculiar circumstances of the day. But its success did Churchill no good in the longer run. No doubt he disarmed to some extent the diehards of the extreme Right who had been the element most hostile to him in the Conservative Party, but he infuriated the parties of the Left and his "image" as an enemy of organized labor and an oppressor of the working class long continued, though a travesty of the truth. However, he had an effective answer to those who accused him of failure to be "impartial": "I decline utterly to be impartial between the fire brigade and the fire."

In 1929 the Conservatives were defeated. The Labour Party did not have an overall majority, but, as in 1924, MacDonald took office at the head of a minority government with Liberal support. Churchill found himself on the Opposition front bench for the first time ever. He soon began to distance himself from his former cabinet colleagues. Two issues were involved. One was the question of India, the other that of tariff reform which suddenly reentered the political scene. Of these, India was the more important. The viceroy, Lord Irwin, better known as Lord Halifax, later foreign secretary and then wartime ambassador in Washington, favored a major step toward Indian independence. He had been appointed by Baldwin but was continued under MacDonald. Baldwin agreed with this change of policy and hoped for a Conservative/Labour consensus. Churchill was bitterly opposed. His attitude to India was conditioned by his experiences as a young cavalry officer in the Fourth Hussars. With the middle, intellectual and professional classes—who in Delhi, Calcutta, and Bombay were the driving force for independence—he had no sympathy or understanding whatever.

Churchill was in America when Baldwin persuaded the Conservative "Business Committee"—it would now be called the Shadow Cabinet—to support Lord Irwin. On his return to London Churchill quickly and publicly registered dissent in a strong article in the *Daily Mail* on November 16, 1929. He could never understand that what the subjects of imperial rule sought was not good government but self-government, and that no amount of argument that the British Raj was just, honest, and efficient—which it was—would have any effect at all on those who wanted to govern themselves whether badly or well. Churchill persistently opposed the idea of even modest steps toward what was called "dominion status" for India. Early in 1931 Gandhi was released from detention and the decision was backed by Baldwin. Churchill promptly resigned from the Business Committee.

He was also on a collision path with Baldwin over the other question—tariffs. Baldwin, in office, had been content to accept free trade. Out of office, he was at once faced with strong Conservative pressure to declare himself in favor of what was called "empire free trade"—imperial tariffs under a different name—backed by the newspaper magnates, Lords Beaverbrook and Rothermere. Baldwin was not averse to some steps in that direction. He was not willing to go the whole way but he made concessions which were a further reason for Churchill widening the gap with his leader.

Churchill now seemed more and more a figure of the extreme Right. He pursued his battle over India to the bitter end. When the economic crisis of 1931 occurred he was not invited to join the MacDonald/Baldwin coalition. He continued to use every parliamentary device to block the India Bill. He had little support among Conservative MPs but considerable backing in the party organization, though never a majority. He made himself very unpopular in April 1934 by accusing Lord Derby, a respected pillar of the party, and Sir Samuel Hoare, secretary of state for India, of a breach of parliamentary privilege by influencing evidence to be given to a joint select committee on India. The charge was quite unjustified and was rejected by the Committee of Privileges two months later.

The tariff issue died away. Churchill's next criticism of his party was concerned with rearmament and foreign policy. There is much mythology about this and Churchill's memoirs have to be read in the light of a brilliant study by last year's Crosby Kemper lecturer, Mr. Robert Rhodes James, *Churchill: A Study in Failure* (1970). Churchill was by no means consistent in his opinions: he spoke well of Mussolini; he was ambivalent at first about Hitler; he was pro-Franco till late in the day; he admired Japan. But he was from the early 1930s onward a consistent advocate of British rearmament against the mounting German threat, and a constant critic of the British government's failure, as he saw it, to cope with the danger.

At first he was given a reasonable degree of access to official information, despite his vigorous attacks on government policy. He was careful in timing these. From October 1935 till March 1936 he held his fire hoping to return to office. No offer came, and he was greatly disappointed. He now began to strike a harsher note of criticism and, although some of his information was wrong and some of his advice doubtful, there can be no doubt that he was far nearer to the truth and reality than were the successive governments of MacDonald, Baldwin, and Neville Chamberlain. This, of course, did not make him popular. Indeed, one is struck throughout this period right up to the outbreak of war by what a lonely figure he had become. He still had no following. His supporters over India were also, for the most part, supporters of the Conservative defense and foreign policies which he was attacking. His right-wing conservatism divided him from Conservative social reformers, and of course made any rapprochement with the Liberals, let alone Labour, out of the question. He had nowhere to go. He was the prisoner of the Conservative Party, however much he disliked its general tone and style.

Nevertheless, he was beginning to make some headway over rearmament and on November 12, 1936, he had an exchange with Baldwin from which he came out triumphant and Baldwin very badly. Then there occurred an unexpected reversal. The crisis over King Edward VIII's decision to marry Mrs. Simpson suddenly broke into the open after months of gossip and rumor. The leaders of all the political parties and the Dominion prime ministers were convinced that the marriage was incompatible with retaining the Crown. Churchill—romantic, loyal, protective, quixotic—convinced himself that the king was being unduly hurried into an irrevocable decision. His wife and friends begged him to keep quiet, but he insisted on issuing a public statement. When he tried to make a speech in the House on the same lines he was for the only time in his life literally shouted down. His popularity sank to zero.

Churchill was quiet during the first half of 1937 but if he had hopes of office under the new prime minister, Neville Chamberlain, who succeeded Baldwin in May, he was to be disappointed. "If I take him into the Cabinet he will dominate it, he won't give others a chance of even talking." The crunch came with Eden's resignation in February 1938 and the Munich crisis in September/October. After Eden's departure there was at last a group of Conservative MPs prepared to cooperate against "Appeasement," but, significantly, they kept aloof from Churchill. They welcomed his independent support, not his membership nor that of his few friends. The Munich settlement inspired one of Churchill's greatest but most resented speeches. One has to remember the enormous sense of relief that war had been averted and of admiration for Chamberlain's diplomacy— "peace in our time." From the outset he was uncompromising: "I will begin by saying the most unpopular and unwelcome thing. I will begin by saying what everybody would like to ignore or forget but which must nevertheless be stated, namely, that we have sustained a total and unmitigated defeat, and that France has suffered even more than we have." Lady Astor shouted "Nonsense"—she often did—and the angry hubbub on the Conservative front benches was so loud that Churchill had to pause for a time before he could continue his marvelously worded but highly provocative indictment of a policy overwhelmingly supported in Parliament and press. Here is an extract: "All is over. Silent, mournful, abandoned, broken, Czechoslovakia recedes into the darkness. . . . This is only the beginning of the reckoning. This is only the first sip, the first foretaste of a bitter cup which will be proffered to us year by year unless, by a supreme recovery of moral health and martial vigour, we arise again and take our stand for freedom as in the olden time." A serious effort was made to force him to resign as a Conservative MP, and it was repeated early in 1939, but he rode out the storm each time, and was supported by a majority of the Epping constituency party.

Then the scene abruptly changed. The German occupation of Prague killed appeasement stone dead. Events, culminating with the German-Soviet Pact, moved relentlessly to war. One of the major criticisms of Churchill—that he appeared positively to enjoy waging war—seemed now an asset. If there has to be a war there is something to be said for putting it in charge of people who will conduct it with enthusiasm. Churchill became once again first lord of the Admiralty. A series of disasters caused a catastrophic fall in Chamberlain's majority and a cry in May 1940, as in May 1915, for a coalition government. Labour was not prepared to serve under Chamberlain. Of the only serious contenders, they would have preferred Lord Halifax and so probably did most Conservatives. Chamberlain and the king also favored Halifax. But he was not willing to accept and thus, in a curiously negative way, Churchill became prime minister on May 10, 1940.

His relations with the party were by no means cordial at first. The leadership was retained by Neville Chamberlain though he offered to resign it. He was the man whom Conservative members cheered on his first entry into the House after his resignation. The cheers for Churchill were almost all from the Labour and Liberal benches. In the House of Lords the announcement of Churchill's appointment was received in dead silence. The old mistrust, suspicion, and hostility were not to disappear at all easily. In October ill health forced Chamberlain to retire. Churchill's prestige had risen greatly, thanks to his leadership and Britain's survival during the Battle of Britain. He was pressed by many people to assume the leadership. His wife, however, implored him not to. She had always been a Liberal and felt at heart deep antipathy to the Conservatives, which she could never eradicate. She believed that the leadership would detract from his status as a great national figure who was above mere party considerations. Churchill did not agree. He remembered the difficulties of Lloyd George—a prime minister without a party after the First World War. He still by no means trusted the Conservatives and he knew that there were those who by no means trusted him. It was safer to be on top. He told the adoption meeting that he accepted "solemnly but also buoyantly."

Henceforth, Churchill was in total control. There were grumbles when things went badly in the war, grumbles after the war when he lost the general election and seemed a rather casual leader of the Opposition, grumbles again when, after 1953, he seemed to cling on too long to office. But they were minor grumbles. There was no question of ousting the most famous Englishman of his day equal in public esteem to Chatham and Wellington rolled into one. He could choose his own time to depart, and he did. But there was a lingering doubt about him. Perhaps I can end by quoting what I wrote in my history of the Conservative Party about his final resignation in April 1955:

And so the greatest statesman to have led the party bowed out. He had been leader for nearly fifteen years, but the relationship was often uneasy, especially after the war. He was a man of genius, energy, vision, a master of the spoken and written word. He had saved England in 1940. But was he really a Conservative and if so in what sense? Perhaps the answer is that he was an anachronism. It was as if time had been warped in some strange way, and an eighteenth-century Whig was leading a twentieth-century Tory party.

PHILIP S. ZIEGLER, official biographer of Earl Mountbatten of Burma and King Edward VIII, is a fellow of the Royal Society of Literature and the Royal Historical Society. After years in the diplomatic service and years as editor-in-chief of the London publishing house of William Collins, he published many books, one of which, *Melbourne*, won the Heinemann Award.

7

❧

The Transfer of Power in India

Philip S. Ziegler

It is now a little over forty years since that moment in August 1947 when power was transferred in the Indian subcontinent, and two new nations, some 450 million human beings, found their independence (the word "some" is used advisedly; statistics in India have an awe-inspiring imprecision—no one would argue if one were to put the figure twenty or thirty million less or more). Two generations of Indians and Pakistanis have not known what it was to live under the British Raj, only the most elderly of surviving elder statesmen exercised any authority before their countries took charge of their own affairs. It is a moot point when, if ever, one is able to survey the past with anything approaching objectivity, but by now it should at least be possible to look back on those years immediately following the Second World War without being swayed too markedly by those passions and prejudices which are bred by personal participation. The transfer of power in India is ripe for reassessment; and Indian historians being no less enterprising, ingenious, and energetic than those of other nations, there has been no shortage of real or self-styled "authorities" from the subcontinent, as well as from Britain and the United States, who are ready and eager to contribute to the task.

The 15th of August 1947 was a day of ecstatic euphoria for the citizens of the two new nations and was hardly less acclaimed in the former imperial power itself. The sternest critics were temporarily muted, the doubters hoped for the best, the optimists anticipated something even better. For the Indians and Pakistanis it was a day of rejoicing at a great victory won; there might be storms ahead but during that day at least there was no need to contemplate them. For the British the triumph was more equivocal, yet they comforted themselves with the reflection that they had made the greatest act of enlightened self-sacrifice in recorded history and by so doing had won the loyalty and affection of those who otherwise might have been expected to become their enemies. A deluge of congratulations descended on Nehru and Jinnah, the leaders of the two new nations; on Mountbatten, the former viceroy, in New Delhi; on Attlee, the Labour prime minister, in London. The British congratulated the Indians, the Indians the British; and above the welter of self-satisfaction rang the trumpet call of that guru of Washington's political commentators, Mr. Walter Lippmann: "Perhaps Britain's finest hour is not in the past. Certainly this performance is not the work of a decadent people. This on the contrary is the work of political genius requiring the ripest wisdom and the freshest vigor, and it is done with an elegance and a style that will compel and will receive an instinctive respect throughout the civilized world. Attlee and Mountbatten have done a service to all mankind by showing what statesmen can do not with force and money but with lucidity, resolution, and sincerity."

It was, of course, much too good to last. Even before the celebrations in New Delhi and Karachi had run their course, the hideous massacres that accompanied partition were already gathering force. The atmosphere reminds one of Byron's Brussels on the eve of Waterloo: "There was a sound of revelry by night," the dance went on, joy was unconfined, until suddenly a deep sound struck like a rising knell. It was, I do not need to remind you, "the cannon's opening roar." That roar, or rather the anguish of the victims in the Punjab gave new heart to the critics of Britain's policy. They have not ceased to be heard today and will no doubt continue so long as the story of the end of the British Empire retains its fascination. Their voices are many and various but in the main they fall into two categories. First, there are the traditionalists who believed, and sometimes still believe, that the surrender of power in India was the betrayal of a sacred trust, at the best premature, at the worst uncalled-for, and in either case disastrous in its consequences. On the other hand are those who are convinced that the transfer of power was essential and long overdue but that its execution was sadly botched; that the unity of India was sacrificed without more than a token effort being made to retain it; that the settlement was biased in one way or the other; that it was handled so precipitately that chaos and bloodshed inevitably ensued; and that it was so ill-conceived that it left behind it a legacy of problems that have haunted the Indian subcontinent ever since. Not surprisingly it was the first group who were most vociferous in the period directly after partition, the second whose criticisms have grown with the years and become more elaborate and sometimes more extravagant. My purpose today is to look back at 1947 and try to conclude whether, viewed from the vantage point of contemporary experience, Britain should have transferred power when she did. If so, could she have handled the transition to greater advantage and in a way that would have avoided such hostile criticism?

In a world in which Europe's empires have almost entirely passed away and lip service at least is paid to the doctrine of self-determination in every country which professes itself democratic, it is hard to remember how substantial a body of opinion in Britain, and indeed elsewhere, believed at the end of the Second World War that imperial rule in India should continue—if not perpetually, then at least for many years. The chief proponent of this point of view was the architect of Britain's victory, the recently dispossessed prime minister, Winston Churchill.

Churchill nourished a romantic veneration for the idea of the Indian empire coupled with a marked lack of enthusiasm for the Indian people. "I hate Indians," he once remarked to Leo Amery. "They are a beastly people with a beastly religion." This showed him at his most petulant, but even when in a more benign mood he was inclined to think that Indian soldiers were good enough to fight and if necessary die for the Raj, and that some of the princes could play a decent game of polo, but that they were not equipped for anything more onerous. It was the sacred duty of the British to rule and educate this lesser breed until such time—perhaps fifty, perhaps a hundred years ahead—when they would be fit to take on the burden themselves. Such an expression of his views is of course a caricature of the case that would have been put forward by that most sophisticated and eloquent of statesmen. But Churchill, like many men of genius, was capable of extraordinary naïveté, and India provoked from him reactions that would have been surprising even in a lesser man.

There was nothing new about his attitude. It was as long before as 1931 that he had resigned from the shadow cabinet in disgust at Baldwin's far-from-radical policy toward India and had fought the government's modestly liberal India Bill clause by clause through the House of Commons. It was India which proved one of the first serious causes of dissension between Churchill and President Roosevelt—when the prime minister objected vigorously to what he regarded as the mischievous activities of Roosevelt's representative in New Delhi, Colonel Louis Johnson. It was Churchill who, having grudgingly agreed that Sir Stafford Cripps should lead a mission to India in 1942 to discuss the grant of dominion status once the war was over, did everything in his power to ensure that the mission did not and could not succeed. Nineteen forty-seven found him still firmly entrenched in his position; deploring any surrender of power but most of all one which was hurried through precipitately:

> In handing over the government of India to these so-called political classes," he protested in the House of Commons, "we are handing over to men of straw of whom in a few years no trace will remain. . . . Many have defended Britain against her foes, none can defend her against herself. But, at least, let us not add—by shameful flight, by a premature hurried scuttle—at least let us not add to the pangs of sorrow so many of us feel, the taint and smear of shame.

In the inflexibility and extremeness of his attitude Churchill was unusual but by no means unique. There were in the Conservative Party many decent and honorable men who could not look on the retreat from empire with anything but anguished disapproval. The maverick genius of their leader often alarmed and sometimes dismayed them. They found a more acceptable expression of their doubts in the voice of the veteran Fourth Marquis of Salisbury who protested to Clement Attlee against a withdrawal from India enforced by weakness. "Is this country to go down in history," he asked, "with the badge upon her of betrayal?" Attlee replied firmly that there had been no weakness and no betrayal, and was fortified in his belief by the support of Conservatives such as R. A. Butler and the former viceroy and ambassador to the United States, the Earl of Halifax. The issue, indeed, was one that to some extent transcended party barriers. Some of the most cogent arguments against an early transfer of power came from the Labour foreign secretary, Ernest Bevin, who in January 1947 told Attlee that the defeatist attitude adopted by the cabinet and the viceroy was undermining British foreign policy and playing into the hands of her enemies. Was the British Empire, he asked rhetorically, to knuckle under at the first blow?

Yet the weakness which Attlee denied had shaped British policy was very plainly apparent to even the most partisan observer. To some Indian historians, indeed, it seems that the transfer of power was no more than a surrender to *force majeure* and in no proper sense of the words a deliberate act of policy on the part of the British government. There are some powerful arguments to support their contention.

Economically, militarily, administratively, politically—the case for a rapid retreat from India was very strong. Economically, Britain's position was pitifully weak. A quarter of her national wealth had been spent in the course of the war and her external liabilities amounted to well over £3,000 million—pettifogging enough by the standards of today's debtor nations, but intimidating in 1946. India, on the other hand, had accumulated sterling balances of over £1,300 million in London. To finance a sustained occupation of the subcontinent against what seemed certain to be fierce local opposition would have strained intolerably Britain's already exiguous resources. Militarily, the situation seemed even worse. The rapid demobilization of Britain's conscript armies was not merely desirable to get the factories and mines fully operational again but essential if growing discontent was to be contained; the servicemen remaining in Southeast Asia would have required some very convincing arguments to persuade them that they should now engage in a full-blooded campaign for the repression of Indian nationalism. The regular army was fully stretched by its responsibilities in Europe and the Middle East—there were more than 100,000 men held down in Palestine alone. The Indian army had on the whole proved astonishingly faithful to the Raj throughout the war, but the one thousand Indian officers who served in it in 1939 had grown to nearly sixteen thousand by 1945, the ideals of nationalism were rife among the younger officers at least, the army's loyalty could no longer be taken for granted. Administratively, the same was true: the proportion of British officials in the Indian civil service fell every year as less and less young Britons felt that the job offered any prospects of a secure career for life. Indianization of the civil service and the judiciary had been proceeding since the First World War. By 1945 the Indians in the higher reaches of the administration were more numerous than the British—within a decade it was clear that they would be in a massive majority. Finally, the political pressure on Britain from the United States to dismantle its Indian empire was already powerful. The substitution of Truman for Franklin Roosevelt had perhaps somewhat muted the stridency of these demands, but the economic power of the United States was so absolute and their views on Indian independence so firmly established that the factor was one which any British government would ignore at its peril.

So potent were all these factors that, even if Churchill had won the 1945 election, it is hard to believe he would have been able to delay the advent of Indian independence by more than a few years at the most. It was the timing and the style of the transfer of power that were in question, not its inevitability. But to those who see it only in terms of a British surrender it should be said that for the Labour leaders, for Attlee and Stafford Cripps in particular, the decision was still made on grounds of principle. It was ten years at least since these Labour leaders had manifested their belief that India should be granted independence. The war had provided reasons for deferring the transition but not for challenging its validity in terms of justice and morality. Now the time was ripe. That it happened also to coincide with British interests was a fact, but the fact did not shape their conclusions.

So much then for those who said that Britain should never have yielded up its empire. What of those who felt the process was due, if not overdue, but that its execution was at fault? Many Indian historians believe in particular that Britain's most precious legacy to Asia should have been a united India and that this heritage was thrown away with no more than a token effort to preserve it. Some would even say that it was willfully destroyed in the interests of securing a quick settlement. Britain, by this argument, was concerned exclusively with its own interests and not those of its former empire. "Mountbatten's mission," wrote B. Krishna, "was not so much to see a united free India as to carry out, as a true Englishman, Attlee's directive—to retreat from India with honour."

That Attlee's directive was, on the contrary, to hand over independence to a truly united India or, failing that, then at least to as closely knit a federation as could be contrived, is evident both from the formal instructions issued to Mountbatten and the viceroy's own testimony. The cabinet mission which had visited India in March 1946 was committed to the achievement of this end. It found an India which had been polarized as never before by the recent elections in which the Congress Party had swept the board in almost all the predominantly Hindu provinces, while the Muslim League, led by Mohammed Ali Jinnah, had captured 90 percent of the Muslim seats. Against this unpromising background the mission had done remarkably well. It had so far overcome Jinnah's resistance as to secure his grudging acquiescence in a form of federation. This would have conceded almost complete internal autonomy to the Muslim provinces, while reserving issues such as defense and foreign policy to a central government. It was the Hindu Congress Party which balked at this solution, in so doing rejecting terms which it would have grasped at eagerly only a year later.

Then came the Muslim League's call for a "Direct Action Day" to mark its disapproval of Hindu intransigence. Riots and massacres followed, leaving more than twenty thousand killed or seriously wounded in Calcutta alone. Attitudes hardened on both sides. By the time Mountbatten arrived in India in March 1947, Jinnah had reverted to the same attitude he had taken up before the arrival of the cabinet mission; he was not interested in discussing the details of the transfer of power, still less of any possible sharing of power between Muslim and Hindu, until the principle of a wholly independent Pakistan had been accepted. And by Pakistan he made it clear he meant not what he called the moth-eaten nation over which he was eventually to rule, but a greater Pakistan to include the whole of Bengal, the whole of the Punjab, and with a corridor sweeping across north India to link the two parts of the country.

The "great men" theory of history tends today to be unfashionable in the ranks of academic historians. Napoleon, Alexander the Great, Washington, perhaps left some mark on the march of events, but to comprehend history properly one must study the agriculture and the trading patterns of the age, the demographic trends, the incidence of plague, the climatic variations. There is more than a little truth in this but, as a biographer by profession, I must plead that there is room for great men too. And even if the role of the individual is often credited by the romantic with greater significance than can be justified, there remains always a handful of men and women who, by a combination of the qualities of their characters and the circumstances of their time, exercise a decisive influence on the destinies of their fellow men. Preeminent among such people was Mohammed Ali Jinnah. Gandhi was the greater man by the standards which the world customarily applies to greatness; Nehru was more attractive and perhaps wiser; but in Jinnah's hands lay the destiny of united India.

It is one of the more curious ironies of Indian history that Jinnah made his name as a member of the Congress Party and a champion of unity between Muslim and Hindu. In 1928 he left the Congress Party in frustration at what seemed to him the exclusively Hindu aspirations of its leaders. By 1940 he was the champion of an independent Pakistan. In 1946 he briefly wavered toward acceptance of some loose and, as he no doubt calculated, temporary form of federation, but the events of that year quickly cured his uncharacteristic weakness. Mountbatten arrived in Delhi to be confronted by a Muslim leader who seemed incapable of even a suspicion of flexibility—chilly, adamant, indifferent to any efforts to change his point of view. Patiently Mountbatten deployed and redeployed what seemed to him the overwhelming economic and political arguments against partition; Jinnah, he wrote, "offered no counterarguments. He gave the impression that he was not listening." It was more than an impression. In any meaningful sense of the word Jinnah was *not* listening, he had made up his mind and closed it, nothing would induce him to reopen the question.

Mountbatten has been accused of abandoning the idea of a united India with undue alacrity; it has been said that he had written it off in his own mind even before he arrived in Delhi and sought only to maneuver the Congress leaders so that it appeared that the initiative toward partition came from them. This is not how Mountbatten saw it. He had been sent to

India to work for a united and independent country and nothing else could in his eyes be counted as complete success. Partition was a defeat to be accepted with reluctance—economically damaging to both new countries, militarily disastrous, politically catastrophic. It was only when it became clear that the imposition of any form of united India would lead to civil war that he accepted the inevitable. He was one of the last to do so. The viceroy found that the Congress leaders acquiesced in the dismemberment of their country with disconcerting alacrity. Nehru himself was to say that partition had become unavoidable a year at least before it happened. Britain can fairly be blamed for helping to create the circumstances in which Muslim nationalism could flourish, but the decision to divide the subcontinent was taken by the inhabitants of that region—and to the deep regret of the former imperial power.

One tantalizing query remains. Jinnah was a dying man. Already the tuberculosis which was to kill him little over a year after independence was gnawing at his strength. If Mountbatten had known, could he so have spun out negotiations that the final decision was taken when the Muslim leader had departed from the scene, and would it have helped if he had? The question is, of course, academic; Mountbatten did not know and so had no reason to seek to delay matters—on the contrary, as we shall see, he had every reason for hurrying them along. My personal view is that even if he had known, or even if Jinnah had died eighteen months earlier than he did, it would have made little difference. It was by then too late. However much some of the Muslim leaders might have doubted the wisdom of partition they would not have dared reject the burden which Jinnah had laid upon them. The Muslim League was by 1947 irrevocably committed to the pursuit of an independent Pakistan, and nothing Mountbatten or anybody else did or said could have deflected them in their crusade.

Another charge frequently leveled against the British is that the terms of the settlement were unfair to Pakistan. Sometimes such accusations relate to the basic equipment necessary to run a state. When the vast omelette of united India had to be divided, there was no question of reconstituting every egg and sharing them out equitably. Rough justice had to be done. To the minds of the Pakistanis the justice was sometimes very rough indeed. When it came to tanks and airplanes for the armed forces, rolling stock for the railways, printing presses for the production of official publications, even typewriters and telephones for the government offices, India took the lion's share. The geography of united India made it inevitable that the bulk of such material should be in the possession of the Hindus on independence day. Human nature being what it is, and possession being nine points of the law, that is where the material remained. There was little the British could do. Mountbatten did his best to see fair play. For instance, at the end of 1947, India proposed to freeze the £30 million due to Pakistan out of the residual capital funds. Mountbatten denounced their attitude as unwise, unstatesmanlike, and dishonorable. He enlisted Gandhi as an ally, and won the day.

He had few comparable victories and got little credit for his attitude from the Pakistanis, who saw him as a puppet of Nehru and one of their most inveterate enemies. They were at their most critical when it came to the drawing of the partition line that was to separate India and Pakistan. The principle was that each state or province should be allotted to India or Pakistan on the basis of whether it was predominantly Hindu or Muslim. In the Punjab and Bengal, however—two vast provinces in which Hindu and Muslim populations were roughly equal—the principle broke down. In these provinces there must be partition within partition. Yet the two denominations did not live in neatly segregated areas but hopelessly intermingled. In the Punjab the problem was still further bedeviled by the existence of fourteen million Sikhs. This warlike and intemperate race had elements of both Hindu and Muslim religions in its faith. They disliked the one almost as much as the other, but their greater fear of the Muslims led them to make common cause with the Hindus. They too had to be accommodated in the final settlement.

To achieve the impossible and divide these provinces on a basis which would both make economic and political sense and appear equitable to both parties, a British lawyer, Cyril Radcliffe, was imported. Radcliffe was a man of formidable intelligence and unquestionable integrity, but his job, as he freely admitted, was that of the butcher rather than the surgeon. In theory, he worked with the help of expert assessors drawn from both groups; in practice, since the assessors were diametrically opposed on any point of contention, he was constrained to make up his own mind. By the application of a pencil to a map he carved up communities that had been one for centuries, severed farms from their markets, fields from their water, arbitrarily created two countries where there had been one before. It was a brutal and thankless task; that he performed it to the best of his ability is accepted by everyone capable of forming an objective opinion.

Whether the British authorities, in particular whether the viceroy, performed their task with equal impartiality is where the historians differ. Radcliffe delivered his recommendations for the partition line on August 13, 1947. Mountbatten—now renewing life as governor-general of independent India but, significantly, not of Pakistan—published them on the 16th of August. Nothing will convince the Pakistani historians that during those three days Mountbatten did not tamper with the findings and, in certain small but vitally important particulars, amend them in favor of India. Above all, they are emphatic that he overruled or overpersuaded Radcliffe so as to ensure that three-quarters of the district of Gurdaspur should be awarded to India, thus providing the Indians with a means of access to Kashmir. The evidence is circumstantial. Radcliffe's secretary a week or so before had indicated to the Punjab government that the final partition line was likely to be somewhat more favorable to Pakistan than in fact it was. Members of Mountbatten's staff recorded that the viceroy was under pressure from Nehru to amend Radcliffe's recommendations and was having energetically to be dissuaded from doing so. Against this we have Radcliffe's flat denial that anyone had sought to influence him or to amend his conclusions. If the main object of such a change was indeed to allow India access to Kashmir and thus to facilitate the accession of that state to India, then indeed Mountbatten would have been behaving eccentrically in bringing it about. At the period he was engaged in a vigorous, though ultimately unsuccessful, effort to persuade the maharajah of Kashmir to follow the wishes of a majority of his people and accede to Pakistan. The matter has never been, and I suspect never will be, decided with absolute certainty one way or the other. My own conclusion, for what it is worth, is that Mountbatten was perhaps tempted to succumb to Nehru's blandishments and redraw the partition line to India's benefit, but that the temptation was resisted. The risk of being caught red-handed was far too great. Whatever else Mountbatten may have been, he was not a fool. To imperil the whole settlement for the sake of winning some small advantage for one side or the other would have been an act of folly.

If Radcliffe had been given more time for the task, the partition line would have been plotted on a more scientific basis. There would still have been shattering disruption to the Muslim, Hindu, and Sikh communities, but some injustices and inconsistencies could have been avoided. The job was rushed. This charge, that the whole operation was conducted at too breakneck a pace and insufficient time left for reflection and preparation, is the one most widely leveled at the British government, above all at the viceroy. It has been voiced by Hindus as well as Muslims, and by many Britons too. "If only, . . ." it said; if only Mountbatten had allowed time to prepare people for the idea of partition; to persuade them to remain in the villages where they had been born; to let those who were determined to move do so in a gradual and orderly fashion; to station troops in the areas where communal trouble was most likely. Then, goes the argument, there need have been no massacres; the great movements of population which triggered the worst of the bloodshed would never have occurred; properly escorted convoys could have moved the hard core of would-be refugees to their chosen homes.

I have said already that the science of statistics in the Indian subcontinent is alarmingly inexact. Many figures have been put forward as to the number of Muslims, Hindus, and Sikhs who died in the communal massacres that followed partition. The nearest approach to a serious analysis that has been made suggests the death toll to have been somewhere between two hundred thousand and a quarter of a million. The total is small compared with the wilder estimates of a million or more. It seems smaller still compared with the million and a half who died in the Bengal famine of 1943. Yet it is horrifying enough. "It seems to me immaterial," wrote Mountbatten's chief of staff, General Ismay, "whether one hundred thousand or a million have actually died: or whether only three percent of the country is in turmoil. The essential facts are that there is human misery on a colossal scale all around one and millions are bereaved, destitute, homeless, hungry, thirsty—and worst of all, desperately anxious and almost hopeless about their future."

Surely, say the critics, nothing could have been worse than this. An operation which ended in such carnage must, ipso facto, have been ill-conceived and botched in its execution. And yet the issue is not as clear-cut as this. Mountbatten was playing from a rapidly weakening hand. All those elements which could normally have been relied on to operate the machinery of partition were being eroded by the day: the police, the judiciary, the civil service were running down and, with the rapid withdrawal of the relatively impartial British element, were disintegrating into hostile factions. The army, the only force that might have been able to control the vast disturbances in the Punjab, was itself falling prey to communalism—many of its regiments could no longer be trusted to hold a fair balance between Muslim, Hindu, and Sikh. Yet simultaneously the fires of religious hatred were burning ever more fiercely. Once the principle of partition had been accepted it was inevitable that communalism would rage. The longer the period which Mountbatten left before severance actually took place, the worse the tension and the greater the fear that violence would spread. As it was, only the phenomenal influence of Mahatma Gandhi checked the spread of the massacres to Bengal; from there they might have enveloped Hyderabad or any of the other areas where Muslims and Hindus lived cheek by jowl. Two hundred thousand dead could have become two million, even twenty million.

The only way to establish with certainty whether any other approach would have proved more successful would be to go back to the beginning and start again, and since this recourse is mercifully denied us one historian's guess will remain as unverifiable as another's. When I myself was working on the biography of Mountbatten I approached the controversy with an open mind suspecting that there must have been bungling somewhere but wholly without a firm foundation of fact on which to base my suspicions. I am by no means confident that I now possess such a foundation and have my doubts whether anybody else does either, but I have been convinced by the unanimity of all those who were in a position to form an opinion at the time. Civil or military, Indian or British, friend or enemy of Mountbatten, all agree that time was not merely not on his side but was his greatest enemy. The view was enunciated most tellingly by Chakravarti Rajagopalachari, the man who was in time to replace Mountbatten and become India's first Indian head of state and who combined wisdom with cunning in a way which is rarely found among us Anglo-Saxons. "If the Viceroy had not transferred power when he did," said Rajaji, "there could well have been no power to transfer." That, in a nutshell, is the case for the way the British handled the transfer of power in India.

It would seem as if I seek to acquit the viceroy and the British government on every charge. Was the transfer of power in India then a model operation planned by wise and far-seeing statesmen, carried through with copybook perfection? The question hardly needs an answer. Power was transferred by desperately anxious men, working in the conviction that a disaster of awe-inspiring proportions was only a few months or even weeks away, believing that an imperfect settlement was far, far better than no settlement at all. In such an atmosphere it was inevitable that there would be grave mistakes made and important decisions left untaken.

Some of these imperfections were to impose a heavy burden on the fledgling nations. Most notable, perhaps, was the division of Pakistan into two uneasy portions separated by more than a thousand miles of hostile country. Racially distinct, economically impoverished, East Pakistan's feeling that it was the poor relation in the Muslim family was encouraged by its Hindu neighbors. It proclaimed itself independent in 1971. No one had been optimistic about the union from the start: Jinnah had believed a corridor linking East and West Pakistan was essential to its survival; Mountbatten had given the union twenty years and had not proved extravagantly pessimistic. Given the troubled history of Bangladesh, one must wonder whether much of this misery could not have been avoided. To accept a divided Pakistan was the path of least resistance. Would it not have been possible instead to make some grandiose deal by which Pakistan might have been compensated in the Punjab for its surrender of a claim to East Bengal? Might Mountbatten have tried for the alternative of a united and independent Bengal? Such options would perhaps have created more problems than they caused but surely some greater efforts should have been made to avoid a so-called solution which solved nothing and merely ensured trouble in the future.

And then there was Kashmir. Mountbatten was convinced that this predominantly Muslim state, ruled by a Hindu maharajah, should follow the wishes of the majority of the people and accede to Pakistan. But he did not devote to the subject a large enough proportion of his energy and persuasive powers to achieve the desired end. The maharajah dithered; the Pakistanis lost patience and sent in the Pathan tribesmen; the maharajah panicked and acceded to India; Indian troops flew in; the long drawn-out imbroglio had begun. It was to bring India and Pakistan to war and today still embitters relations between the two countries. Mountbatten should somehow have contrived that the maharajah of Kashmir took the natural course and opted for Pakistan; failing that he should have aimed for partition, with predominantly Hindu Jammu going to India and the Muslim Vale of Kashmir to Pakistan. He had an awful lot else on his mind—there is no shortage of excuses for him—yet in the last analysis, he failed.

Bangladesh, independent and in perpetual economic crises; Pakistan under military rule; India having had its own experiments with authoritarian rule and plagued by the problem of the Sikhs: the history of the Indian subcontinent since independence has not been wholly triumphant. And yet how much worse it might have been. The direst prognostications of Winston Churchill and the other opponents of the transfer of power have not been fulfilled. The area has not disintegrated into an ill-stitched patchwork of warring fiefs. It has not moved into the communist camp. The essential principles of democracy and equality before the law are still observed in India and there is reason to hope that Pakistan has not finally abandoned them. Perhaps most striking of all, the individual from the West, above all the English speaker, is welcome throughout the subcontinent and can feel at home in a way he will hardly experience in any other country with so different an ethnic and cultural background.

I do not come here to argue the pros and cons of imperialism. There is no lack of far better qualified historians who can and do contest whether the British presence in India was justified at the outset and, given that the empire had come into being, whether and when it should have been brought to an end. All I would say is that the history of the subcontinent since 1947 suggests that the servants of the Raj did not do too bad a job, and that the legacy they have left India is not one of which Britain need feel ashamed. And though the details of the transfer of power have been justly criticized and the settlement which it introduced has been modified in important aspects, the essentials have withstood the tests of time. Perhaps Walter Lippmann went too far when he described it as a "work of political genius requiring the ripest wisdom and the freshest vigour," but at the least it was the work of honorable men toiling to the best of their abilities in conditions of almost impossible difficulty. Of their labors, too, Britain has no cause to feel ashamed.

SIR MICHAEL HOWARD, a fellow of the Royal Historical Society, the Royal Society of Literature, and the British Academy, was cofounder and president of the International Institute for Strategic Studies and vice president of the Council on Christian Approaches to Defense and Disarmament. He received the Duff Cooper Memorial Prize for his *The Franco Prussian War* and has served as professor or visiting professor in European history at British and American universities.

8

⧒⧓

Churchill
Prophet of Détente

Sir Michael Howard

Y ou have built here at Fulton a memorial to a very great man, but you have done something more. This glorious church in which we meet is a symbol of more than Churchill's own greatness, or even of the genius of the incomparable Christopher Wren. It is a monument, as any Englishman must recognize, to the unique qualities of the American people—your imagination in conceiving the project, your energy, your ingenuity, your technology, your craftsmanship, and above all your generosity in implementing it. These were the qualities that saved Europe in two world wars and made it possible to rebuild the free world after the second, qualities to which Winston Churchill himself constantly paid tribute and on which we all continue to rely—even in a world which has changed so much, and so incomparably for the better, since the dark days of 1946.

It was then, just over forty-four years ago, that Winston Churchill came to Fulton on March 5 and warned his audience here that: "From Stettin in the Baltic to Trieste in the Adriatic, an iron curtain has descended across the Continent." Behind that barrier, he said, Soviet occupying forces were gradually extinguishing all elements of independent opposition and imposing totalitarian control. In front of it, and throughout the world, communist fifth columnists "constitute a growing challenge and peril to Christian civilization." The Soviet Union did not, he believed, desire war. "What they desire is the fruits of war and the indefinite expansion of their power and doctrines." To counter their expansion it was necessary that the Western democracies, especially the United States and the British Commonwealth, should stand together in strict adherence to the principles of the United Nations charter. "If however they become divided or falter in their duty and if these all-important years are allowed to slip away then indeed catastrophe may overwhelm us all."[1]

This was not what his audience wanted to hear. The war was over. The boys, in their hundreds of thousands, were coming home. Barely nine months had passed since the Allied leaders had met, to all appearances amicably, among the enemy ruins at Potsdam. Their foreign ministers were busy in London and Paris thrashing out the framework of a peaceful new order under the auspices of the United Nations. What was this call for a new entangling alliance against America's wartime ally? "The United States wants no alliance, or anything that resembles an alliance, with any other nation" editorialized the *Wall Street Journal* (205). President Truman had to deny that his presence on the platform in any way indicated official endorsement of Churchill's remarks. And in England, ninety-three members of Parliament (including future Prime Minister James Callaghan) tabled a vote of censure against their former prime minister on the grounds that his proposals were "calculated to do injury to good relations between Great Britain, the USA and the USSR and are inimical to the cause of world peace" (208).

We all know what happened. In 1947 the disintegrating economies of Western Europe provoked the imaginative generosity of Marshall Plan aid. In 1948 the Soviets consolidated their rule with the coup d'état in Czechoslovakia and the Berlin blockade. And in 1949, four years after Churchill had delivered his warning here at Fulton, the United States signed the North Atlantic Treaty, creating exactly that alliance for which Churchill

---

1. Martin Gilbert, *Never Despair: Winston S. Churchill, 1945–1965* (London: Heinemann, 1988), 200–202. References to this work will hereafter be given in the text by page number.

had called; an alliance for mutual support, threatening no one, but pledged to uphold the peaceful principles of the United Nations charter.

And now? Within the last six months, the Iron Curtain has dissolved. The captive peoples of Central and Eastern Europe are free once more—free, most of them, for the first time in fifty years. The two halves of Germany are coming together under a government which, however it may be constructed, will be firmly democratic as no government of a united Germany has been since 1933. The Soviet Union itself has entered on a period of turbulent and open-ended transformation that is likely to make it, for the time being at least, a cooperative partner on the international scene. Could any of us have foreseen this a year ago? or last July when you invited me to deliver this lecture? I understand that you have also invited President Gorbachev, when he visits the United States later this year, to come here and formally proclaim the end of the dark era whose opening was heralded in this place forty-four years ago. I hope he will come, for there could be no more appropriate messenger for such good news; unless it could have been Winston Churchill himself.

And it is sad that it cannot be Winston Churchill himself. No event would have given him greater joy. Certainly it was with no pleasure that he carried out his self-imposed task all those years ago and gave warning of the bleak years ahead. This was not the peace for which he and his people had struggled for so long. Churchill was no cold warrior. Wary as he had been of Soviet ambitions and objectives, he had gone to extreme lengths—in the eyes of some, too extreme—to conciliate his wartime ally. He had established—so he had believed—a warm relationship with Marshal Stalin. He was sensitive to the security needs of the Soviet state. Most of all, he had a deep respect and affection for the Russian people and a grateful recognition for all they had suffered in the common cause. In his speech here he movingly conveyed the "deep sympathy and good will" of the British people "towards the peoples of all the Russians, and a resolve to persevere through many differences and rebuffs in establishing lasting friendships. "We understand," he said, "the Russian need to be secure on her Western frontiers by the removal of all possibility of German aggression. We welcome Russia to her rightful place among the leading nations of the world. We welcome her flag upon the seas. Above all, we welcome constant, frequent and growing contacts between the Russian people and our own people on both sides of the Atlantic" (200).

Churchill's desire to establish, or rather to reestablish, good relations with the Soviet peoples (who to the end of his life he persisted in calling Russian) was not eroded by the hostility of their leaders. A few months after his Fulton speech he stressed, before the House of Commons, the "earnest desire (of the West) to dwell in friendly cooperation with the Soviet government and the Russian people" (238). For him, Western rearmament was a cruel necessity, but not one that should inhibit an unwearying search for accommodation with the Soviet Union: "We arm," as he once put it, "to parley." His deepest hope was that the frost of the Cold War should be temporary, and that the world was not entering another political ice age.

When he spoke at Fulton, Churchill was of course no longer prime minister. For another five years he remained in Opposition; years in which he continually stressed the need for Allied strength and unity, but no less his goodwill toward the Russian people if only they could be reached through the carapace of oppression imposed by the apparatus of party rule. Then in 1951, shortly before his seventy-seventh birthday, Churchill became prime minister for the second time.

The Cold War was now in full swing. The invasion of South Korea eighteen months earlier had convinced the Western world that the Soviet Union had moved from subversion to armed aggression. The organizational bones of the Atlantic Alliance were being clothed with military flesh. The Federal German Republic had been created, and the search was on for means to integrate her into the Western military alliance. In the United States an anticommunist witch-hunt was being conducted by Senator Joe McCarthy which the Democrats could not and the Republicans would not do anything to check. In Britain, Soviet spies were tumbling out of the woodwork. Never had détente appeared less feasible—or indeed less to be desired.

Sixteen more months were to pass before Churchill saw, or thought that he saw, a gleam of light in the darkness. Then, on March 5, 1953, Josef Stalin died. Within a week Churchill was writing to his old wartime colleague, now President Eisenhower, suggesting that they should test the intentions of the new regime by a personal meeting with its leaders. "I have the feeling that we might both of us together or separately be called to account if no attempt was made to turn over a leaf so that a new page could be started" (806). Eisenhower, more cautious in the White House than he had been out of it, was unresponsive, but Churchill continued to hammer away. "Great hope has arisen in the world," he wrote again on April 11, "that there is a change of heart in the vast, mighty masses of Russia, and that this can carry them far and fast" (813).

Ten days later, on April 21, Churchill suggested a formal summit meeting of "the three victorious powers who separated at Potsdam" (819). Undeterred by the president's discouraging reply, he went on to suggest sending a personal message to the Soviet foreign minister, Mr. Molotov, inviting himself to Moscow "so that we could renew our own wartime relation and so that I could meet Mr. Malenkov [the new Soviet leader] and some others of your leading men" (827). To this suggestion Eisenhower, advised by his secretary of state John Foster Dulles, returned a very firm negative indeed. Such a move, he warned, could be misinterpreted as weakness or overeagerness—especially any suggestion that a Western leader might visit Moscow. But it was only in Moscow, Churchill replied, that he could really learn what was going on and influence the main decision makers. "I am very anxious to know these men and talk to them as I think I can, frankly and on the dead level. . . . I find it difficult to believe that we shall gain anything by an attitude of pure negation, and your message to me certainly does not show much hope" (828).

It was not only to Eisenhower that Churchill was expressing his desire for a meeting at the summit. On May 11th he made one of his most memorable speeches in the House of Commons. He was anxious, he said, that "Nothing in the presentation of foreign policy by the NATO powers should, as it were, supersede or take the emphasis out of what may be a profound movement of Russian feeling." It was now desirable, he suggested, that a conference should take place at the highest level. Such a conference "should not be overhung by a ponderous or rigid agenda, or led into mazes and jungles of technical details, zealously contested by hordes of experts and officials drawn up in vast, cumbrous array." It should be confined to the smallest number of powers and persons possible, meeting privately and informally. "At the worst, the participants in the meeting would have established more intimate contacts. At the best we might have a generation of peace" (831–32).

Churchill's speech, perhaps the most significant he had made since Fulton, delighted the House of Commons as much as it appalled the British Foreign Office. "It must be long in history," the Foreign Secretary Anthony Eden was to write in his diary, "since any one speech did so much damage to its own side" (832). Poor Eden. For the past five years the Foreign Office had been engaged on the delicate and difficult task of putting together an alliance of mutually suspicious powers who had only just finished fighting one another, and persuading their war-weary peoples that it was necessary once again to rearm. Success still hung in the balance. The French were still strenuously opposing all plans for recreating the German army which both the Americans and the British believed to be necessary to Western defense. Détente now might destroy everything that had so far been achieved. The view of the officials was well expressed by Eden's secretary, Evelyn Shuckburgh, who in his diary condemned "this sentimental illusion that peace can be obtained if only the 'top' men get together. It seems an example of the hubris which afflicts old men who have power, as did Chamberlain when he visited Hitler." At most, Shuckburgh considered, Churchill might achieve "a momentary and probably illusory 'relaxation of tension.' After that splendid achievement he would die in triumph and we should all be left behind in a weaker position than before" (868 and n. 2). As at the time of Munich fifteen years earlier, Whitehall considered Churchill to be a loose cannon on the deck, capable of doing a great deal of harm.

Churchill was still pressing the idea of a summit meeting on an unwilling and increasingly impatient Washington when, on June 23, 1953, he suffered a disabling stroke which put him out of action for several weeks. In his absence Eisenhower agreed that there should be an exploratory meeting with the Russians, not, however, of heads of government but of foreign ministers. But this was exactly the kind of formal, official contact that Churchill wanted to avoid. "They have botched things up", he growled. From his sickbed he wrote again to Eisenhower urging that before the officials got together there should first be an informal meeting at the summit: "I am sure that gives a much better chance than if we only come in after a vast network of detail has been erected." But the President was firm: "I do not like talking informally," he replied somewhat curtly, "with those whose only wish is to entrap and embarrass us" (863–65).

Churchill made an astonishingly rapid recovery from his stroke, which had only increased his sense of urgency. He was now seventy-eight. In the nature of things he could not go on much longer. But he felt all the more stubbornly that only he, with all his talents and experience, could make the breakthrough that would ultimately bring about world peace. "I don't like being kicked out until I have had a shot at settling this Russian business," he told his doctor. "I'm playing a big hand—the easement of the world, perhaps peace over the world" (869). He said the same to the Conservative Party conference the following October: "If I stay on it is because I have a feeling that I may through things that have happened have an influence on what I care about above everything else, the building of a sure and lasting peace" (896). And in the first speech he made to the House of Commons after his recovery, on November 3, he made yet more explicit his reasons for hope:

> It may well be that there have been far-reaching changes in the temper and outlook of the immense populations, now so largely literate, who inhabit "all the Russians" and that their mind was turned to internal betterment rather than external aggression. . . . The only real sure guide to the actions of mighty nations and powerful governments is a correct estimate of what are and what they consider to be their own interests. Applying this test, I feel a sense of reassurance. . . . [Given Western strength] I do not find it unreasonable or dangerous to conclude that internal prosperity rather than external conquest is not only the deep desire of the Russian people, but the long-term interest of their rulers. (907)

This was the message that he took when he met with President Eisenhower and the French prime minister in Bermuda the following month. Soviet policy might well have changed, he suggested, as a result of the strong stand of the United States and the need to hold out some hope of economic improvement to their own peoples. "We should not repulse every move for the better," he urged. "There should not be a question of finding a reason full of suspicion for giving evil meaning to every move of the Soviets." There should be, he suggested, "a two-fold policy—of strength, and readiness to look for any hope of an improved state of mind, even if it were necessary to run a slight mental risk." The more contact between the peoples, the more trade and infiltration of Western ideas, the better. "He would not be in too much of a hurry to believe that nothing but evil emanates from this mighty branch of the human family or that nothing but danger and peril could come out of this vast ocean of land in a single circle so little known and understood" (921–22).

Eisenhower's reaction to these somewhat anodyne remarks was quite remarkable. He exploded with anger. He expressed in the most vehement terms his disagreement with the prime minister. The Soviet Union, he said, was simply the same old woman of the streets, however much she might have been tarted-up. "Despite bath, perfume and lace, it was still the same old girl. . . . He did not want to approach this problem on the basis that there had been any change on the Soviet policy of destroying the capitalist free world by all means, by force, by deceit, by lies. That was their long-term purpose." He then stormed out of the meeting, leaving the rest looking at each other aghast. John Colville, Churchill's private secretary, commented: "I doubt if any such language has ever been heard before at an international conference" (923).

Churchill's own conclusion was that Eisenhower was little more than a ventriloquist's doll for John Foster Dulles, whom he cordially disliked. Dulles, considered Churchill, was "clever enough to be dangerous on a rather large scale" (867). Discussing the results of the meeting with his confidante Lord Moran he grumbled, "This fellow preaches like a Methodist Minister and his bloody text is always the same: that nothing but evil can come out of a meeting with Malenkov." He went on rather pathetically: "Ten years ago I could have dealt with him. Even as it is, I have not been defeated by this bastard. I have been humiliated by my own decay" (936).

It was alas true that after his stroke Churchill often seemed to be trembling on the verge of senility. He was deaf, forgetful, and repetitive. His personal staff lived in a constant dread of a total and public collapse. The White House had little patience with what were seen as an old man's maunderings. Dulles had none whatever. Dulles had inherited none of the wartime camaraderie that still made Eisenhower treat Churchill with respect and affection. He was contemptuous of the attempt to maintain Britain's status as a major power coequal with the United States. He was apprehensive of the effect on public opinion of Churchill's attempt to break ranks. And his view of the Soviet Union was exactly as Churchill had described: it was an empire of evil. If there was indeed a change in Soviet attitude, Dulles considered, this could only be the result of American pressures, so this was the time to intensify, not relax them.[2]

In fact Eisenhower's instincts were very much the same as Churchill's, but his respect for Dulles's expertise and his unwillingness to tangle with the activists in the Republican Party inhibited him from saying so openly. But he did hope to use the new atmosphere to take some initiatives in the field of disarmament, and immediately after the Bermuda conference he made his great "Atoms for Peace" speech to the United Nations—a speech which gained him a standing ovation in which the Russians joined.[3] His outburst at Bermuda indicated rather a mood of momentary exasperation than of settled policy, and over the next two years he began cautiously to distance himself from Dulles's stubborn negativism and listen more attentively to the voices of those who, like Churchill, argued that limited accommodation with the Soviet Union might now indeed be possible.

As for Churchill, he continued in season and out of season to urge a direct approach to the Soviet leadership. He told his colleague R. A. Butler on March 12, 1954, that "the only political interest he had left was in high-level conversations with the Russians" (958). A new and chilling event lent yet greater urgency to his desires; the revelation in 1954 of the imminent development of thermonuclear weapons whose range and destructiveness would turn war into mutual suicide.

This led him to make a new approach to Eisenhower, suggesting that they should frankly discuss the situation with the Russians: "Perhaps we

2. Townsend Hoopes, *The Devil and John Foster Dulles* (Boston and Toronto: Little, Brown, 1973), 271.
3. Stephen E. Ambrose, *Eisenhower: The President,* vol. 2 (New York: Simon and Schuster, 1984), 149.

are reaching the moment when both sides know enough: to outline the doom-laden facts to one another. . . . Men have to settle with men, no matter how vast, and in part beyond their comprehension, the business in hand may be. I can imagine that a few simple words, spoken in the awe which may at once oppress and inspire the speakers, might lift this nuclear monster from the world" (960).

When he visited Washington in June, Churchill found Eisenhower very much more flexible over the question of high-level talks. Dulles of course remained as dourly obdurate as ever, but when Churchill suggested that once more he might himself make a preliminary "reconnaissance in force" Eisenhower did not object in principle; requiring only that such a meeting should not take place on Soviet or Soviet-controlled territory. This acquiescence may have been simply courtesy toward a very old man, combined with an assumption that there would be further consultation before anything actually happened; but Churchill took it as the green light for which he had been waiting so long. So on his return voyage to England on the *Queen Elizabeth* he dispatched a telegram to the Soviet foreign minister, Molotov, proposing the initiation of talks in which the United States would not participate, at which there would be no agenda, and which would have "no object but to end a reasonable way of living side by side in growing confidence, easement and prosperity" (1013).

Eisenhower's reaction when informed of this was philosophical. He complained mildly that he might have expected to receive some advance warning of such an initiative, but "that is now past history," he told Churchill, "and we must hope that the steps you have started will lead to a good result" (1013). "Personal trust based upon more than a dozen years of close association and valued friendship," he said in a later message, "may occasionally permit room for amazement but never for suspicion" (1027). But Churchill's own colleagues in the cabinet were less amenable. He had really been very naughty. He had sent the message over the protests of his own foreign secretary, Anthony Eden, and before there had been time for the cabinet to give the matter any consideration. On his return they called him to account. At least one member threatened to resign. Churchill argued first that the action lay entirely within his competence as prime minister, and second, it committed the British government to nothing. The cabinet disagreed. Such an initiative, they maintained, engaged their collective responsibility, and they did not like it. Warned that if he persevered the government would probably break up, the prime minister backed down. A Soviet proposal for a general meeting to discuss European security got him off the hook, and he did not follow up his initiative. After this confrontation most of his colleagues felt that it was time for Churchill, now approaching eighty, to go.

Churchill hung on through the winter of 1954–1955, to the unconcealed exasperation of Eden, his designated successor, hoping that a summit might yet take place before he finally retired. "It is the hope of helping forward such a meeting," he confessed to Eisenhower in December, "that I am remaining in this office longer than I planned" (1082). But by March 1955 he realized that it was not likely to happen in his time, and he made way, with the worst conceivable grace, for the unfortunate Eden. But before he finally retired he made one last magnificent speech in the House of Commons, looking forward to the coming of the day for which he had worked so long. "The day may dawn," he proclaimed in his peroration, "when fair play, love for one's fellow men, respect for justice and freedom, will enable tormented generations to march forth serene and triumphant from the hideous epoch in which we have to dwell. Meanwhile never flinch, never weary, never despair" (1100).

Was Churchill right to press, as he did, for an easing of relations with the Russians? Was this the far-sighted statesman of Munich and Fulton, or the rash adventurer of Gallipoli? Was he no more than a stubborn, egocentric old man living in the past, blind to the realities of a new and harsher age? Historians will differ in their assessments. Certainly his expectations were premature. Stalin might be dead, but the grip of Marxist-Leninist idealogy remained unshaken in Moscow. Even if expectations of revolution in Western Europe were beginning to fade, the spread of revolutionary socialism in the Third World would, within a few years, hold out hopes of a far richer prize. Certainly the Soviet leadership did not want war, but no less certainly they still looked, under Khrushchev, for the fruits of war. They still believed, in Khrushchev's own words, that "We will bury you."

On the other hand, it was Churchill rather than Dulles who discerned the long-term processes at work; who looked beyond the hostile ideology of the Soviet state to the evolution of the Russian people themselves. His perception of their growing restiveness at the deprivation enforced by the regime, a restiveness only likely to increase as their contacts with the West multiplied, was one day to be triumphantly vindicated. Meanwhile it was Churchill who formulated the "two-track" strategy which NATO was to adopt a few years later as its own: the maintenance of military strength combined with a continuing search for agreement and the persistent infiltration into the Soviet Union of Western models, Western influence, Western ideas; the strategy which, two decades after his death, was to bring about all he desired, and the collapse of the barriers to freedom that the Soviet Union had erected in the closing stages of the Second World War.

Churchill made his last speech to his constituents in Essex on April 20, 1969, in his eighty-fifth year when, in the shadow of a new crisis over Berlin, relationships with the Soviet Union were as sour as they had ever been. Let me quote from it in conclusion:

> I seek, and have always sought, nothing but peace with the Russians. . . . Both Russia and England have all to gain and nothing to lose by peace. The Soviets hope that the doctrines of Karl Marx may eventually prevail. We on our side trust and believe that, as the mild and ameliorating influence of our prosperity begins at last to uplift the Communist World, so they will be more inclined to live at peace with their neighbours. This is our hope. We must not be rigid in our expression of it; we must make allowances for justifiable Russian fears; we must be flexible and firm. (1291)

This was the lesson Churchill bequeathed to the West: this and his last words to the House of Commons: "Never flinch. Never weary. Never despair." Never despair of victory. Never despair of peace. That is the Churchill we celebrate here today. May God rest that great and noble soul.

THE LADY SOAMES, D.B.E., the youngest and only surviving child of Winston and Clementine Churchill, has published several books on her esteemed family, including a prizewinning biography of her mother. Among many posts of distinction, she served as chair of the Royal National Theater Board and as a member of the Winston Churchill Memorial Trust Council.

9

Winston Churchill
The Great Human Being

The Lady Soames

Winston Churchill has passed beyond us into history: his record and achievements must stand the test of time. I think his will be a remembered name and his words ring true and heartening wherever and whenever men look and strive for freedom.

But even during his lifetime, and increasingly from the hour of his death, contemporary historians, strategists, literary critics, and, of course, muckrakers, had started on the inevitable continuing reassessment which all figures of public stature must undergo. Apart from the historic record, tales and anecdotes—true or untrue—multiply, often with little regard for accuracy, and often slanted (if not invented) to suit the storyteller's own purpose. And now I find that often with both his faults and virtues out of focus, Winston Churchill's character and personality risk becoming embalmed in his fame, and in the legend which attaches already to this hero-figure.

Because it has fallen to my lot to be Winston Churchill's child—and now of my parents' five children, sadly, the only survivor—I have a testimony which I feel duty- and honor-bound to give, and I am grateful for the opportunity given me to do so.

But I have imposed upon myself strict rules: I am loath to stray beyond the frontiers of my daughterly knowledge; not for me is the luxury of imagined conversations or apocryphal jokes and anecdotes; nor will I allow myself to be lured into the tempting pastures of what-would-your-father-think-of-so-and-so or of such-and-such. And as in Parliament, I must plead "interest": I look back on my parents through eyes of love and gratitude and admiration. But if the lenses of my vision are adjusted to love, I hope I can say it is not blind love.

But of course, my perception of my parents has changed with the passing of years: "When I was a child, I spake as a child, I understood as a child, I thought as a child."

For me, clear, consecutive memories of my father begin with the opening of that decade, which, in the chronology of Winston Churchill's life, has come to be called "The Wilderness Years." In 1929 he had ceased to be chancellor of the Exchequer with the defeat of Stanley Baldwin's government and for the next ten years he was to be out of office, although fully involved in active political life.

Winston was now in his mid-fifties: Clementine, his wife, ten years younger, and myself, aged eight, trailing along well behind Diana, Randolph, and Sarah. Politics kept my parents much in London. But Chartwell was the center of their family life, and the place my father—both then and later—most liked to be in the whole world.

Chartwell was bought in 1922, in the week that I was born in London; and from the age of two until I was seventeen I knew no other home: educated at a local school, I was indeed the "Chartwell child," and, never confined to the nursery wing, participated fully in my parents' life there.

Long before I was aware of my father's fame or that he was an important public personage, he was of course famous and important to me—as for a fleeting and felicitous time all parents are to their children.

His spontaneous enjoyment of so many things and his varied and numerous occupations made him a convivial and enthralling companion to people of all ages, as many who knew him well or worked closely with him have often recounted.

But to have been his child was an enrichment beyond compare. I was blessed indeed in the love of my parents and siblings. I was then the unconscious, even careless, acceptor of the golden dower of love and security, which is the rightful heritage of all children, and which certainly encircled my childhood years. As with my older brother and sisters, I, in my turn, was soon admitted to a grown-up world of interest, variety, excitement, and fun.

Chartwell was my parents' home for forty years: their London abodes changed several times, but Chartwell was their sure base and refuge—and was a veritable playground for my father. The place bears visible testimony to my father's love of construction and his skill as a bricklayer in the extensive wall around the vegetable garden, which he built largely with his own hands.

He loved directing outdoor works: tree clearing; or channeling the meager trickle from the Chartwell through various courses, and transforming it into rushing streams and cascades by skillfully placed pumps and stop-cocks.

Once, in my mother's absence, he converted a peninsula, which jutted out into the lower lake, into an island: this turned out to be a more extensive operation than he had originally anticipated—the digging works requiring the services of a giant mechanical digger and a system of skips on tracks to remove the large quantities of earth, which transformed our green and pleasant valley for one whole winter into a scene which looked like a film set for *All Quiet on the Western Front*. Occasionally my father's enthusiasms outstripped practical bounds. But all these activities afforded him immense satisfaction.

After the Second World War he addressed himself to farming, finding new preoccupations in the lives of the cattle and pigs and in the output of a market garden. The basic logic of farming, however, caused Winston some difficulty—for he could not bring himself to devour livestock with whom (in his own words) "I have established social relations."

Later still, he took up racing and derived enormous pleasure from the triumphs of his brilliant grey horse, Colonist the Second, and other rather good horses he acquired and also bred in a small stud farm not far from Chartwell.

Animals were extremely important in his scheme of things: his faithful chocolate poodle, Rufus, was a constant companion; the beautiful marmalade Chartwell cat a cossetted friend. For several years a blue budgerigar called Toby accompanied him even abroad, and visitors to my father in his room, where Toby flew free, were at risk from the bird's indiscretions.

And of course, from human company Winston derived the utmost stimulation and pleasure. Happy hours were passed round the dining room table with his family, friends, and colleagues, when conversation and repartee and argument flashed to and fro, or long-remembered lines of verse and prose poured forth like a torrent. Mealtimes, thus, would often last two or three hours. My mother would presently make a move. I can see now, so well, my father looking at her across the table: "Ah Clemmie," he would say, "It is so nice. . . . Do not go. Let us command the moment to remain." Ah, if only that were possible.

And then, of course, there was painting. Taken up almost by accident during the First World War when he was forty, it took the role of therapy, which distracted his mind from the traumatic debacle of the Dardanelles campaign, the concept for which he bore a major responsibility, and whose failure had resulted in such grievous loss of life and precipitated a political crisis and his own resignation from Asquith's government. Long years later, Clementine would tell his biographer, Martin Gilbert, "I thought he would die of grief." But from that grim summer of 1915 for over forty years more, Winston found hours of pleasure and occupation in painting. When problems of perspective and color gave him respite from dark worries, heavy burdens, and the clatter of political strife: "Happy are the painters," he wrote, "for they never shall be lonely: light and colour, peace and hope will keep them company to the end—or almost to the end of the day." And these were happily to prove prophetic words for him personally.

As I advanced through my girlhood, of course, I came to realize my father played a public role and that my parents' lives were governed by public events and obligations in which I more and more became interested. My mother's life, our family life, and that of our guests and household were geared around my father's massive program of work and of his enjoyments. It seemed quite natural that this should be so—and indeed it still does.

As my perspective altered as I grew up, I came to see that my father's whole political life had been and was a dramatic procession of great issues.

He saw events and people, as on a stage, lit by his own knowledge of history and his burning sense of destiny and the march of events. I was brought up to take the nobler, larger view of life: "to do one's duty" was not an archaic phase to me; "to serve one's country" I accepted should be a natural element of one's life. My father often quoted Marvell's lines on the execution of Charles I: "He nothing common did or mean / Upon that memorable scene." And living at Winston Churchill's side in those fatal years one was constantly in mind that we were indeed upon "a memorable scene" and that much would be expected of us all.

As a child I took my father's giant program of work and play completely for granted. And what a prodigious worker he was. I think he wrang from each twenty-four hours half as much time's-worth again.

Chartwell was a veritable factory, and the lights gleamed from his upstairs study late into the night as, padding up and down the long room with its high-vaulted, raftered ceiling, he dictated to one of his secretaries hour after hour his books, newspaper articles, and speeches. I soon became aware of the immense pains he devoted to his written works; he spent hours also correcting proofs and galleys. His speeches made him quite broody: "You must not disturb your father," my mother would say: "He is with speech."

Winston Churchill was an essentially natural person and almost totally lacking in hypocrisy. Even as his fame and standing grew, his public and private persona remained much the same. He was a being blessed in that for him the boundary line between work and play was smudged. His main life's work was a natural expression of his gifts for heroic action, oratory, and writing. But when I ponder again his life and the wide range of his interests and activities, even I am always amazed anew by their variety.

His zest for life was one of his most attractive characteristics, of which those of us who were fortunate enough to be close to him were the luckiest beneficiaries. For he was such fun to be with, and his spontaneous enjoyment of so many things was infectious. In a life packed with action and arduous work, my father nearly always found time for what he called "my toys."

Because our generation's most immediate image of Winston Churchill is of the older man, it is easy to forget the dash and brilliance of his younger

days. His cavalry training had made him a good horseman; he had been
a brilliant polo player (playing his last game in 1923); he was a good shot
and loved a day with hounds, fox- or boar-hunting.

But, of course, the demands of politics and his writing, which he did
always up against sharp deadlines, keeping his family by his pen relegated
both sport and social life to the margins of his existence.

But where sport and painting were in competition, painting won an
easy victory. In a letter to his wife in 1921 when he was staying in Scotland
with the Duke of Sutherland, he wrote: "It is another splendid day: & I am
off to the river to catch pictures—much better than salmon."

I find it touching and attractive that, in those earlier days especially,
the fun-loving and convivial side of his nature caused him an occasional
glance at another sort of world: the glittering beau monde to which he and
Clementine naturally belonged, the world which would be swept away a
few years later in the First World War.

On one occasion in the early years of their marriage, in December 1910,
Winston was staying with a fashionable house party at Warter Priory in
Yorkshire for shooting. He wrote to Clementine, who had stayed at home
because of a heavy cold: "A nice party—puissant, presentable, radical in
preponderance—a rare combination. I wish you were here. . . . Tomorrow
pheasants in thousands—the vy best wot ever was seen. Tonight Poker—
I lost a little—but the play was low." He continued reflectively, "On the
whole survey, how much more power and great business are to me, than
this kind of thing, pleasant tho it seems by contrast to our humble modes of
entertainment. I expect I will have a headache tomorrow night after firing
so many cartridges. All the glitter of the world appeals to me: but thank God
not in comparison with serious things." One receives the impression of a
spectator looking in on a brilliantly lighted scene but turning resolutely—
indeed gladly—back to the blustery weather outside.

And how fortunate indeed he was in the woman he had married. How
different might have been the course of Winston Churchill's life and career
had he married a socially eager or trivial-minded woman. Churchill would
always, through his talents and thrusting nature, have been to the forefront
of political life but his energies might have been distracted or, who knows,
the rapier of the purpose of his destiny blunted or tarnished, had the

woman he loved lacked the dedication, the high principles, and the fiery courage of Clementine Hozier.

Any consideration of Winston Churchill's life and emotional makeup must recognize the role his beloved Clemmie played throughout the fifty-seven years they lived together—through a period as cataclysmic and changing as any time in our history, and always in the glare of public interest.

As of great events, so of his marriage, Winston took the romantic's view. He ended his autobiography, *My Early Life,* with the words: "In 1908 I married, and lived happily ever after."

Of course it wasn't quite as easy as that. Winston and Clementine's partnership was not always equable: both had high-mettled natures: Clementine did not hesitate to differ from him on political questions; they often did not agree on friends; but love and loyalty never failed. Each had a deep love for the other and an unquestioning commitment to their marriage. Their relationship ever reminds me of Shakespeare's lines: "Let me not to the marriage of true minds / Admit impediments."

Winston early recognized his deep need of Clementine. In January 1913, when he was first lord of the Admiralty, he wrote to her from the Admiralty yacht *Enchantress* (they had evidently had quite a sharp disagreement before Winston had left home), "I was stupid last night—but you know what a prey I am to nerves and prepossessions. It is a great comfort to me to feel *absolute* confidence in your love and cherishment. . . . Don't be disloyal to me in thought. I have no one but you to break the loneliness of a bustling and bustled existence."

On the eleventh anniversary of their marriage in 1919 Winston wrote to Clementine: "How I rejoice to think of my great good fortune on that day! There came to me the greatest happiness and honour of my life. My dear it is a rock of comfort to have yr love and companionship at my side." And to the end of their correspondence, spanning as it did over half a century, their letters to each other, to the last one, breathe tenderness.

Reflecting on my parents' life together (and their correspondence is a revealing witness corroborating the evidence of those who knew them well), I am convinced that it was in the security and happiness of their marriage that Winston found sanctuary from the depressive side of his nature which he had christened "black dog." After his marriage, and with growing confidence in Clementine's steadfastness, "black dog" was largely banished—and certainly lost his malign power. Their marriage was the great stabilizing element in his emotional life, from whose citadel he could confront the demands and vicissitudes of his public life.

If one considers Winston Churchill's long life, one cannot fail to be struck by the salient characteristic in his makeup of magnanimity.

Someone once said of him: "Winston is a very bad hater." I would say he *could* be a very good hater, but he could never keep it up for long!

On the flyleaf of each volume of his *War Memoirs,* as on the pediment of his statue here, are inscribed these words:

> In War: Resolution
> In Defeat: Defiance
> In Victory: Magnanimity
> In Peace: Good Will

And these words appropriately sum up the theme of his whole life's work. After the First World War, he wanted food ships run in to Germany to relieve the starving civilian population while the public cry was to "squeeze the orange till the pips squeak."

In 1946 when Europe lay prostrate and divided by hatreds, in a famous speech at Zurich University in which he sounded a clarion call for European unity, he spoke of the necessity for there to be "an end to retribution. . . . There must be an act of faith in the European family and an act of oblivion against all the crimes and follies of the past."

And this same generous outlook in public affairs was very much present in his private life. My father would often quote the biblical injunction: "Let not the sun go down upon your wrath." And he truly practiced what he preached for he was ever a quick forgiver.

What of my father's philosophy of life? He certainly had faith in the indomitable spirit of man. Taking leave of his government ministers in 1955, he used the phrase, "Man is spirit."

But what of his faith in God? Winston Churchill was not religious in a conventional sense—and certainly no regular churchgoer. I saw him once greatly embarrassed when a visiting divine addressed him as a "pillar of the church." My father, one of whose endearing qualities was candor, replied, "Well, I don't think that could be said of me. But I do like to think of myself as a flying buttress."

He had a strong underlying belief in a providential God. When the call to him came in 1940, he later was to write: "I felt as if I were walking with destiny, and that all my past life had been a preparation for this hour and this trial." And indeed when one looks back upon the hazards and dangers through which he had passed—the illnesses and accidents he suffered in his youth, the numerous close encounters with death in his soldier-of-fortune days—it is hard not to see a guiding and a guarding hand, and he himself felt this element increasingly.

On death, I have heard him express different thoughts. The concept of a "deep velvet sleep" at times seemed a pleasing option. But this was among the musings of an old man. To Clementine, in his prime, when life and love and ambition throbbed in his veins, he revealed a belief in which valiant hope and a certain tinge of uncertainty seem to be mingled. In July 1915, he wrote a letter marked "To be sent to Mrs. Churchill in the event of my death": "Do not grieve for me too much. I am a spirit confident of my rights. Death is only an incident, and not the most important wh happens to us in this state of being. On the whole, and especially since I met you my darling one, I have been happy, and you have taught me how noble a woman's heart can be. If there is anywhere else, I shall be on the lookout for you."

Winston Churchill's outlook in the main was profoundly stoical. In *Thoughts and Adventures* written in the thirties he seems to have expressed his overall view:

> Let us be contented with what has happened to us and thankful for all we have been spared. Let us accept the natural order in which we move. Let us reconcile ourselves to the mysterious rhythm of our destinies, such as they must be in this world of space and time. Let us treasure our joys but not bewail our sorrows. The glory of light cannot exist without its shadows. Life is a whole, and good and ill must be accepted together. The journey has been enjoyable and well worth making—once.

And I do not think he would have sought to alter a word of this after a
further thirty years or so of his life's long and eventful journey.

How do I see him now as I myself, nearing seventy, look back upon this
truly extraordinary man, who is a world-hero and who was my father?

I, too, see Winston Churchill with infinite pride and wonder as a hero-
figure . . . for am I not an Englishwoman? Do I not cherish liberty more
than life?

But also I see him as I knew him, as a supremely blessed and happy
human being—despite the anguish of the dramas through which he lived
and which he felt in every fiber of his being and in which he played so
great a part. Yet for these epic times and events how magnificently was he
equipped in mind and spirit.

Dowered with a stalwart constitution, his manifold talents found expression in the varied and exciting events and political conflicts of his life.
In his writing and painting and in numerous lesser occupations, he found
endless employment and enjoyment. So I believe that until his very last
years he did not know the meaning of the word *boredom.*

Just after his retirement as prime minister in 1955 when he was in
his eighty-first year, he told a visitor to Chartwell: "I look forward to a
leisure hour with pleasurable agitation: it's so difficult to choose between
writing, reading, painting, bricklaying, and three or four other things I
want to do."

When at long last the pace slowed, and his good companion of forty
years, the Muse of Painting, had gently taken her leave, and that seemingly
unquenchable well of his zest for life ran dry, the long daylight hours did
indeed hang heavy. Yet from those muted sad years, I treasure a precious
and, to me, infinitely moving picture. As a young cavalry officer in Cuba
and then in India, Winston had been fascinated and amazed by the size
and beauty and variety of the butterflies he saw there. Years later, he
caused plants and shrubs which attract butterflies to be planted in quantity
at Chartwell.

I remember my father on summer days in these twilight years sitting in his chair strategically placed before the opulently flowering bud-
dleias, watching with rapt enjoyment the vivid, quivering splendor of the

butterflies—the Red Admirals, the Peacocks, and the Painted Ladies—as they fluttered and feasted on the purple, honey-laden flowers. And remembering him thus, I recall Walter Savage Landor's lines: "I warmed both hands before the fire of life / It sinks, and I am ready to depart."

REGINALD V. JONES, C.B., C.B.E., F.R.S., the first living member elected to the Electronic Warfare Hall of Fame in Washington, D.C., was a professor of Natural Philosophy for thirty-five years at Aberdeen University in Scotland. His work in scientific intelligence during World War II is described in Sir Winston Churchill's *The Second World War*. Among Mr. Jones's several publications are *Some Thoughts on "Star Wars"* and *Reflections on Intelligence*.

10

Churchill as I Knew Him

Reginald V. Jones

In 1946, Sir Winston Churchill gave one of the greatest speeches of the twentieth century. His words have ever since echoed down the years and round the world.

I have never been, of course, in such a position of unique authority as he was to survey the world scene, and so it would be impertinent, though tempting, to speculate on what he would have said in 1992, with all the remarkable changes brought about by the global scene-shifters who raised the infamous Iron Curtain. He would be soberly cheered by the triumph of Western, indeed Christian, ideals; and he would be gratified that at last his generous words of 1946 were coming true. Despite the descent of the Iron Curtain, he said, "Above all we welcome constant, frequent and growing contacts between the Russian people and our own people on both sides of the Atlantic." And he would be relieved by the fulfillment—so far at least—of the optimism he expressed in 1955 after the first hydrogen bombs had been exploded: horrific though their consequences might be, "It may well be that we shall by a process of sublime irony have reached a stage in this story where safety will be the sturdy child of terror and survival the twin brother of annihilation."[1]

1. " 'Iron Curtain' Speech," Westminster College, 5 March 1946; Martin Gilbert, *Never Despair: Winston S. Churchill, 1945–1965* (London: Heinemann, 1988), 1100.

He himself had, of course, faced many grave situations, above all in 1940 when we in Britain were standing alone against the Nazi threat, and when he became prime minister. A few weeks after he had taken over, he called me in to advise him on a new development in the threat that we were about to face from the Luftwaffe, and so I saw him at close quarters at that vital time; ever afterward he would call on me when a new threat developed. I am therefore privileged to share some aspects of his actions and character as I saw them at the time, and as I have come to recall with an appreciation that has been enriched over the years by the treasures I have since found in his books and speeches.

I will start with his courage, for he himself wrote: "Courage is rightly esteemed the first of human qualities, because it is the quality that guarantees all others."[2] The facts that Churchill served with honor in no less than eight British regiments, from the northwest frontier of India to the mud of Flanders, and before the outbreak of war in 1914 had made nearly 140 flights while learning to fly, testify to his supreme physical courage. Flying was at that time very dangerous, but he only gave it up because his wife was so worried: he gave her the news in a most moving letter:

> This is a wrench, because I was on the verge of taking my pilot's certificate. It only needed a couple of calm mornings; & I am confident of my ability to achieve it vy respectably. . . . But I must admit that the numerous fatalities of this year wd justify you in complaining if I continued to share the risks—as I am proud to do— of these good fellows. So I give it up decidedly for many months & perhaps for ever. This is a gift—so stupidly am I made—wh costs me more than anything wh cd be bought with money. So I am vy glad to lay it at your feet, because I know it will rejoice & relieve your heart.[3]

Courage shines even brighter when it marches with humor, and this, too, bubbled in abundance through Churchill's phrases. Even, for example, when exposing to Parliament in 1936 the weakness of our air defenses, he

---

2. *Great Contemporaries* (reprint, London: Fontana, 1962), 177.

3. Randolph S. Churchill, *Young Statesman, 1900–1914* (London: Heinemann, 1967), 704.

could leaven the gravity of the occasion with a telling touch of levity: "A friend of mine the other day saw a number of persons engaged in peculiar evolutions, genuflections and gestures. . . . He wondered whether it was some novel form of gymnastics, or a new religion . . . or whether they were a party of lunatics out for an airing. They were a searchlight company of the London Territorials, who were doing their exercises as well as they could without having the searchlight."[4]

Again, when describing how he just scraped into the Royal Military Academy at Sandhurst, where budding officers are trained, at his third and final attempt, he said that his fate hung on the mathematics paper where he happily found that one question concerned:

> cosines and tangents in a highly square rooted condition which must have been decisive on the whole of my life. It was a problem. But luckily I had seen its ugly face only a few days before and recognised it at first sight. . . . If this aged, weary-souled Civil Service Commissioner had not asked this particular question . . . the whole of my life would have been altered, and that I suppose would have altered a great many other lives.[5]

After service in the army in India and the Sudan, he would have liked to go to Oxford but his prospective entrance there encountered a new difficulty. Latin had been the bête noire among his school subjects but now, for Oxford, "I could not see why I should not have gone and paid my fees and listened to the lectures and argued with the professors and read the books that they recommended. However, it appeared that this was impossible. I must pass examinations not only in Latin, but even in Greek. I could not contemplate toiling at Greek irregular verbs after having commanded British regular troops."[6]

This barrier from Oxford, though, inhibited neither the breadth of his reading nor the brilliance of his writing. One of the best of his early books was *The River War*, in which he shaped his prose, he said, to effect "a

---

4. Speech in the House of Commons, 12 November 1936.
5. *My Early Life* (reprint, London: Fontana, 1959), 34.
6. Ibid., 209.

combination of the styles of Macaulay and Gibbon, the staccato antitheses of the former and the rolling sentences and genitival endings of the latter; and I stuck in a bit of my own from time to time."[7]

Unaware that he had said this, I was talking to him at Chartwell in 1946 while he was in bed with a cold. This was a marvelous opportunity to ask him many questions, and I finally summoned enough nerve to ask him what he really thought of Macaulay, for by that time I had read that he had called Macaulay a liar because Macaulay had said that the great Duke of Marlborough had obtained his first preferment in the army by selling his sister Arabella to King James II. I said, "I know what you have said about Macaulay, and I understand why you said it; but it has also struck me that your style is very like Macaulay's." "You have hit the nail on the head," he replied, "If I had to make my literary will and my literary acknowledgements I should have to own that I owe more to Macaulay than to any other English writer. When I was a boy at Harrow there was a prize that you could win if you could recite 800 lines of any poet, or 1200 of Macaulay. I took the 1200 of Macaulay, and won!"

The River War described the British expedition that culminated in the Battle of Omdurman in which Churchill himself took part in the Charge of the Twenty-first Lancers. His description of the battle, and indeed of all other actions in the campaign, was meticulous. More than that, it was magnanimous. Struck by the sight of the Dervish dead after the battle he wrote: "When the soldier of a civilized Power is killed in action . . . his body is borne by friendly arms reverently to the grave. . . . But there was nothing dulce et decorum about the Dervish dead; all was filth and corruption. Yet these were as brave men as ever walked the earth . . . destroyed, not conquered, by machinery."[8]

Time after time he could not help recognizing bravery, even in an enemy. Speaking of the Boers in his first speech in Parliament in 1901, when the South African War was still raging, he said, "The Boers who were fighting in the field . . . and if I were a Boer, I hope I should be fighting in the field." And my own generation remembers his tribute to Rommel, even

7. Ibid., 217.
8. *The River War*, vol. 2 (London: Longmans, 1899), 162.

when he himself was being subjected to a vote of censure in Parliament for our failures in North Africa: "We have a very daring and skilful opponent against us, and, may I say across the havoc of war, a great General."[9]

Reverting to the Dervishes at Omdurman, his tribute continued with sublime prescience:

> "Mad fanaticism" is the depreciating comment of their conquerors. I hold this to be cruel injustice. . . . Why should we regard as madness in the savage what would be sublime in civilized men? For I hope that if evil days should come upon our own country, and the last army which a collapsing Empire could interpose between London and the invader were dissolving in rout and ruin, that there would be some—even in these modern days—who would not care to accustom themselves to a new order of things and tamely survive the disaster.

So wrote Churchill in 1899: Could he already hear the sirens of 1940?

Long before then, of course, the First World War had occurred, and Churchill had played many parts in it, from first lord of the Admiralty, when he had brought the Royal Navy to immediate readiness for war, to commanding a Scottish battalion in the trenches of Flanders. Among the many lessons that he drew from the war, two were outstanding. The first arose from his zest for action in the front line, which led him virtually to desert his post as head of the Admiralty to take command of the Royal Marine Brigade in the defense of Antwerp against the Germans in 1914.

The prime minister, Asquith, had great difficulty in getting him to come back to London, and noted in his diary Churchill's remonstration and his request to be given a military command:

> His mouth waters at the thought of Kitchener's new armies. Are these "glittering commands" to be entrusted to "dug-out trash" bred on the obsolete tactics of 25 years ago, "mediocrities who have led a sheltered life mouldering in military routine etc. etc.?" For about a quarter of an hour he poured forth a ceaseless cataract of invective and appeal, and

---

9. Speeches in the House of Commons, 18 February 1901, 27 January 1942.

I much regretted that there was no shorthand writer within hearing, as some of his unpremeditated phrases were quite priceless. He was, however, three parts serious and declared that a political career was nothing to him in comparison with military glory.[10]

Reflecting in 1931 on this same episode in one of his essays, "A Second Choice," Churchill recognized that "I ought, for instance, never to have gone to Antwerp. I ought to have remained in London. . . . Those who are charged with the direction of supreme affairs must sit on the mountain-tops of control; they must never descend into the valleys of direct physical and personal action."[11]

It may be questioned, though, whether Churchill henceforth restrained himself in accordance with this dictum. He continued to find refreshment in front-line action; indeed, in one instance the refreshment was physical as well as moral. This was when he was in Flanders with the Grenadier Guards, the elite regiment in which his great ancestor, the Duke of Marlborough, had first been commissioned. Churchill later related:

> When the Second-in-Command went home on leave, I was invited temporarily to undertake his duties. This was certainly one of the greatest honours I had ever received. The offer emboldened me to make a suggestion to the Colonel. I said that I thought I should learn of the conditions in the trenches better if I lived with the Companies actually in the line instead of at the Battalion Headquarters. The Colonel considered this a praiseworthy suggestion, and made arrangements accordingly. I must confess to the reader that I was prompted by what many will think a somewhat inadequate motive. Battalion Headquarters when in the line was strictly dry. Nothing but the strong tea with the condensed milk, a very unpleasant beverage, ever appeared there. The Companies' messes in the trenches were, however, allowed more latitude. And as I have always believed in the moderate and regular use of alcohol, especially under conditions of winter war, I gladly moved my handful of belongings from Ebenezer Farm to a Company in the line.[12]

10. H. H. Asquith, *Memories and Reflections,* vol. 2 (London: Cassell, 1928), 45–46.
11. *Thoughts and Adventures* (London: Odhams, 1947), 6.
12. Ibid., 72.

Churchill's enjoyment of good living was, of course, famous. He even overcame an original distaste for whisky when, with little else to drink in the heat of the northwest frontier, he found that "The very repulsion of the flavour developed an attraction of its own; and to this day, although I have always practised true temperance, I have never shrunk when occasion offered it from the main basic refreshment of the white officer in the East." At the same time, reflecting on the overindulgence of the Oxford and Cambridge undergraduates of his day, he said:

> They even had clubs and formal dinners where it was an obligation on everyone to consume more liquor than he could carry. . . . I had been brought up and trained to have the utmost contempt for people who got drunk—except on very exceptional occasions and a few anniversaries—and I would have liked to have the boozing scholars of the Universities wheeled into line and properly chastized for their squalid misuse of what I must ever regard as a good gift of the Gods.[13]

Churchill's own appreciation of that gift throughout his long life has recently prompted an eminent geneticist to suggest that nature had endowed him with a protective gene that gave him exceptional resistance to its harmful effects.[14]

Reverting to Churchill's unflagging enthusiasm to see for himself what was happening in the front line, he wanted in 1944 to sail with the British and American armada for the D-Day landings in Normandy, despite his own verdict on his Antwerp episode in 1914. The news that he had booked himself a berth in a British cruiser, *H.M.S. Belfast,* alarmed those who knew of his intention, and ultimately General Eisenhower told him that he should not go. The supreme Allied commander, though, received very short shrift: Churchill told him that he might be supreme commander, but that gave him no right to regulate the complement in one of His Majesty's ships, and Churchill still intended to go. What power on earth could now stop him? I have sometimes told my American friends that we have one shot in the locker that they do not possess, for when King George VI

13. *My Early Life,* 133.
14. *The Times,* February 1992, 1, 19.

heard of Churchill's intention, he was indignant, and told his family that "I was a naval officer. I was at Jutland. And if Winston can go, I can go!" But when Churchill told him that he was sure that the cabinet would not recommend the king to go, the king replied that if it was not right for him to go, neither was it right for Churchill. Finally, the king wrote: "I ask you most earnestly to consider the whole question again, and not let your personal wishes, which I very well understand, lead you to depart from your own high standard of duty to the State."[15] Churchill, still protesting, gave way.

He was still protesting in his memoirs eight years later, where he gave perhaps his final view on one of the fundamental problems of command, over which his theory and practice had sometimes appeared at variance.

> I may here set down the view I have formed over many years on this sort of thing. A man who is to play an effective part in taking, with the highest responsibility, grave and terrible decisions of war may need the refreshment of adventure. He may need also the comfort that when sending so many others to their death he may share in a small way their risks. His field of personal interest, and consequently his forces of action are stimulated by direct contact with the event. As a result of what I saw and learned in the First World War, I was convinced that Generals and other high commanders should try from time to time to see the conditions and aspect of the battle scene themselves. I have seen many grievous errors made through the silly theory that valuable lives should not be endangered. No one was more careful of his personal safety than I was, but I thought my view and theme of the war were sufficiently important and authoritative to entitle me to feel freedom of judgement as to how I discharged my task in such a personal matter.[16]

The second lesson that Churchill drew from the 1914 war concerned what may be termed the hierarchical attenuation of front line experience

---

15. Winston S. Churchill, *Closing the Ring* (London: Cassell, 1952), 549.
16. Ibid., 551.

as the battle situation is reported upward through a chain of command. While commanding the Sixth Battalion of the Royal Scots Fusiliers in the trenches Churchill had noted that generals rarely came up to the front line to see the conditions for themselves. On one occasion when he was being visited by a general from some rear headquarters, Churchill teased him by asking whether he would care to step across the parapet so that the two of them could take a stroll in no-man's-land. "Wouldn't that be dangerous?" asked the general, to which his delighted soldiers heard Churchill reply, "Sir, this is a very dangerous war!"[17]

Afterward, Churchill noted that the insulation of generals from seeing conditions at the front for themselves was one of the factors leading to the disaster of the Somme in 1916, because there had been too much uncritical reliance on optimistic reports coming up through the chain of command. "Sir Douglas Haig was not at this time well served by his advisers in the Intelligence Department of General Headquarters. The temptation to tell a chief in a great position the things he most likes to hear is the commonest explanation of mistaken policy. Thus the outlook of the leader on whose decisions fateful events depend is usually far more sanguine than the brutal facts admit."[18]

He pointed to a similar attenuation of front line experience in the naval field, when the British admirals in 1917 refused to adopt the convoy system, and it was only forced on them by the insistence of Churchill himself and Lloyd George. It was an even more remarkable example because, although generals rarely had to go into the front line, admirals did from time to time go to sea.

> No story of the Great War is more remarkable or more full of guidance for the future than this. . . . The astonishing fact is that the politicians were right, and the admiralty authorities were wrong . . . in the naval service . . . the firmly inculcated doctrine that an admiral's opinion was more likely to be right than a captain's, and a captain's than

17. A. D. Gibb, "Captain X," in *With Winston Churchill at the Front* (London: Gowans and Gray, 1924).
18. *The World Crisis: 1916–1918*, abridged ed. (London: Macmillan, 1941), 653.

a commander's, did not hold good when questions entirely novel
in character, requiring keen and bold minds unhampered by long
routine, were under debate.[19]

And it was partly because Churchill had talked with junior officers who had
been serving at sea and therefore appreciated the conditions at first-hand
that he was able to overcome the opposition of the admirals. He was to keep
this lesson constantly in mind when he became prime minister in 1940.

Far better than most politicians in the thirties Churchill recognized the
growing importance of science in national and international affairs, and
this presented him with a problem: How could he keep in touch with
the front line of science from which many threats and benefits were likely
to develop? Although science had not figured largely in his education at
school, chemistry was, next to English, his best subject; and in the Flanders
trenches one of his officers noted that "Winston had a flair for a good man
of science"[20] from his eagerness to get his battalion medical officer to talk
on his own subject.

After the war, in 1921, he found his own man of science when
Mrs. Churchill was partnered in an exhibition tennis tournament for
charity by the newly appointed professor of Experimental Philosophy at
Oxford, F. A. Lindemann, who, besides being an outstanding physicist,
was a Wimbledon player and had been tennis champion of Sweden. At
first sight, Churchill and Lindemann would have appeared unlikely friends,
for Lindemann was a total abstainer, a non-smoker, and a vegetarian; but
there could be no doubt of his courage for he was the first man to work
out the aerodynamics of what was happening when an aircraft got into the
near-fatal condition of spinning and then devise what its pilot should do
to recover it. To test his theory, Lindemann learned to fly himself, put his
aircraft into a spin, and brought it out again and again: the procedure he
devised became a standard drill for aviators.

Churchill respected Lindemann both for his courage and his keen brain,
and his gift for expressing the recent discoveries of science in everyday

19. *Thoughts and Adventures*, 92.
20. Gibb, "Captain X."

terms; and the two men became the firmest of friends. Besides courage and humor, they shared a love of good language—I have known a wartime defense meeting in the cabinet room held up over the exact meaning of a particular word, and only resumed when the *Oxford English Dictionary* was sent for to settle the question.

Each excelled in his chosen sport—Churchill at polo and Lindemann at tennis—and their friendship lasted on the closest terms right up to Lindemann's death in 1957 when Churchill despite growing infirmity, insisted upon accompanying the coffin to the grave. This friendship provided Churchill with a means of keeping contact with advances in science, one of the frontiers of human endeavor in which he knew that he himself could never serve in the front line.

As early as 1924, in an essay entitled "Shall We All Commit Suicide?" Churchill had drawn on Lindemann's briefing on nuclear energy to write:

> Has Science turned its last page on them? May there not be methods of using explosive energy incomparably more intense than anything heretofore discovered? Might not a bomb no bigger than an orange be found to possess a secret power to destroy a whole block of buildings—nay, to concentrate the force of a thousand tons of cordite and blast a township at a stroke? Could not explosives even of the existing type be guided automatically in flying machines by wireless or other rays, without a human pilot, in ceaseless procession upon a hostile city, arsenal, camp, or dockyard? As for Poison Gas and Chemical Warfare in all its forms, only the first chapter has been written of a terrible book. . . . And why should it be supposed that these resources will be limited to Inorganic Chemistry? A study of Disease—of Pestilences methodically prepared and deliberately launched upon man and beast—is certainly being pursued in the laboratories of more than one great country. Blight to destroy crops, Anthrax to slay horses and cattle, Plague to poison not armies only but whole districts—such are the lines along which military science is remorselessly advancing.[21]

21. Churchill, *Thoughts and Adventures,* 188–89.

This essay was followed by another in 1931 entitled "Fifty Years Hence" which pointed to the energy that could be released by the fusion of hydrogen into helium nuclei: "There is no question among scientists that this gigantic source of energy exists. What is lacking is the match to set the bonfire alight, or it may be the detonator to cause the dynamite to explode. The Scientists are looking for this."[22]

Churchill was clear about his dependence on Lindemann in the Second World War as he explained in *Their Finest Hour*:

> He had two qualifications of vital consequence to me. First as these pages have shown, he was my trusted friend and confidante of twenty years. Together we had watched the advance and onset of world disaster. Together we had done our best to sound the alarm. And now we were in it, and I had the power to guide and arm our effort. How could I have the knowledge?
>
> Here came the second of his qualities. Lindemann could decipher the signals from the experts on the far horizons and explain to me in lucid, homely terms what the issues were. There are only twenty-four hours in the day, of which at least seven must be spent in sleep and three in eating and relaxation. Anyone in my position would have been ruined if he had attempted to dive into depths which not even a lifetime of study could plumb. What I had to grasp were the practical results, and just as Lindemann gave me his view for all it was worth in this field, so I made sure by turning on my power-relay that some at least of these terrible and incomprehensible truths emerged in executive decisions.[23]

As Churchill said, he and Lindemann had together watched the advance and onset of world disaster, and had done their best to sound the alarm. Their efforts earned them little but scorn as warmongers by their contemporaries, until Hitler invaded Poland on September 1, 1939; a disillusioned government in Whitehall then promptly recalled Churchill as first lord of the Admiralty. The Anglo-French disaster of the next few months, with the

22. Ibid., 208.
23. *Their Finest Hour* (London: Cassell, 1949), 338.

German advances into Denmark, Norway, and the Low Countries resulted in a public reaction which led to Churchill becoming prime minister on May 10, 1940. He later wrote of this appointment: "I felt as if I were walking with destiny, and that all my past life had been but a preparation for this hour and for this trial."[24]

Indeed, his past life had qualified him uniquely. He had been in politics for forty years. He had served in the front line, and he had been head of the three service ministries—of the Home Office, the Colonial Office and the Board of Trade—and he had been chancellor of the Exchequer. Yet he had been out of office for more than ten years, and even this was a further qualification, for as he wrote of Moses, "Every prophet has to come from civilisation, but every prophet has to go into the wilderness. He must have a strong impression of a complex society and all that it has to give, and then must serve periods of isolation and meditation. This is the process by which psychic dynamite is made."[25] And that was what he now provided.

He never overclaimed his part in 1940. Disaster had united rather than disrupted the people of Britain as he knew it would. Although as a nation we were alone, as individuals we were all in it together. He felt our temper exactly: "There is no doubt that had I at this juncture faltered at all in the leading of the nation, I should have been hurled out of office. . . . It fell to me in these coming days and months to express their sentiments on suitable occasions. This I was able to do, because they were mine also!" All this was true, but there was much more. Churchill could turn even a minor occasion into a memorable one by happy phrase or a humorous comment. Here he had one of the big occasions of history, and it called for the summit of language, for "There was a white glow, overpowering, sublime, which ran through our island from end to end."[26] In speech after speech he helped us to see where we stood in history, he convinced us that the direction at the center was now firm and good, and he called from us our supreme effort.

24. Winston S. Churchill, *The Gathering Storm* (London: Cassell: 1948), 526–27.
25. *Thoughts and Adventures*, 219.
26. *Their Finest Hour*, 88.

But it was not to his eloquence or even to his humor alone that we responded; disaster had struck the scales from our eyes, and suddenly we saw the towering courage that had been Churchill's all his life. We all knew, in that instinctive way that tells true from false, that here was a man who would stand to the last; and in this confidence we could stand with him.

I myself was fortunate enough to be summoned by him to the cabinet room in June 1940, and so I saw him at close quarters at the hour of his— and our—greatest trial. I of course felt the elation of a young man at being noticed by any prime minister, but somehow it was much more. It was the same whenever we met in the war—I had the feeling of being recharged by contact with a source of living power. Here was strength, resolution, humor, readiness to listen, to ask the searching question, and, when convinced, to act. He was rarely complimentary at the time, handsome though his compliments could be afterward, for he had been brought up in sterner and more admirable days when: "At Sandhurst and in the Army compliments are few and far between, and flattery of subalterns does not exist. If you won the Victoria Cross or the Grand National Steeplechase or the Army Heavyweight Boxing Championship, you would only expect to receive from your friends warnings against having your head turned by your good luck." In 1940 it was ample compliment itself to be called in by him at the crisis; but to stand up to his questioning attack and then to convince him was the greatest exhilaration of all.[27]

The reason why Churchill had summoned me was that Lindemann, who incidentally had been my professor at Oxford, had told him that I had found convincing evidence that the Luftwaffe had developed systems of radio beams to guide their bombers to attack targets by night and through clouds when our defenses would be powerless to shoot them down. As I presented the evidence in the cabinet room, so Churchill told me, it was for him one of the blackest moments of the war. He had reckoned that we should just be able to win the coming Battle of Britain by day, but then he had this young man come and tell him that even if that battle were won,

---

27. *My Early Life,* 212; Winston Churchill, *The Malakand Field Force* (London: Longmans, 1901), 172. He himself had written "Nothing in life is so exhilarating as to be shot at without result."

the Luftwaffe would be able to strike our cities accurately by night when we had virtually no defense. He felt the clouds gathering about him, but then they were as quickly lifted when the young man told him that it would be alright, we could do something about it by radio countermeasures.

I could see at the time how deeply he was absorbing my words, and the episode made a lasting impression on him—all the more so, fortunately, when it transpired that the radio countermeasures we then instituted had blunted the blitz to the extent that only one bomb in five fell on their intended targets. Ever afterward he would summon me when Lindemann told him that I had perceived a new threat, most dramatically, of course, in the German development of the V-1 and V-2 weapons in 1943 and 1944. And once again he sent for me to settle the great internal battle of whether or not we should use "Window" or "Chaff" to protect bomber command and the Eighth Air Force against detection by German radar.

When all these battles, and many others, were ultimately won and the European war came to an end, Churchill's Conservative government was rejected in the 1945 Election, and he was no longer prime minister. He felt the shock deeply—it was a sharper change of fortune than any man might expect to face. But no political misfortune could detract from the universal admiration for what he had done in the war. And so, after a moment of uncertainty in which he contemplated graceful retirement "in an odour of civil freedom," his confidence returned. "Many people," he said to me a year later, "say that I ought to have retired after the war, and have become some sort of Elder Statesman, but how could I? I have fought all my life and I cannot give up fighting now!" And so he led the Opposition at home and was feted abroad; and, for all his tiredness, he made some of his best speeches—humorous, wise, prescient and magnanimous. And it is the most acclaimed of those speeches that we celebrate here today.

The many honorary degrees that he received gave him occasions for reflecting on his education. A few days before Fulton he had been at the University of Miami where he quipped: "I am surprised that in my later life I should have become so experienced in taking degrees when, as a schoolboy I was so bad at passing examinations. In fact one might almost say that no one ever passed so few examinations and received so many degrees." And, recalling his own development he went on to plead for the late starter. Long before, in *My Early Life,* he had made a similar point when in what he called his "Socratic" mood and planning his republic he would make drastic changes in the education of the sons of well-to-do citizens: "It is only when they are really thirsty for knowledge, longing to hear about things, that I would let them go to the University. It would be a favour, a coveted privilege, only to be given to those who had either proved their worth in factory or field or whose qualities and zeal were pre-eminent."[28] Those of us who experienced the sense of purpose of the ex-service student who had fought in the Second World War, will understand the enthusiasm of the mature students who were determined to make the fullest use of the chance of education that was now offered them.

At Aberdeen, about a month after he was here in Fulton, he expressed his renewed enthusiasm for the humanities.

> But as my life has rolled out, I have regretted very much that I had no knowledge of the Classics, but have been compelled to read them only in translation. I have had to make my way through all the arguments and debates of forty or fifty years with just a handful of trusty, well-proved and frequently-exercised quotations, which have had to go out in all weathers to stand the battle and the breeze.
>
> There would be a danger to education if it assumed in these formative years—the late teens and early twenties—a purely technical or specialized aspect. Without a knowledge of the humanities, without the great record and story of the past and of the ancients laid out before one, without having the lives of the noble Greeks and Romans and the writings of antiquity in one's mind, it is not possible to form those broad and inspiring views which should ever be the guide of men as they advance to serve in a country as great as ours.[29]

As I read these speeches, I wondered whether he was himself putting into practice the advice he had given me when I was leaving my Whitehall post for a university chair at Aberdeen in natural philosophy, the old title

28. Gilbert, *Never Despair,* 193; Churchill, *My Early Life,* 119.
29. R. V. Jones, *Winston Leonard Spencer Churchill: 1874–1965,* vol. 12, biographical memoirs of Fellows of the Royal Society, 1966.

for physics: "Praise up the Humanities my boy—that'll make them think you are broadminded." And in an expansive mood he said, "Socrates said that there would only be good government when philosophers were kings and kings philosophers. During the war I had the power of a king, and with my power and your philosophy, we won!"

For all his appreciation of science, though, he became impatient with the postwar pressure for scientists to have a large say in government: "There have been theocratic governments, military governments and aristocratic governments. It is now suggested that we should have scientistic—not scientific—governments. It is the duty of scientists, like all other people, to serve the State and not to rule it because they are scientists. If they want to rule the State they must get elected to Parliament."[30]

His postwar distrust of science, perhaps in revulsion to the slaughter and destruction in the Second World War, led him once again, in 1953, to commend instruction in the humanities. "This," he told our Trades Union Congress, "ranks in my opinion far above science and technical instruction, which are well sustained and not without rewards in our present system."[31]

But some of us could see that the standard of science teaching in our schools was already falling, and both Lindemann and I represented this fact to him as strongly as we could. I was able to produce figures for the production of engineers in Russia which outstripped our own; and the fact that the Russians had matched the Americans in producing a hydrogen bomb gave dramatic confirmation of our fears.

When, therefore, Churchill retired in 1955 and took a holiday in Messina with Lindemann and John Colville, his principal private secretary, he reviewed his second premiership and told Colville

> how much he regretted that owing to so many other preoccupations he had not, while prime minister, devoted more of his energies to procuring an increase in facilities for giving the highest possible technological training. He was sure that for Great Britain, whose future depended on the brains of her inhabitants this was a vital

30. Speech in the House of Commons, 7 November 1945.
31. Jones, *Churchill, 1874–1965.*

necessity. It appalled him to think that we, who had contributed
more than any other nation by our inventiveness in the past, should
now apparently be falling behind in the race.[32]

Colville has recorded how, starting from Churchill's expression of such
concern, he suggested that part of the public fund raised to commemorate
Churchill's eightieth birthday might be used to inaugurate a further fund
for an institute for higher instruction in technology, on the example of
M.I.T. Ultimately the idea came to fruition in the foundation of Churchill
College at Cambridge with its special emphasis on technology.

As the years advanced, Sir Winston gradually drew back from public
affairs, and death finally came on January 24, 1965. In a sense it was no
shock for his years were many; but there was a surge of feeling at his funeral
as though the nation, besides mourning the individual, was parting with
the brightest treasure of its own greatness. For when he was born, Britain
stood at a peak of progress and influence; and although he called us back
to sublimity from malaise in 1940, we had since seemed to lose our drive.

He had seen weapons advance from the muskets of Malakand to the
bomb at Bikini, and military transport from the horse to the supersonic
aircraft. His zest for war was not based on distant enchantment—he had
too often been in the thick of hot action and had too often afterward
helped to bury his mangled friends. War has its uttermost miseries as he
well knew; but it has a fineness, too, when "men are facing fearful odds,"
and this exhilarated his romantic courage. His delight in the imaginative
unconventional showed itself in a thirst for new weapons and for the
unexpected counterstrike—a flank attack would always appeal to him, all
the more if it evoked some resounding phrase.

Yet we must remember that for years as a young politician he set himself
to social reform, to the cutting of arms expenditure and not to the making
of war. He genuinely did more for peace than many who claimed peace
as their sole aim; and he was the first to speak for the vanquished and
to make friends of enemies who had fought well. For him, writing was
companion to fighting all through, from *The Malakand Field Forces* to *Their
Finest Hour*. He loved the English language and he always had something

32. John Colville, deposition in Churchill College Archives, July 1959.

to write about, evoked by first-hand experience, by ancestral loyalty, by reflection on the past, or by contemplation of the future. And while in most of his activities he was a brilliant amateur, in writing he was supremely professional. Time after time he returned to the theme of education—how he might have been led to learn more at school, how much he missed the chance of a university, how he taught himself in India, how important it was that students should genuinely want to learn, how classics had too great a place, and yet, toward the end, how important they were as part of a common culture.

To technology he seemed drawn by subconscious fascination and by his own flair for invention. Appreciative of science in both world wars, he seemed to recoil after 1945, apprehensive that "the Stone Age may return on the gleaming wings of science."[33] But he came again to its lasting support, and especially to the encouragement of technology, as soon as he had time to reflect in 1955. His most tangible memorial in Britain is Churchill College, devoted to the advancement of learning and technology.

The minds of his countrymen whom he led in 1940 hold another memorial, less tangible but no less precious—the memory of what he said and did in the fight that to reason looked so forlorn but to emotion so right. He seemed to be standing for us at the bar of history at the very moment of judgment, when it was almost beyond hope to purge past faults with present merits. But with sure faith he called forth our old merits in new measure and led us to save the day.

Half-American and honorary citizen of the United States, ardent for closer bonds both with his mother's land and with Europe, born in an English palace and buried in the village churchyard nearby, he was at one with all men of courage and goodwill no matter what their rank, race or nation. He once said of Clemenceau, "As much as any single human being, miraculously magnified can ever be a nation he was France."[34] In those terms, can there be any doubt that he himself was Britain?

33. " 'Iron Curtain' Speech."
34. *Great Contemporaries*, 246.

EDWINA SANDYS, M.B.E., an accomplished painter and sculptress whose works are situated in museums and private collections throughout the world, is the granddaughter of Sir Winston Churchill. Her sculpture made from the collapsed Berlin Wall, "Breakthrough," was dedicated by President Ronald Reagan and rests in Fulton at the site of Churchill's "Iron Curtain" speech.

11

⊘⊱

Winston Churchill
His Art Reflects His Life

EDWINA SANDYS

S tanding in the snow in St. Petersburg, Russia, last month, I watched
the eternal flame flickering at the Tomb of the Unknown Warrior.
Something about that scene—the violet shadows on the snow—
made me think of one of my grandfather's paintings, a winter scene at
Chartwell. I thought about the nine-hundred-day siege of Leningrad and
the brave Russians who once again turned back an invader inside their own
territory. *What if* the Allies had ignored Russia's pleas for aid? *What if* the
Allies had stood by and left Russia to fight it out alone with the Germans?
"What if" is a wonderful game to play with the benefit of hindsight.

If an unaided Russia had been defeated then, think what the world might
have looked like today! I am an artist, not a historian, but occasionally I
look at a map. History is shaped by geography. Picture Hitler's empire
stretching from Munich through Vienna, through Moscow all the way
across Siberia to Vladivostok—to join up with his allies in Tokyo. A belt
of terror encircling the globe. No wonder Churchill and Roosevelt banded
together to prevent it.

History is the reason for gathering in Fulton, in a Christopher Wren
church plucked from a bomb site in London. In a chain of events which
began in 1946, my grandfather stood here to deliver his "Sinews of Peace"

speech. That was the *first* link in the chain. The famous phrase "the Iron Curtain" had stayed in people's minds until the building of the Berlin Wall became the physical embodiment of that "curtain."

The *second* link of the chain, of course, is this beautiful church, brought here stone by stone. The love and imagination of the people of Fulton, and their skill and determination in reconstructing it here to celebrate an ideal, stands as one of the miracles of modern days.

Since these larger than life events, others have followed. Many individuals have given their time and effort to build a memorial and library in which my grandfather would surely have felt at home.

Now, I enter the picture for a moment. One thing leads to another. Life inspires art. When the Berlin Wall fell in 1989, I read that people were chipping away pieces of the wall for souvenirs. I knew in a flash what had to be done. It was an opportunity of a lifetime. I called Dr. Saunders, then president of Westminster College, and said, "Harvey, if I can get a piece of the Berlin Wall, and make a sculpture out of it, would you like to have it in Fulton at the site of the "Iron Curtain" speech?" "Wonderful idea!" he said.

My grandfather's speech was in my mind all the time I was planning what the sculpture would be. I wanted to portray freedom—breaking through the Iron Curtain, breaking through the Wall.

On the first anniversary of the fall of the Wall, my sculpture, "Breakthrough," was dedicated here by Ronald Reagan, the man who had said, "Mr. Gorbachev, tear down that wall!" We had come full circle. Or so we thought. But, lo and behold, last year Mikhail Gorbachev, drawn inextricably by this chain of events, decided to make his major speech in the USA right here at Fulton. Newly thrown out of office, like Churchill in 1946, the deposed Russian leader walked through the "Breakthrough" sculpture, from the drab communist side of the wall to the colorful freedom side, to the cheers of 15,000 enrapt admirers. Life had indeed inspired art—and art, in turn, had returned the compliment by inspiring life.

Winston Churchill was unusual as a grandfather. What was unusual, from my point of view, was that whereas he belonged to us as a family, he belonged to everyone else as well. The world over, people felt intensely about him. Even today, he is as much yours as he is ours.

Some of my most vivid memories of my grandfather are of him as a painter. He was the first artist I ever knew. As a child I would stand behind him and watch, spellbound by the magic he was creating. As he was the "expert" in the family, I would sometimes show him some small effort of my own.

How do you get to know someone? How did you first become attracted to your wife or husband? A glimpse across a crowded room, an intriguing snippet of conversation? At first you get to know a small part of a person, which gives you an appetite for more. Later you find that this small thing is part and parcel of the whole person.

You can see Winston Churchill in the little things of life—by the way he enjoys his dinner, by the way he plays at cards, by the way he pats his poodle, and by the way he puts paint onto his canvas.

His art reflects his life. Not that Churchill mixed politics with his paint. There was art in his politics, but no politics in his art. Some artists like to bring in a "message," or make a political statement with their art. Some just concentrate on the statement and don't bother with the art at all, creating "works" solely consisting of the message. Not he! Unashamedly, he painted for pure pleasure, channelling his joie de vivre onto the canvas.

There are five descriptive words that are often used to characterize Churchill. Please imagine with me now how these five descriptions of him in his public life show up repeatedly in his paintings—that is to say his private life.

He was PRODIGIOUS.

He was BOLD.

He was filled to the brim with a LOVE OF LIFE.

He was IRREPRESSIBLE.

And finally he was INSPIRING, that quality of his which, more than any other, shaped world history. These five words help me to re-create him.

PRODIGIOUS

Nearly seventy out of his ninety years were spent in public life. There was hardly anything that was going on in the world between 1890 and 1960 in which he was not vitally involved. In 1893 he was fighting the Dervishes at Omdurman in the last cavalry charge in history. In 1915 he was planning the first tank, and in 1945 he was laying the ground rules for the United Nations. He was literally "into everything."

He was prodigious as a painter, as well. During a span of forty-five years, from 1915 to 1960, he produced more than five hundred paintings.

Today many of these paintings hang in museums and private collections from Buckingham Palace to Brunei.

Although he gave away about a hundred paintings during his lifetime, he hated to part with them—every artist does. The only ones we don't mind parting with are the bad ones—and those we daren't give away.

The list of owners of his paintings reads like a thumbnail *Who's Who* of his life. Apart from members of the family, there were: Beaverbrook, Eden, F. E. Smith, Eisenhower, Harriman, Heath, Vivien Leigh, Montgomery, Onassis, Roosevelt, Smuts, Truman, and on and on.

In spite of these gifts, there were still plenty of paintings to keep for himself. My grandmother hung them in the main rooms at Chartwell, but more kept coming. She dealt with these in a novel way—wall to wall Winstons. The hallways and passages were stacked with canvasses, two or three high, like a page of postage stamps. Very effective, very exciting, very democratic really. Viewing for all sizes and ages—high enough so the lofty General de Gaulle would not have to stoop his head—low enough so the small grandchild would not have to stand on tiptoes.

BOLD

A wonderfully descriptive word for Churchill is bold—bold in all the battlefields of life. One could fill a library with examples of his daring.

One particular episode that I'm fond of happened in 1916. Churchill was commanding a battalion of the Royal Scots Fusiliers, stationed in a village called Plugstreet, just over the French border into Belgium, less than a mile away from the front line. His battalion was in and out of action—by turns in the 'trenches and by turns "resting." Within earshot, eyeshot, and gunshot of the enemy, Churchill set up his easel and painted the scene around him. A group of farm buildings increasingly riddled with shells appeared on his canvasses. One of these paintings, *Plugstreet Under Shell-Fire,* shows men running to escape the bombardment. Churchill had stayed at his easel and caught the danger of the moment.

Laurence Farm, done at the same time, is another example of his sangfroid. This painting shows the elegant figure of his friend Archibald Sinclair casually reading a newspaper, oblivious to the destruction happening around him—the epitome of the Scottish gentleman. "If you can keep your head about you, when all around are losing theirs." I'm sure both artist and sitter had these lines from Kipling in mind while this scene was being painted.

He was bold as a man and bold as a painter. Churchill was already forty when he first began to paint. It was 1915. He had left the Admiralty, cruelly forced out of office, in the middle of the Dardanelles disaster. Inactivity was intolerable. He cast about for a way to channel his energies. In his book, *Painting as a Pastime,* he describes his first efforts:

> Everyone knows the feeling with which one stands shivering on a spring-board, the shock when a friendly foe steals up behind and hurls you into the flood, and the ardent glow which thrills you as you emerge breathless from the plunge. . . . This beginning with Audacity, or being thrown into the middle of it, is already a very great part of the art of painting. For a joy ride in a paint-box, Audacity is the only ticket.

He was bold in his choice of colors. So bold were they that many people, including Clementine, would sometimes suggest that he cool them. In particular, Clementine promoted the friendship and influence of the eminent painter Sir William Nicholson, encouraging her husband to tone down his brilliant colors to the cooler and more subtle hues of Sir William.

Whatever the advice, and from whatever quarter, Winston could not bear to give up his bold colors. He insists:

I must say I like bright colours. I cannot pretend to feel impartial about the colours. I rejoice with the brilliant ones, and am genuinely sorry for the poor browns.

When I get to heaven I mean to spend a considerable portion of my first million years in painting, and so get to the bottom of the subject. But then I shall require a still gayer palette than I get here below. I expect orange and vermillion will be the darkest, dullest colours upon it, and beyond them there will be a whole range of wonderful new colours which will delight the celestial eye.

IRREPRESSIBLE

He was irrepressible in public and in private life.

During the Boer War, as a civilian press correspondent not under military command, he simply took over a derailed troop train en route to Ladysmith, issuing orders and rescuing the soldiers.

During the General Strike of 1926 he exulted in running what turned out to be more or less his own newspaper—the *British Gazette,* which briefly had a circulation of more than a million.

Look at the photographs of Churchill during the gravest days of the Second World War. Anyone can see, within that resolute man with the bulldog face, there's a cheeky little red-haired boy bursting to come out. "I do not need to be prodded," he said. "If anything, I am a prod."

He was irrepressible as a painter.

Whereas statesmen today will grab an hour or two on the tennis court or golf course to refresh themselves after long hours of negotiating, Churchill would don his own peculiar form of leisure clothing and his latest hat and escape like a naughty schoolboy with his paints and brushes. Wherever he was and whatever he was doing, he always tried to make it fun. On a trip to Egypt in 1921, he paints *Cairo from the Pyramids.* In this majestic landscape with purple mountains and billowing clouds, he has been unable to resist puckishly inserting a tiny "Winston" in the foreground.

His sense of humor never deserted him. After his election defeat in 1945, he was offered the Order of the Garter, which he refused with the quip,

"Why should I accept the Order of the Garter from His Majesty, when the people have just given me the Order of the Boot?"

LOVE OF LIFE

No one loved life more than he did. He loved his work, he loved his family.

Most men keep their work in the office. Whenever possible, Churchill brought his home. No time or place was exempt. Wherever *he* was, was "where it was at." The dinner table at Chartwell was the mecca to which all were attracted. It was always the hub of the household, and frequently the hub of the world. It was the center both in time and place for family and friends, where discussion with a grandchild about the nesting habits of the black swans was as important as an argument with Monty about the Battle of Alamein. The guiding light on these occasions was my grandmother, who was always ready with a word or a look to keep things under control.

Love of life shone in his painting and how he felt about it.

"Just to paint," he wrote, "is great fun. The colours are lovely to look at and delicious to squeeze out."

He had a physical affinity with his materials, like a good workman with his tools. In a *Painter's Painting,* he did what most artists do sooner or later. He painted his own paints—the result, a tactile still life of squidgy tubes of color.

To me, one painting sums up his love of life—his love for the good things in life. This painting, *Bottlescape,* which still hangs at Chartwell, takes me back to my childhood. A fine array of decanters and bottles mostly opened, and a fine disarray of half-filled glasses, all bathed in orange light, evoke the warmth of the dining room. It is painted in rich reds and browns with bold white highlights on all the shiny objects—quite loosely painted, but you know exactly what each bottle holds and how it tastes. You can almost smell the cedarwood cigar boxes stacked up on the side of the painting.

Through his painting, Churchill also achieved a heightened awareness of the beauties of nature. He explains that he has discovered "a tremendous new pleasure and interest which invests every walk or drive with an added object. . . . I found myself instinctively as I walked noting the tint and character of a leaf, the dreamy, purple shades of mountains, the exquisite lacery of winter branches, the dim, pale silhouettes of far horizons. And I had lived for over forty years, without ever noticing any of them except in a general way, as one might look at a crowd and say, 'What a lot of people!' "

Scapes: landscapes, seascapes, skyscapes—he loved to capture on canvas scapes of all kinds. When asked why he preferred landscape painting to portraiture, he replied, "A tree doesn't complain that I haven't done it justice."

After his initial baptism with turpentine, Churchill discovered that the whole world was open with all its treasure. Painting became a spur to travel and he actually sought out what he called "paintatious" landscapes. It was total immersion. Painting was now a positive pleasure rather than simply a release from tension and the affairs of the state. In the south of France he would stand at his easel, without tiring, for three or four hours at a stretch, totally absorbed in *Sunset at Cannes*. Cigar and brush were both so much a part of Churchill that it's not hard to picture him putting the paintbrush in his mouth and stabbing the canvas with his cigar.

INSPIRING

Throughout his public life, Churchill was an inspiration to people— through his actions and through his words.

The sort of thing that makes a speech good also makes a painting good. Contrast, imagination, clarity. There was nothing wishy-washy in his speeches or his paintings. The French painter Paul Maze gave him this advice: "Paint like you write or speak. You can do it—every stroke of the brush must be a statement felt and seen."

And in some ways his painting started to affect his words. He uses vivid imagery gained with his new painter's eye. His World War II "Finest Hour" speech ends with the painterly metaphor: "I see a day when men and women walk together in broad sunlit uplands."

Churchill's joy in painting has become an inspiration to others to take up the paintbrush and "have a go!" What he did for his own pleasure also gave pleasure to others—at first to those around him, and later to a wider circle through exhibitions both in Britain and abroad.

In 1958 his great exhibition at the Royal Academy drew crowds. The art critic John Russell wrote: "Nearly all of us are pleased when an amateur outdoes the professionals." My Aunt Mary Soames recalls a woman standing next to her in the gallery, saying to her companion, "He must have had such lovely holidays!"

Last summer, a show of Churchill's paintings was held at Hyde Park, the home of his friend and ally Franklin D. Roosevelt. The director of the Vassar Art Gallery, James Mundy, commented, "His best stuff is his earlier stuff, and if he'd stayed with it he could have had a major career in art." This was also the view of Picasso, who once said, "If that man were a painter by profession, he would have no trouble in earning a good living."

Modest though he was about *this* particular activity, Churchill *did* want his paintings to survive and be known to future generations. David Coombs, who compiled the definitive catalog did so on the instructions of this cryptic 1950 memo: "Mr. Churchill wants a catalogue of his pictures made."

Three times in his life, the Muse of Painting came to Churchill's rescue—twice when he was thrown out of office (in 1915 and in 1945), and then again in 1955, when he finally retired from office. On this occasion, at the age of eighty, he said, "If it weren't for painting, I couldn't live; I couldn't bear the strain of things."

Painting was only a thread in the tapestry of his life, but in these descriptions, I've tried to illustrate how my grandfather's art and life were intertwined: His Art Reflects His Life.

The paintings of Winston Churchill endure, and like a ripple in a pond are enjoyed by an ever-increasing circle of people. We are all the inheritors of his art. His paintings are a tangible part of his life, made by his own hands and touched by his spirit.

So, the ending is not the ending—the spirit of Winston Churchill lives on, in us and in ours. It will never die. The paint is dry on the canvas, but the image lingers on.[1]

1. I gratefully acknowledge the following sources of information: Winston S. Church-ill, *Painting as a Pastime* (reprint, New York: Cornerstone Library, 1965); Mary Soames, *Winston Churchill: His Life as a Painter* (London: Collins, 1990); Martin Gilbert, *Church-ill: A Life* (London: Heinemann, 1991).

THE RT. HON. LORD AMERY, a Member of Parliament for over twenty
years, and Sir Winston Churchill's personal representative to Generalissimo
Chiang Kai-shek in 1945, is the author of several books, including a biography of
Joseph Chamberlain. His honors and awards include: Knight Commander of the
Order of Phoenix (Greece), Grand Cordon of the Order of Skanderbeg (Albania),
and Order of Oman.

12

Memories of Churchill and How He Would Have Seen the World Today

THE RIGHT HONORABLE LORD AMERY

I suppose I have always known Winston Churchill because he was a close friend of my father's. Since he lived for the most part, while not in office, in his country house in Kent and my father lived in London, he was a frequent visitor to our home. I suppose I grew up not realizing quite who he was or what he was, but he was a familiar figure with a gold watch chain and very often a spotted necktie.

My first conscious memory of him was at school when he came to judge a competition in oratory and he didn't give me the prize, which I rather resented. But he called me over afterward and said, "You dropped your voice at the end of the sentence—same mistake as Anthony Eden makes." Who was corrected? I must say I was very touched. I was sixteen or seventeen, and Anthony Eden was the rising star in the Conservative Party, and I thought I had been admitted to the magic circle by being asked not to make the same mistakes as this rising figure.

My next and first grown-up meeting with him was in February, I think it was, of 1939. My father had invited Count Coudenhove-Kalergi, the first prophet of united Europe, to meet Churchill at lunch. My father had to go out to an early board meeting and he said to me as he left, "Julian, make sure that Churchill has enough liquid refreshment." It was to me a memorable occasion. Not only did Count Coudenhove-Kalergi talk about united Europe, all of which Churchill received very well and he wrote a powerful article that evening in support of it, but Coudenhove-Kalergi also said, "You do realize, Mr. Churchill, that Hitler and Stalin are just about to conclude an agreement." And Churchill was shocked, and he said, "Not possible. I see the Soviet Ambassador Mr. Maisky quite often. I don't think this can happen." Coudenhove said, "This is what I learned from my sources in the Vatican." Well, the Vatican have a habit of being rather well informed. And so Churchill was silenced for a moment by this. Not many things silenced him. That is my principal memory of the conversation at lunch that day.

Next time I saw him was the last big dance or ball given in England before the war. It was at Hever Castle, and Churchill had very kindly asked me to stay in his house for the occasion. We were mostly a gathering of young people, perhaps eight or ten. But he had just received visitors from Czechoslovakia, for they were still with him, because to Mrs. Churchill's dismay an hour after dinner he hadn't yet finished. He was not the most considerate of men where the clock was concerned; but as he came out he was in a rather gloomy and grumpy mood and rather quiet at dinner, as was his way until he had eaten and had a little champagne. By then he had cheered up, and we all went to the ball, which was the last big social occasion before the outbreak of war, which all of us thought by now was inevitable.

Then came the war. I was abroad. I was in Yugoslavia at this time. I had no further contact with him for a bit. As I remember very well after the fall of France, the people of Eastern Europe lost hope, particularly those who were democrats and who feared the advance of Nazi Germany. I went to a village in Serbia trying to study agricultural conditions in the old Yugoslavia and was taken to a small farm. There was a small and impoverished farmer who showed me over his farm and there was a pretty cross-looking pig. Then he pointed to his pig and he said, "I call him Churchill." I was a little offended. I was a young attaché at our embassy then, and I said, "Why do you call your pig after our Prime Minister?" He said, "He is my last hope of getting through the Winter alive!"

There followed for me months of excitement in the war, sometimes months of boredom, but mostly interesting work, until Marshall Rommel, the great German commander, came to the gates of Cairo. He was only about a day's march away, or his tanks an hour's drive away. My job was then in the secret service, and we had to make plans how to deploy the network of secret agents we had in case the Germans took over. Otherwise, all of these men would have been in real danger. Some were shipped off to South Africa, some even to India, but there was no certainty that we would survive. And I went home to London in what was regarded as very privileged position—in the belly of a Liberator bomber—anxious that the pilots shouldn't press the lever that would drop me out like a bomb. However, I got home safely and I went to my father's home and found my father having lunch with Harold Macmillan, then a very young minister. And they said to me, "What is going to happen?" I said, "It is a very dangerous position. The army is low in morale." And they said, "How do you know that?" "Well," I said, "I have to go up to the front quite often and to the forward air fields. We've taken a hell of a pasting from the Germans. We have lost several hundred tanks, and their replacement is coming 'round Africa, but it won't be here for two or three weeks." "What is to be done?" "Well," I said, "you can't get the tanks any quicker to the desert. The only idea I have, and you may think it a foolish thing for a young man to propose, is if Churchill, himself, were to go out and show himself to the troops and speak to them. It just might make the difference and give us a few more days." Having said my piece, I went off to my own office in the secret service headquarters and I was at a meeting with my boss while the telephone rang, and he said, "I am terribly sorry, this is Downing Street on the line, I may have to ask you to leave the room for just a moment while I just check." Then his face fell, and he said, "The call is not for me. It is for Julian Amery." And the call was an order from Churchill to come at once to Downing Street. I was with him in a few minutes, since the traffic was pretty thin in London in the wartime years.

I was shown into the cabinet room where he was dressed in that familiar air force blue siren suit, smoking a cigar with what looked like a sort of weak whiskey in front of him. On his right hand was Sir Alan Brooke, the chief of the general staff. He said, "Tell me what you have to say. I have heard about your lunchtime conversation." So I repeated it. Alan Brooke did not like the idea or a junior officer criticizing the morale of an army which was under the command of friends of his. But Churchill said, "Let him have his say. Let him talk." And so Alan Brooke kept quiet, and I finished what I had to say. Then he asked me a series of questions about the journey. Had I stood up to it easily? Had it been very cold in the air? Was it very hot in Cairo? He asked me one question after another, showing a keen interest in the journey, and then he thanked me and bade me good afternoon.

I left, thinking I have done my bit for what it was worth. Two or three weeks later, his private secretary, Mr. Martin, telephoned and said, "I thought you would like to know Churchill left for Cairo this morning. So your words have borne fruit." It led to the big change in the high command, and Field Marshal Montgomery was appointed to lead the battle with General Alexander as his field commander. So that was my contribution to the battle of El Alamein. Coming as it did at about the same time as the battle of Stalingrad, this reassured us that victory was now certain. The United States and the Soviet Union had both become involved in the war, and the Germans could no doubt put on a tough fight still but they were cornered. Churchill's problem was, "Alright, we're no longer going to be defeated, but how are we going to win and what are we going to do with our victory?" Already, the shadow of the Soviet advance into Eastern Europe could be seen, and there was a big conference at Teheran, where President Roosevelt, Marshal Stalin, and Churchill were all there. At that conference Churchill deployed the strategy he wanted to pursue. This was that the Anglo-American army, then in Italy, should halt its operations halfway up Italy. If you think of it, Italy is very narrow. It was the most uncomfortable place to fight a war. There is not much room for maneuver. He said, "Let's send the army across the Adriatic and bid for the Danube and try to get there and cut off the Germans from Eastern Europe." He put forward this plan, but it was vetoed by Stalin and Roosevelt. Stalin, of course, already had ambitions in Eastern Europe. Roosevelt guessed that what Churchill was after was keeping the road to the Middle East open to the British Empire. And so his plan failed and he came back to Cairo, increasingly suspicious about the ambitions of the Soviet Union.

Mr. Casey, a great mining magnate, had a villa just under the pyramids. At a dinner on one of the evenings after Churchill came back, he said, "Oliver Cromwell was a very great man, but he made a very great mistake. Obsessed with the power of Spain, he failed to observe the rise of France. Will they say this of me?" meaning that the Germans were already really defeated and the Russians would take over unless something was done.

There was a dinner a couple of nights later at the British Embassy. He was celebrating his birthday, and all the great men were there— Montgomery, Alexander, Smuts—but he also invited what he called "the boys," young men like me who were operating behind the lines in Greece, Albania, and Yugoslavia. After dinner he took "the boys" aside and he said, "I think what I am going to do is to support the Communists in Yugoslavia, and the King in Greece." Having said this, he went around and asked what we thought about it. When it came to me, I said, "It may be a bit awkward because Yugoslavia and Albania have a common border with Greece." And he looked at me and he said, "Well, Julian, you may think I am being inconsistent, but I still have some influence here and this is my policy." So I shut up pretty quickly. What he meant, of course, was that Eastern Europe was going to fall to the Soviets. Was there any chance of peace before then?

Your Professor Charmley, who was here, has written a book called *The End of Glory,* in which he said, "Churchill could have made peace at the end of 1940 or '41." I think this is a good example of an academic not understanding politics. We had not a card in our hand in '40 and '41. Our whole army had been destroyed at Dunkirk. Our air force had just survived the Battle of Britain, and not much of it was left. The Germans still had a good deal in order to prosecute their war, which was just coming with the Russians. So I don't think there was any chance of peace when Professor Charmley thought it might have happened.

It was just conceivable, it seemed to me, that in the end of '42, the beginning of '43, after the Battle of Stalingrad and El Alamein, that the German generals might have attempted to overthrow Hitler and accept terms that we might have thought possible. But we had all signed up the agreement on unconditional surrender. Germany was to surrender totally. And this was something that both President Roosevelt and Marshal Stalin were committed to. And Churchill, by now the junior partner in the Great Western Alliance, was in no position to say "No." So we went on for another fifteen months to fight the war at considerable cost.

In 1945 we could at least say peace was here. We had avoided defeat. We had won the war. Then there was a general election in Britain. And, for the first time in my life, I ran for office. I have never seen such enthusiasm. The British are a fairly phlegmatic people, but I have never seen such enthusiasm as there was for Churchill. I accompanied him on the long drive to my constituency and people came out with flags tied to their crutches—veterans from World War I. They threw flowers at his car. I was absolutely convinced. I fought twelve elections since, but the only time I have been absolutely convinced of victory, we lost. Largely, I think, because of the overseas vote of the army. They all wanted to come home and they felt Churchill would continue the war, the war against Japan particularly. Anyway, there he was—defeated.

He wasted no time in futile regret or feeble reproaches. He pulled himself together and, according to his old maxim, he said, "Who is now the enemy?" He was convinced by this time that the Soviets had become the enemy, but no other statesman of the front rank had yet reached this conclusion. It was here in Fulton, and later in Zurich, that he denounced the danger of the "Iron Curtain" dividing Europe and leading to an even greater danger than the Germans had presented.

I, of course, sympathized and applauded what he said at Fulton and at Zurich. I got involved in the European Movement. I had been to visit the Count Coudenhove-Kalergi, who I have already mentioned to you, at his villa in Gstaad. On the second day I was staying with him, a telegram arrived from Churchill saying, "I am going to start a European Movement. I understand you have got one, too. Please let me have full details of your organization." And Coudenhove-Kalergi replied, "Julian Amery is returning to London tomorrow, and he is fully briefed."

So I found myself a couple of days later lunching at Chartwell with Churchill, Robert Boothby, Duncan Sandys, and my father. Churchill was in very good spirits. He said, "I have decided to simplify my drinking, nothing but champagne and brandy." We talked over lunch, and he was quite clear that he wanted to launch a movement for the unity of Europe, and he wanted Britain to play a full part in it. There have been a lot of arguments since as to how far he wanted to commit Britain. I can tell you, as I was with him then and in the remaining development of the European Movement, I have no doubt whatever that he expected Britain to join fully. But, when I say to join fully, he was not a federalist. He had seen the British Commonwealth and independent countries fight through the First World War and the Second World War alongside of us, and so he did not think federation was the answer. He thought the answer lay in a close union of sovereign states. General de Gaulle, in exile in London, watching how the Commonwealth operated, came to the same conclusion. And that was what led him to proclaim "a union of States" for Europe. He said, in rather cynical terms, "I want a Europe to evolve on British lines, but, hopefully, without the British!"

Then came the question of what to do about the threat of the Soviet Union. Churchill had managed to maintain good relations with Marshal Stalin, though in no way was he taken in by him. And there is perhaps a story here I can tell. Possibly you have heard it before. After one of their conferences, Stalin said to Churchill, "Come and have a bite of something to eat and a drink in my flat in the Kremlin. I will just have an interpreter." And so they went off. Churchill drank a lot of whiskey, and Stalin drank a lot of red wine. When Churchill got back to the British Embassy at two or three in the morning, he went to sleep. When he awoke in the morning, he said to himself, "I wonder what I agreed to." And so he rang for his secretary and he dictated a letter: "Dear Generalissimo: I very much enjoyed our evening. I think we agreed to the following points," and he put down the points he would have liked to be agreed upon. Two hours later, the reply came back: "I also enjoyed our evening. My recollection of the conversation is completely different than yours, but do not worry. We were both drunk, and the interpreter has been shot."

Gradually the relationship with the Russians deteriorated, and I see a Mr. Ponting has said in a book that Churchill wanted to launch a nuclear war against the Russians. This is quite untrue. But what is true is that he did recommend that, while the United States had the monopoly of nuclear weapons which was until 1950 or 1951, we should put an ultimatum to the Russians and ask them to withdraw from Eastern Europe. This was not done, so presently they developed their own nuclear power. Once they had done that, the prospect of a major war faded away as far as he was concerned. The consequences would have been too dreadful for any advantage either side might have secured.

In 1953 Marshal Stalin died, and Churchill recalled that when the great Khan, Ghengis Khan, had died in Karakorum in the thirteenth century, I think it was, all his generals had saddled up and ridden home as fast as they could to be in on the succession. And he thought, well now there may be a chance to penetrate the totalitarian armor of the Russians. And he called for a summit meeting on the United States, Britain, and France with the Russians. Everybody was against him, including his own foreign office, so he embarked on some secret diplomacy and began a negotiation, the venue of which strangely was my own house in London, with the Russian Ambassador to see if such a negotiation could take place. He had some reasons for thinking it might work. There were clear signs the Soviets were going to withdraw from Austria. But I think it was premature. They did withdraw from Austria, and the result was that Hungary blew up in their face, and they had to invade Budapest.

Churchill, of course, as you know, was a lifelong friend and ally of the United States. He knew without the United States, we could not have won the war. Anyway, he was half-American by birth and he had many friends in the United States, but he did resent American anticolonialism and, more particularly, their criticism of our policy in India, which was still under the British Raj. I remember before I paid my first visit to the United States (I had some lectures then arranged), he said to me to be sure and tell them that under British rule the population of India has risen three or four times. The same cannot be said for the Indian population in the United States.

At the end of his life a shadow was cast over his friendship with the United States, in the shape of American pressure on us to withdraw from the Suez Canal base. And Anthony Eden, his foreign secretary, agreed with the American line, while Churchill, himself, rejected it.

I made a speech one day in the House of Commons criticizing Anthony Eden in the sort of rather unmannerly terms that a young man sometimes uses. The telephone rang the next morning, and it was Number Ten Downing Street. I thought I'd be getting a rocket. It was the prime minister's private secretary, who said, "Prime Minister has read your speech. He wants me to say he agrees with every word of it" (the speech attacking his own foreign secretary). This was in 1953. He left office in 1955, so he was not there when Eden launched his attack with France against Colonel Nasser. I often wondered whether the American response might have been friendlier than it was, if he still had been in office and had been able to fly to Washington and tell President Eisenhower what was in his mind. His own verdict on the Suez operation was simply this: "I don't know whether I would have dared to start; I would never have dared to stop." You may think this has some application to the recent crisis in the Gulf!

But then he left office. He was over eighty, his hearing was very bad, his physical capacities were beginning to decline. And having once left government, he didn't make any effort to intervene in the conduct of affairs. But he used to come to the House of Commons quite a lot. I was sitting next to him one day and on the bench behind us a distinguished Conservative member, Sir Bernard Braine, was speaking, and Churchill said to me, "Who is that?" And I said, "Braine." "James?" he queried. "No," I said, "Braine." "Drain? You can't be called Drain. No one is called Drain." So I wrote it down. "Braine." "Oh!" he said, "is he well known?"

He spent those last declining years painting, taking an interest in his racing horses—he had never been interested in that before. And he very much befriended Mr. Onassis, the Greek shipping magnate, who found a key to conversation with him (Churchill). It is perhaps difficult for people today to realize that Churchill's authority was such that nobody, certainly not a young man who knew him as well as I did, would have dared to argue much with him. Certainly not criticize him. Onassis had no such inhibitions. I remember a dinner where Onassis turned to him and said, "You let Roosevelt down very badly," over some issue and Churchill said, "What did you say?" So Onassis repeated the criticism, and he got in reply a five- or ten-minute vintage speech from Churchill. Onassis had the effect of slapping him in the face, as it were, and making him respond.

The last time I saw him was at dinner at the Other Club, a club he had founded, and I was just about opposite to him. He was too deaf for any conversation, but I scribbled one or two notes to him. The first one had no reply. The second drew a real Churchillian response. It was about de Gaulle for whom he had a great regard. At dinner after some oysters, he had some roast beef and a big pudding, and he drank champagne throughout and then two or three glasses of brandy. That was early in the new year before he died. But the sparkle never left him, and his son, Randolph, told me that a day or two before he died Randolph went in to see him in his bedroom and Churchill said, "I would like to see the press, the newspapermen," and Randolph said, "But you're not well enough to do that." "Yes," he said, "I would like to see some of the top commentators." "Oh," said Randolph, "What do you want to say to them?" He said, "I want you to say to them that my Doctor, Lord Moran, is sinking fast." It was typical of the sense of humor that never left him, even in the hour of death.

His legacy—well, that would mean writing a book, and I won't attempt to inflict it on you now. I see somebody has said that he was not really a democrat. His idea of democracy was perfectly simple. He said, "Every government must give the people the chance every five years or so to get rid of it, if they want to." But he didn't believe in framing your policy from day to day in the light of public opinion polls.

He once said, "A politician, with his ear to the ground, must inevitably have his bottom in the air. This is a vulnerable and undignified position and should be avoided."

Basically, I suppose he was a free trader and a free market man. His views on religion were simple. Once he said to me, "I am a buttress of the church, rather than a pillar," by which he meant that he thought religion had an important part to play in peoples' lives, even if not entirely in his own. He was incapable of resentment. You might say the opposite of what he believed in to him. He never held it against you. Working with him was fun, enlivened by refreshment and excitement at the feeling that you were working with history, living with history.